The Economics of
Public Issues

29641461

The Pearson Series in Economics

Abel/Bernanke/Croushore
Macroeconomics*

Acemoglu/Laibson/List
Economics*

Bade/Parkin
Foundations of Economics*

Berck/Helfand
The Economics of the Environment

Bierman/Fernandez
Game Theory with Economic Applications

Blanchard
Macroeconomics*

Boyer
Principles of Transportation Economics

Branson
Macroeconomic Theory and Policy

Bruce
Public Finance and the American Economy

Carlton/Perloff
Modern Industrial Organization

Case/Fair/Oster
Principles of Economics*

Chapman
Environmental Economics: Theory, Application, and Policy

Daniels/VanHoose
International Monetary & Financial Economics

Downs
An Economic Theory of Democracy

Farnham
Economics for Managers

Froyen
Macroeconomics: Theories and Policies

Fusfeld
The Age of the Economist

Gerber
International Economics*

Gordon
Macroeconomics*

Greene
Econometric Analysis

Gregory/Stuart
Russian and Soviet Economic Performance and Structure

Hartwick/Olewiler
The Economics of Natural Resource Use

Heilbroner/Milberg
The Making of the Economic Society

Heyne/Boettke/Prychitko
The Economic Way of Thinking

Hubbard/O'Brien
Economics*

InEcon

Money, Banking, and the Financial System*

Hubbard/O'Brien/Rafferty
Macroeconomics*

Hughes/Cain
American Economic History

Husted/Melvin
International Economics

Jehle/Reny
Advanced Microeconomic Theory

Keat/Young/Erfle
Managerial Economics

Klein
Mathematical Methods for Economics

Krugman/Obstfeld/Melitz
International Economics:
Theory & Policy*

Laidler
The Demand for Money

Lynn
Economic Development: Theory
and Practice for a Divided World

Miller
Economics Today*

Miller/Benjamin
The Economics of Macro Issues

Miller/Benjamin/North
The Economics of Public Issues

Mishkin
The Economics of Money, Banking,
and Financial Markets*

The Economics of Money, Banking,
and Financial Markets, Business
School Edition*

Macroeconomics: Policy and
Practice*

Murray
Econometrics: A Modern
Introduction

O'Sullivan/Sheffrin/Perez
Economics: Principles, Applications
and Tools*

Parkin
Economics*

Perloff
Microeconomics*

Microeconomics: Theory and
Applications with Calculus*

Perloff/Brander
Managerial Economics and Strategy*

Pindyck/Rubinfeld
Microeconomics*

Riddell/Shackelford/Stamos/
Schneider
Economics: A Tool for Critically
Understanding Society

Roberts
The Choice: A Fable of Free Trade
and Protection

Scherer
Industry Structure, Strategy, and
Public Policy

Schiller
The Economics of Poverty and
Discrimination

Sherman
Market Regulation

Stock/Watson
Introduction to Econometrics

Studenmund
Using Econometrics: A Practical
Guide

Todaro/Smith
Economic Development

Walters/Walters/Appel/Callahan/
Centanni/Maex/O'Neill
Econversations: Today's Students
Discuss Today's Issues

Williamson
Macroeconomics

The Economics of
Public Issues

Twentieth Edition

Roger LeRoy Miller
Research Professor of Economics
University of Texas—Arlington

Daniel K. Benjamin
Clemson University, South Carolina
and PERC, Bozeman, Montana

Douglass C. North
Washington University St. Louis, Missouri

 Pearson

New York, NY

Vice President, Business Publishing: Donna Battista
Director of Portfolio Management: Adrienne D'Ambrosio
Specialist Portfolio Manager: David Alexander
Editorial Assistant: Nicole Nedwidek
Vice President, Product Marketing: Roxanne McCarley
Senior Product Marketer: Tricia Murphy
Executive Field Marketing Manager: Carlie Marvel
Product Marketing Assistant: Marianela Silvestri
Manager of Field Marketing, Business Publishing: Adam Goldstein
Vice President, Production and Digital Studio, Arts and Business: Etain O'Dea
Director of Production, Business: Jeff Holcomb
Managing Producer, Business: Alison Kalil
Content Producer: Christine Donovan

Operations Specialist: Carol Melville
Creative Director: Kathryn Foot
Manager, Learning Tools: Brian Surette
Content Developer, Learning Tools: Sarah Peterson
Managing Producer, Digital Studio, Arts and Business: Diane Lombardo
Digital Studio Producer: Melissa Honig
Digital Studio Producer: Alana Coles
Digital Content Team Lead: Noel Lotz
Digital Content Project Lead: Courtney Kamauf
Project Manager: Kathy Smith, Cenveo® Publisher Services
Interior Design: Cenveo® Publisher Services
Cover Design: Cenveo® Publisher Services
Cover Art: E+/Getty Images
Printer/Binder: LSC Communications/Crawfordsville
Cover Printer: Phoenix Color/Hagerstown

Library of Congress Cataloging in Publication Control Number: 2017021881

 Pearson

1 17
ISBN 10: 0-13-453198-1
ISBN 13: 978-0-13-453198-4

To

Max and Sara,

Strong climbers make strong leaders.

Continue on!

R.L.M.

To

Gini Ozenne,

With admiration for your extraordinary courage,

and gratitude for your kindness and steadfast friendship.

D.K.B.

CONTENTS

SUGGESTIONS FOR USE

At the request of our readers, we include the following table to help you incorporate the chapters of this book into your syllabus. Depending on the breadth of your course, you may also want to consult the companion paperback, *The Economics of Macro Issues,* 8th edition, which features macroeconomic topics and a similar table in its preface.

Economics Topics	Recommended Chapters in The Economics of Public Issues, 20th Edition
Introduction to Economics	1, 6, 7, 9, 10, 12, 13, 27, 28
Opportunity Costs and Scarcity	1, 3, 5, 7, 10, 19, 20, 23
Demand and Supply	6, 7, 8, 15
Demand and Supply Applications	1, 8, 9, 10, 12, 13, 16, 17, 18, 20, 22
The Public Sector and Public Choice	1, 2, 4, 6, 9, 10, 11, 12, 14, 17,18, 19, 20, 21, 22, 23, 24, 25, 26, 27, 28, 31
Taxes, Transfers, and Public Spending	11, 12, 14, 19, 20, 21, 22, 23, 27
Consumer Behavior	3, 5, 10, 17, 19, 20, 21
Elasticity of Demand and Supply	6, 7, 8, 9, 10, 11, 18, 19, 20, 22, 27, 28, 30, 31
Rents, Profits, and the Financial Environment of Business	2, 4, 11, 16, 18, 27, 31
Firm Production and Cost	1, 2, 3, 12, 13, 15, 20, 27
Perfect Competition	23
Monopoly	15, 16, 17
Monopolistic Competition	3, 15, 18
Oligopoly	3, 15, 16
Regulation and Antitrust	1, 3, 13, 15, 18, 21
Unions and the Labor Market	11, 12, 13, 14, 15, 31
Income, Poverty, and Health Care	2, 4
Environmental Economics	8, 9, 20, 21, 25, 26, 27, 28
International Trade	30, 31
International Finance	29, 30

PREFACE

The times are certainly changing. It was true when Nobel Prize winner Bob Dylan said so almost fifty years ago and it's true today. But changes in who occupies the White House and which party has the majority in Congress do not alter the way economists think about the world around them. You will discover in this short, but jam-packed volume that economic analysis applies to the public issues, the policies, and the politics of all times and in all places.

Take, for example, our analysis of the Affordable Care Act (ACA), passed in 2010. This act, otherwise known as Obamacare, upended our healthcare industry. Right after the ACA was enacted, we laid out in an earlier edition of this book the features of the law that would lead to its failure. Then and now we have analyzed its impact using simple, straightforward economic analysis. We show how people, whether they are healthcare consumers or providers or government officials, have reacted to the alterations in the *incentives* facing them. The new President and Congress have said they will change the ACA for the better. Change they may bring, but whether this change yields improvement will hinge on whether the politicians recognize and heed the incentives people face. The beauty of economics is that it enables us to see what is and will be, regardless of what we or anyone else might wish for or want things to be.

The guiding principle that ties together the issues in this new edition is that they illustrate the power of economics in explaining what goes on around us. Along the way, we have sought to make the application of economic science to public issues entertaining.

NEW TO THIS EDITION

Selecting new public issues for each edition of our book presents a recurring challenge. After all, there are literally hundreds, if not thousands, of important public issues from which to choose. What we have done is to select those topics that possess a sense of immediacy. As a consequence, we believe that they will be of most interest to our readers.

- The Economics of Obesity *(the economic causes and consequences of packing on the pounds)*
- The Platform Economy *(why Super Bowl tickets can cost $25k)*
- Student Loans *(why you borrow, who will pay)*
- What to Do About the Climate? *(what does—and doesn't—make sense)*

- The Death of Recycling *(the rise and fall of our favorite environmental program)*
- Numerous chapters have undergone major updates that reflect new evidence and explain how the incentives people face have changed.

CHAPTERS THAT HAVE UNDERGONE MAJOR REVISIONS

The following chapters have been extensively revised, either to bring in important new evidence on the issue, or to incorporate recent legal or institutional changes that have altered the incentives people face, and thus the decisions they make.

- Chapter 1: Death by Bureaucrat
- Chapter 6: Sex, Booze, and Drugs
- Chapter 8: Kidneys for Sale
- Chapter 11: *Das Kapital* in the Twenty-First Century
- Chapter 13: The Effects of the Minimum Wage
- Chapter 19: Health Insurance for All . . . Or Maybe Not
- Chapter 26: Save That Species
- Chapter 30: Globalization and the Wealth of America

And of course, all remaining chapters have been updated so that your students will see the most current evidence on each topic in this book.

END-OF-CHAPTER QUESTIONS

We continue to provide a significant set of end-of-chapter questions because instructors have told us they use them extensively. The range of difficulty remains wide, but we always include questions about the basics of the material covered in each chapter.

SELECTED READINGS

As with previous editions, we have included a list of selected readings for each chapter at the back of the book. These selected readings include those that we found useful in our research as well as others.

GLOSSARY

There is a glossary at the back of the book, as usual. Within each chapter, terms included in the glossary are boldfaced the first time that they are used.

INSTRUCTOR'S MANUAL

An Instructor's Manual accompanies this 20th edition. It is available online to all adopters of the book from the Instructor's Resource Center (**www.pearsonhighered.com**). We have attempted to incorporate the very best of the teaching aids that we use when we teach from *The Economics of Public Issues*.

For each chapter, this manual contains:

- A synopsis that cuts to the core of the economics issues presented in the chapter.
- A concise exposition of the "behind the scenes" economic foundations of the text. Often this exposition is supplemented with one or more diagrams.
- Answers to all of the end-of-chapter discussion questions. Most suggest new avenues of discussion.

SPECIAL THANKS AND ACKNOWLEDGMENTS

First, we would like to thank the reviewers from the last edition whose comments were helpful in preparing this edition. In addition to Cyril Morong, who is a steady source of suggestions and improvements, they are: Ninos Malek, San Jose State University and Tina Esparza, Hartnell College. Of course many other users of the last edition offered valuable suggestions and will see many of their comments included in this 20th edition.

We also thank David Alexander, Christine Donovan, and Kathy Smith for all of their efforts in shepherding this project. We thank Sue Jasin for her expert manuscript preparation and Robbie Benjamin, whose editorial skills once again have improved the final product. All errors remain, of course, solely our own.

R.L.M.
D.K.B.
D.C.N.

The Foundations of Economic Analysis

Part One

The Foundations of Economic Analysis

CHAPTER 1

Death by Bureaucrat

How would you rather die? From a lethal reaction to a drug prescribed by your doctor? Or because your doctor failed to prescribe a drug that could have saved your life? If this choice sounds like one you would rather not make, consider this: Employees of the U.S. Food and Drug Administration (FDA) make that decision on behalf of millions of Americans many times each year. More precisely, FDA bureaucrats decide whether or not new medicines (prescription drugs) should be allowed to go on sale in the United States. If the FDA rules against a drug, physicians in America may not legally prescribe it, even if the drug is saving thousands of lives each year in other countries.

A Brief History of the FDA

The FDA's authority to make such decisions dates back to the passage of the Food and Drug Safety Act of 1906. This law required that medicines be correctly labeled as to their contents and that they not contain any substances harmful to consumers' health. Due to this legislation, Dr. Hostatter's Stomach Bitters and Kickapoo Indian Sagwa—along with numerous rum-laden concoctions, cocaine-based potions, and supposed anticancer remedies—disappeared from druggists' shelves. In 1938, the law was expanded with the passage of the Food, Drug, and Cosmetic Act, which forced manufacturers to demonstrate the safety of new drugs before being allowed to offer them for sale. (This law was prompted by the deaths of 107 people who had taken Elixir Sulfanilamide, an antibiotic that had been errantly mixed with poisonous diethylene glycol, a chemical cousin of antifreeze.)

The next step in U.S. drug regulation came after a spate of severe birth defects among infants whose mothers during pregnancy had taken a sleep aid known as thalidomide. By the time these birth defects first became apparent, the drug was already widely used in Europe and Canada, and the FDA was nearing approval for its use in the United States. In fact, about 2.5 million thalidomide tablets were already in the hands of U.S. physicians as samples, though none had been distributed. The FDA ordered the samples destroyed and prohibited the drug's sale in the United States. This incident led to the 1962 Kefauver–Harris Amendments to the 1938 Act, radically altering the drug-approval process in the United States.

THE IMPACT OF THE 1962 AMENDMENTS

Before the 1962 amendments, the FDA was expected to approve a new drug application within 180 days, unless the application failed to show that the drug was safe. The 1962 amendments added a "proof of efficacy" requirement and also removed the time constraint on the FDA. The FDA was given free rein to determine how much and what type of evidence it would demand before approving a drug for sale, and thus could take as long as it wanted before either granting or refusing approval.

The 1962 amendments drastically increased the costs of introducing a new drug and markedly slowed the approval process. Before 1962, for example, the average time between the filing and approval of a new drug application was seven months. By 1967, it was thirty months, and by the late 1970s, it had risen to eight to ten years. The protracted approval process involved costly testing by the drug companies—now more than $2.5 billion for each new drug—and delayed the receipt of any potential revenue from new drugs. Because the delays and the higher costs reduced the expected profitability of new drugs, fewer of them were brought onto the market.

Debate continues over how much FDA regulation is needed to ensure that drugs are both safe and efficacious, but there is little doubt that the 1962 amendments resulted in a U.S. "drug lag." In short order, drugs took far longer to reach the market in the United States than they did in Europe, a lag that grew and then persisted for more than three decades. Admittedly, it takes time to ensure that patients benefit from, rather than are harmed by, new drugs, but regulation-induced drug lag can itself be life threatening. Dr. George Hitchings, a winner of the Nobel Prize in Medicine, estimated that the five-year lag in introducing Septra (an antibiotic) to the United States killed 80,000 people. Similarly, the introduction of a class of drugs called beta blockers—a drug used to treat heart attack victims and people with high blood pressure—was delayed nearly a decade in America relative to its approval in Europe. According to several researchers, the lag in the FDA approval of these beta-blocker drugs cost the lives of at least 250,000 Americans.

TERRIBLE TRADE-OFF

In effect, the law requires FDA bureaucrats to make what is truly a terrible trade-off. One the one hand, lives can be saved because unsafe or ineffective drugs are kept off the market. On the other hand, the regulatory process delays (or even prevents) the introduction of some safe and efficacious drugs, thereby forfeiting lives. Let us now take a more systematic look at this trade-off.

Every time a new drug is introduced, there is a chance that it should not have been—either because it has adverse side effects that outweigh the therapeutic benefits (it is not safe) or because it really does little to help the individuals who take it (it is not effective). When such a drug is introduced, we say that a **Type I error** has been committed. Since 1962, the incidence of Type I error—the thalidomide possibility—has been reduced by the added testing required by the FDA. Other people, however, have been the victims of what is called a **Type II error.** Their cost is the pain, suffering, and death that occur because the 1962 amendments have prevented or delayed the introduction of safe, efficacious drugs. A Type II error—as with Septra or beta blockers—occurs when a drug *should* be introduced but is held back by FDA regulation.

Eventually, outcries over the harm caused by the drug lag brought about important policy changes. For example, the FDA moved to accelerate approvals when the costs of Type I errors are small relative to the damages due to Type II errors—as with terminally ill patients. One famous example involved azidothymidine (AZT), which emerged as a possible treatment for AIDS. Gay men, among whom AIDS was most prevalent at the time, took the lead in pressuring the FDA to approve the drug quickly. As a result, the agency approved AZT after only eighteen months of testing. Similarly, Taxol, an important drug used to treat breast cancer, received an expedited review by the FDA because of pressure applied by women who had a family history of breast cancer.

THE USER FEE REVOLUTION

The most important change to U.S. drug regulation came in 1992, with the passage of the Prescription Drug User Fee Acts. These laws mandated FDA performance goals in reviewing and acting on drug applications within set time periods, in return for charging fees on drug manufacturers' submissions. The FDA has used these fees to expand its drug review staff and facilities, and the fees now comprise more than half of the agency's drug review budget.

The results have been stunning. Approval times for new drugs have been cut to ten months and the drug lag has been reversed. In the 1980s, less than 10 percent of new drugs were introduced first in the United States before anywhere else in the world. Today, more than two-thirds of new drugs are approved in the United States first. Indeed, for the last decade, the FDA has approved drugs more quickly than any other regulator in the world.

The acceleration in the drug review process has stimulated a major increase in pharmaceutical research and development, along with a consequent increase in pharmaceutical innovation. There has been an outpouring of new drugs, most notably for the treatment of cancer and the prevention and treatment of heart disease, but also extending across the board to many other diseases. Despite having to pay for FDA review, pharmaceutical firms have earned higher profits. Most importantly, the lives of many thousands of people have been saved or extended. In addition, because drug approval elsewhere is likely to come sooner once the FDA has approved a drug, people in other nations have benefitted, too.

Lessons from the FDA Story

What can we learn from the FDA regulation of new drugs that will guide us in thinking about other public issues of our time? There are several key principles:

1. *There is no free lunch.* Every choice, and thus every policy, entails a **cost**—something must be given up. In a world of **scarcity,** we cannot have more of everything; so to get more of some things, we must give up other things. Although the FDA review of drugs saves lives by preventing the introduction of unsafe or ineffective drugs, the cost is delayed availability of safe and efficacious drugs, resulting in the deaths of other people.

2. *The cost of an action is the alternative that is sacrificed.* Economists often express costs (and benefits) in dollars because this is a simple means of accounting for and measuring them. But costs need not be monetary, and economics is capable of analyzing costs and benefits that are quite human. The costs that led to the 1938 and 1962 amendments were the very visible deaths caused by sulfanilamide and the terrible birth defects due to thalidomide. Subsequent

revisions to the FDA process for reviewing drugs, as with the user fee acts, have been in response to the deaths and other adverse health effects caused by the regulation-induced drug lag.

3. *The relevant costs and benefits are the marginal (incremental) ones.* The relevant question is not whether safety is good or bad; rather, it is *how much* safety we want—which can only be answered by looking at the added (marginal) benefits of more safety compared to the added (marginal) costs, a topic fully explored in Chapter 3. One possible response to the sulfanilamide poisonings or thalidomide birth defects was to have outlawed new drugs altogether. Such a response would have guaranteed that no harm would ever occur to anyone because of a new drug. But surely this "solution" would not be sensible, because the marginal cost (more Type II errors) would exceed the marginal benefit (fewer Type I errors).

4. *People respond to incentives.* This is true for consumers, suppliers, and even government bureaucrats. Here, the incentive to amend the law in 1938 and 1962 was the very visible death and disfigurement of individuals. The passage of the 1992 user fee acts resulted from intense lobbying by individuals and firms who believed (correctly, as it turned out) that many thousands of people could benefit from a speedier drug review process.

5. *Things are not always as they seem.* Many analyses of the effects of government policies fail to account for the actions that people would otherwise have taken. Pharmaceutical manufacturers, for example, have strong incentives to avoid introducing drugs that are unsafe or ineffective because the companies are subject to loss of reputation and to lawsuits. For similar reasons, physicians have strong incentives to avoid prescribing such drugs for their patients. Even without FDA regulation, there would thus be extensive testing of new drugs before their introduction. Hence, it is incorrect to ascribe the generally safe and effective nature of modern drugs entirely to FDA protection. The flip side, however, is that the drug development process is inherently long, complicated, and costly. Even without FDA oversight, some people would die waiting for new drugs because self-interested manufacturers would insist on some testing and cautious physicians would proceed slowly in prescribing new drugs.

FDA employees are publicly castigated when they "allow" a Type I error to occur—especially when it is a drug that kills people. Thus, FDA bureaucrats have a strong incentive to avoid such errors.

But when testing delays cause a Type II error, as with Septra, it is almost impossible to point to specific people who died because the drug was delayed. Hence, officials at the FDA are rarely attacked directly for such delays. Because the costs of Type II errors are much more difficult to discern than the costs of Type I errors, there is an inherent bias at the FDA in favor of being "safe rather than sorry"—in other words, excessive testing.

6. *Policies always have unintended consequences, so their net benefits are almost always less than anticipated.* In the case of government regulations, balancing incremental costs and benefits (see Principle 3) fails to make good headlines. Instead, what gets politicians reelected and regulators promoted are *absolute* notions such as safety (and motherhood and apple pie). Thus, if a little safety is good, more must be better, so why not simply mandate that drug testing "guarantee" that everyone is free of risk from dangerous drugs? Eventually, the reality of Principle 3 sinks in, but in this instance, not before the drug lag has killed many people.

As is often true with important public issues, our story has one more interesting twist. Thalidomide is back on the market. In 1998, the FDA approved its use in treating Hansen's disease (leprosy), and in 2006, the FDA gave physicians the OK to use it in treating bone marrow cancer. In each instance, there are strong protections to prevent pregnant women from taking the drug. So ironically, perhaps the very drug that brought us the deadly drug lag will turn out to be a lifesaver for a new generation of patients.

DISCUSSION QUESTIONS

1. Why don't individuals simply force the FDA to do what is best for consumers of prescription drugs?

2. Why don't FDA employees accurately balance the marginal benefits to drug consumers against the marginal costs to those consumers?

3. Does the structure of the drug industry have any bearing on the types of errors that drug firms are likely to make? That is, would a drug industry made up of numerous highly competitive firms be more or less likely to introduce unsafe drugs than an industry consisting of a few large firms?

4. How could the incentives provided to the FDA be changed to reduce the incidence of Type II errors? (*Hint:* Is it possible to compare

the FDA approval process with the drug-approval process in other nations?)

5. What would be the advantages and disadvantages of a regulatory system in which, rather than having the FDA permit or prohibit new drugs, the FDA merely published its opinions about the safety and efficacy of drugs and then allowed physicians to make their own decisions about whether or not to prescribe the drugs for their patients?

6. Suppose for simplicity that both Type I and Type II errors resulted in deaths only. Keeping in mind that too little caution produces Type I errors and too much caution produces Type II errors, what would be the best mix of Type I and Type II errors?

CHAPTER 2

Innovation

Would you be better off without your smartphone and other digital devices? Would you be better off without access to the world's greatest library—the Internet? Would you be better off without social media?

Most of you will answer these questions with a resounding, "no." The Internet and rapid telecommunications have changed most people's lives, in the United States and around the world, for the better. But none of what is technologically available today came out of the blue. Rather, someone in the past created an **invention.** As the saying goes, however, inventions are "a dime a dozen"—they have little value in their raw idea form, just by themselves. Rather, **innovation** is necessary—that is, the transformation of something new, such as an invention, into something that benefits us. The technical novelty of the invention must be developed into the practical application that creates value for human beings. Innovations can either reduce the cost of producing what we already have—think telephone calls—or provide new goods and services—think the Internet.

INVENTION TO INNOVATION TO WIDESPREAD USE—NOT ALWAYS FAST

Just because someone has invented something that seems useful does not guarantee a quick transition from invention to widespread use. The incandescent light bulb was originally invented by Humphrey Davy in 1802. But it took more than 75 years, plus the considerable technical and commercial talents of Thomas Edison, to implement a practical application for the bulb. Even then, the widespread diffusion of the light bulb took additional decades—and has not yet occurred in many locations around the world.

Consider also the transistor, which is the fundamental building block of modern electronic devices. When it was invented in 1947, its creators thought that it might help make a better hearing aid. The *New York Times* thought the invention merited no more than a tiny article buried deep in the newspaper's back pages. Now the transistor is the basis for the billions of computers instrumental to the operation of devices ranging from the smartphone to the airplane.

When the laser was invented, nobody knew what to do with it. Indeed, people told the inventor that it was "a solution in search of a problem." One early application was in chemical research. Then people realized it could be used for measurement and navigation. Today, lasers are used in optical data transmission, surgery, printing, reproduction of music, retail sales, telecommunications, and much more.

The pattern of the light bulb, transistor, and laser is repeated for virtually all inventions that have been transformed by innovation. The initial perceived and actual applicability of the invention is narrow—ludicrously so in hindsight. Only after significant technical refinements and the development of ingenious and previously unforeseen applications—the process of innovation—does the invention add substantively to human welfare.

RESEARCH AND DEVELOPMENT AND YOUR STANDARD OF LIVING

Innovations do not arise spontaneously. To paraphrase Edison, they emerge only after substantial inspiration and even more perspiration. As a practical matter, both inventions and innovations are closely tied to how much we spend on research and development (R&D).

Large companies and the federal government are well known for spending billions on the R&D process. A typical large company may see many hundreds of inventions come out of its R&D laboratories each year. Only a few of these inventions are developed into formal proposals for new processes or products. Of these, a carefully chosen select group is further developed, yielding either more efficient production processes or novel new products. Of those, perhaps one or two may "make it" commercially.

Of course, not all R&D is done by large firms and the government. Much R&D is undertaken by single individuals or small start-up companies whose sole initial assets may be no more than the glimmer of an idea in the inventor's mind. Most of these ideas go nowhere. Even so, a large and steady stream of innovations comes to market through the efforts of small companies. Indeed, in some fields, such as pharmaceuticals and computers, the large firms of today were originally founded on a single idea that, over years of research and development, eventually became transformed by innovation into a highly successful product.

INNOVATION AND GROWTH

There is no doubt that the amount of resources devoted to the R&D process (regardless of who undertakes the work) has an important impact on our future standard of living. **Economic growth** is the annual increase in the amount of goods and services produced per person each year. The rate of such growth is what determines our future standard of living. For example, if Country A grows by just one percentage point per year faster than neighboring country B, its prosperity will *double* relative to that of its neighbor in the course of a single human life span.[1]

Innovations are essential to economic growth for two reasons. First, they are the principal source of new products and of resource-conserving cost reductions for existing products. Second, the prospect of profits from those innovations is a chief motivator of the new investment needed to produce more output in the future.

We need only look back to the years before the Industrial Revolution to see the importance of innovation. For most of history until about 1750, the pace of innovation was slow, relatively little new investment took place, and the standard of living hardly moved from one decade—or even century—to the next. Since then, the rate of innovation has been high and the standard of living has soared. Thus, innovation is not just a minor aspect of our economy. It is a fundamental basis of economic growth and prosperity.

INCENTIVES AND INNOVATION

By definition, the innovative process is unpredictable. To the outside observer, then, innovation seems to be totally random. In fact, it is driven by **incentives.** Innovation does not arise spontaneously. It is the result of purposive behavior, motivated by the prospect that the rewards will exceed the costs.

---

1 The Rule of 72 tells us that the doubling time, measured in years, of a growing process is found by dividing the number 72 by the annual growth rate, measured as a whole number. Thus: $72/1 = 72$ years. Life expectancy in the world is 72.

Three elements must be present for sustained, widespread innovation to emerge. First, there must be protection for the ideas that are the source of both inventions and innovation. Second, there must be the prospect of commercial success for the innovation. And finally, this commercial success must actually yield rewards to the innovator.

The Importance of Patents

Many innovative ideas are protected by secrecy. For example, the Coca-Cola Company is the only firm that may produce its flagship product, because it is the only company that knows the formula for that product.

Much of the time, however, the innovative process begins when an inventor applies for a **patent** for her invention. A patent is the protection that the government gives an inventor for the exclusive right to make, use, or sell an item for a limited period of time. This period of time is currently twenty years in the United States. Once the patent is granted, the owner of the patent can sell or license the invention without fear of someone using it without payment.

The American patent system, which dates back to our nation's founding, is generally regarded as the most effective in the world. It is relatively cheap and simple to use, and it offers superior levels of legal protection for patent holders. Hence, the U.S. patent system is acknowledged as playing a crucial role in stimulating innovation in America over the last two centuries.

Although the average rate of innovation in the United States has been high, the emergence of new ideas, at least as measured by patents, has been extremely uneven over our history. For example, from 1800 to 1900, new patents grew at a rate of about 6.5 percent per year. From 1900 to 1980, the growth slowed sharply to just over 1 percent per year. World Wars I and II, plus the Great Depression, no doubt played important roles in slowing patent growth, for these events all greatly reduced normal commercial activities, and thus the incentive to invent. Since 1980, the inventive process has again accelerated, with patent growth averaging about 4.5 percent per year.

Is There a Market?

Innovations are inherently unexpected and thus disruptive. They may pose a threat to existing ways of doing business, as Uber and Lyft have done in the personal transportation market (see Chapter 18), thereby threatening the profits of existing businesses. Or they may raise the prospect of possible threats to human health or safety, as many people feel that genetically modified organisms have done (see Chapter 21).

Politicians and bureaucrats often respond to disruption by attempting to suppress it—the simplest way being to prevent the innovative process by sharply limiting the commercial introduction of new goods and services. This type of political or regulatory suppression clearly reduces the potential rewards to innovation and thus cuts the incentives to undertake it. Many observers believe that European efforts to stifle disruptive innovation have played a key role in reducing both innovation and economic growth on that continent in recent decades.

WHO GETS THE PROFITS?

Even if an innovation is legally protected and makes it to the market, there remains a further hurdle. All governments need tax revenues to operate, and taxes on profits and on the incomes of business owners are an important source of government revenue. Higher taxes mean less after-tax profits, and this in turn means reduced incentives to innovate.

Consider again Europe, where overall taxes are generally much higher than in America. One French economist has estimated that had Bill Gates—the founder of Microsoft Corporation—started that company in France, he would have ended up with only 20 percent of his accumulated wealth. Now, you may say, Gates made so many billions that billions less would not have mattered. Yet would Gates have worked twelve hours a day, seven days a week, for the first twenty years of his career had he thought the government was going to take away an extra 80 percent of what he earned? How many other would-be innovators have simply not bothered to try at all in the face of high tax rates, knowing that 100 percent of the hard work will fall on them, but only 20 percent of the benefits—if any—will be theirs?

HAVE ALL THE EASY INVENTIONS BEEN DISCOVERED?

The six most basic "simple machines," including the wheel, the pulley, the lever, and the screw, were all invented thousands of years ago. Their profound positive impact on human welfare can never be repeated. More recently, the automobile, the telephone, and the electric light bulb were all invented more than one hundred years ago, yielding benefits not easily replicated by other innovations.

Examples such as these have led some observers to argue that "all the important stuff has already been invented." According to this view, from now on it is going to become harder and harder to invent anything that matters very much. There will not be anything like the discovery of electricity or antibiotics in the future. Given this, the benefits of future innovation will likely be far less than in the past. If this pessimistic view of the world is correct, we might thus expect future rates of economic growth to be far lower than the ones we have enjoyed in the past.

But not everyone agrees that the future is so bleak. Consider the automobile, invented late in the nineteenth century. Pessimists argue that cars today are really just refinements of that initial invention. The "big bang" of the car is gone, and something of comparable magnitude cannot realistically be expected again. But this ignores the fact that the first auto was no more than an existing engine bolted onto a wagon frame, using a method of transmitting engine power to wheels that had been adapted from other processes. Even the original steering system was borrowed from wagons. In short, the automobile was simply a new idea built on the platform of old ideas—with a twist. If we fast forward 130 years, "automobiles" are still with us, but their transformation—one innovation at a time—is nothing short of staggering.

Indeed, the automobile episode characterizes a fundamental feature of every innovation: commercial, artistic, intellectual, or otherwise. *All* of them have built on the ideas of the past. But this means that with the creation of each new idea (invention or innovation), the stock of ideas on which still more new ideas can be built is increased. For this reason, the optimists argue, we can actually expect *more* innovation in the future than in the past, because the foundation for it grows with each new idea.

What Does the Future Hold?

Because innovations are, by their very nature, unexpected, neither we nor anyone else can know the future of innovation. But the principles of economics *are* able to make some predictions about how government policies will influence that future.

As we noted above, just as innovations are the engine of economic growth, so too are incentives the engine of innovation. If property rights to new ideas are protected, if fear does not cause us to suppress novelty, and if innovators are allowed to keep the fruits of their labor, then the future of innovation is bright. But if these conditions are not met, innovation will languish and with it the possibility of a more prosperous future. Thus, even if few of us may individually be responsible for important innovations of the future, it is within the power of all of us to encourage government policies that will make such innovations possible.

DISCUSSION QUESTIONS

1. If you had the choice of living today or one hundred years ago, which would you prefer and why? What about the choice between now and one hundred years in the future?

2. Why is it true that inventions are "a dime a dozen"?

3. Are those resources that are spent on R&D but do not yield profitable innovations wasted? Why or why not?

4. Why does it matter to you if the long-run economic growth rate falls from its historical 2.1 percent to, say, only 0.9 percent? How does your answer differ depending on whether you are looking ahead to the end of this year or are looking ahead to the entirety of your working career?

5. Suppose you are about to start an innovative, high-tech company in one of two states. You expect before-tax profits to be about $100,000 per year. Both states have similar living conditions, climate, and other amenities, but the tax rate in state A is 17 percent, while the tax rate in state B is 7 percent. By how much will your annual after-tax profits differ between the two states? From a business perspective, which state is a preferred location?

6. What are the innovations from the last five years that you think are the most important in your life and why? Can you put a rough dollar value on the personal loss you would suffer if these innovations had *not* occurred, perhaps because they were suppressed or discouraged by government policies?

CHAPTER 3

Flying the Friendly Skies?

Most of us hop into our car with little thought for our personal safety, beyond perhaps the act of putting on seat belts. Yet even though travel on scheduled, commercial airlines is safer than driving to work or to the grocery store, many people approach air travel with a sense of foreboding, if not downright fear.

If we were to think carefully about the wisdom of traveling six hundred miles per hour in an aluminum tube seven miles above the earth, several questions might come to mind. How safe is this? How safe should it be? Because the people who operate airlines are not in it for fun, does their interest in making a buck ignore our interest in making it home in one piece? Is some form of government regulation the only way to ensure safety in the skies?

THE ECONOMICS OF SAFETY

The science of economics begins with one simple principle: We live in a world of **scarcity,** which implies that to get more of any good, we must sacrifice some of other goods. This is just as true of safety as it is of pizzas or haircuts or works of art. Safety confers benefits (we live longer and more enjoyably), but achieving it also entails **costs** (we must give up something to obtain that safety).

As the degree of safety rises, the total benefits of safety rise, but the marginal (or incremental) benefits of additional safety decline. Consider a simple example: Adding exit doors to an airplane increases the number of people who can escape in the event of an emergency evacuation. Nevertheless, each *additional* door adds less in safety benefits than the previous one. If the fourth door enables, say, an extra ten people to escape, the fifth may enable only an extra six to escape. (If this sounds implausible, imagine having a door for each person. The last door added will enable at most one more person to escape.) So we say that the marginal (or incremental) benefit of safety declines as the amount of safety increases.

Let's look now at the other side of the equation. As the amount of safety increases, both the total and the marginal (incremental) costs of providing safety rise. Having a fuel gauge on the plane's instrument panel clearly enhances safety because it reduces the chance that the plane will run out of fuel while in flight.[1] It is always possible that a fuel gauge will malfunction, so having a backup fuel gauge also adds to safety. Because having two gauges is more costly than having just one, the total costs of safety rise as safety increases. It is also clear, however, that while the cost of the second gauge is (at least) as great as the cost of the first, the second gauge has a smaller positive impact on safety. Thus, the cost per unit of additional (incremental) safety is higher for the second fuel gauge than for the first.

HOW SAFE IS SAFE ENOUGH?

How much safety should we have? For an economist, the answer to such a question is generally expressed in terms of **marginal benefits** and **marginal costs.** The economically *efficient* level of safety occurs when the marginal cost of increasing safety just equals the marginal benefit of that increased safety. Put somewhat differently, if the marginal benefits of adding (or keeping) a safety feature exceed the marginal costs of doing so, the feature is worthwhile. If the added benefits of a safety device do *not* exceed the added costs, we should refrain from installing the device. Note there are two related issues here: How safe should we *be*, and how should we *achieve* that level of safety?

Both of these issues took on added urgency on the morning of September 11, 2001, when terrorists hijacked and crashed four U.S. commercial jetliners. This episode revealed that air travel was far less safe than had been previously believed. Immediately, it was clear that we should devote additional resources to airline safety. What was not

---

1 Notice that we say "reduces" rather than "eliminates." In 1978, a United Airlines pilot preoccupied with a malfunctioning landing gear evidently failed to pay sufficient attention to his cockpit gauges. When the plane was forced to crash-land after running out of fuel, eight people died.

clear was how *much* additional resources should be thus devoted and precisely *what* changes should be made. For example, almost everyone agreed that more careful screening of passengers and baggage at airports would produce important safety benefits. But how should we achieve this? Should carry-on bags be prohibited or just examined more carefully? How thoroughly should checked luggage be screened for bombs? Even now, our answers to these questions are evolving as we learn more about the extent of the threat and the costs of alternative responses to it. Nevertheless, throughout the process, economic principles can help us make the most sensible decisions.

In general, the efficient level of safety will not be perfect safety because perfection is simply too costly to achieve. For example, to be absolutely certain that no one is ever killed or injured in an airplane crash, we would have to prevent all travel in airplanes—an unrealistic and impracticable prospect. Hence, if we wish to enjoy the advantages of flying, we must be willing to accept *some* risk— a conclusion that each of us implicitly accepts every time we step aboard an airplane.

The Importance of Circumstances

Changes in circumstances can alter the efficient level of safety. For example, if a technological change reduces the costs of bomb-scanning equipment, the marginal costs of preventing terrorist bomb attacks will be lower. It will be efficient to have more airports install the machines and to have extra machines at large airports to speed the screening process. Air travel will become safer because of the technological change. Similarly, if the marginal benefits of safety rise for some reason (perhaps because the president of the United States is on board), it could be efficient to take more precautions, resulting in safer air travel. Given the factors that determine the benefits and costs of safety, the result of a change in circumstances will be some determinate level of safety that generally will be associated with some risk of death or injury.

Airplanes are complex systems, and an amazing number of components can fail. Over the century or so that humans have been flying, airplane manufacturers and airlines have studied every one of the malfunctions that has occurred thus far and have put into place design changes and operating procedures aimed at preventing recurring error. The efforts have paid off. Between 1950 and 2017, for example, the fatal accident rate on U.S. commercial airlines was cut by more than 97 percent.

DOES THE GOVERNMENT KNOW BEST?

Consumers have the greatest incentive to ensure that air travel is safe, and if information were free, we could assert with some confidence that the actual level of safety supplied by firms was the efficient level of safety. Consumers would simply observe the safety offered by different airlines, the prices they charge, and then select the degrees of safety best suited to their preferences and budgets, just as with other goods. Information is not free, however. It is a **scarce good,** costly to obtain. As a result, passengers may be unaware of the safety record of various airlines or the competence of the pilots and the maintenance procedures of an airline's mechanics. Indeed, even the airlines themselves may be uncertain about the efficient level of safety, perhaps because they have no way of estimating the true threat of terrorist attacks, for example. Such possibilities have been used to argue that the federal government should mandate certain minimum levels of safety, as it does today through the operation of the Federal Aviation Administration (FAA). Let's look at this issue in some detail.

One argument in favor of government safety standards rests on the assumption that if airlines were not regulated they would provide less safety than passengers want. This might happen, for example, if customers could not tell (at a reasonable cost) whether the equipment, training, and procedures employed by an airline are safe. If passengers cannot cheaply gauge the level of safety, they will not be willing to reward airlines for being safe or punish them for being unsafe. If safety is costly to provide and consumers are unwilling to pay for it because they cannot accurately measure it, airlines will provide too little of it. The conclusion is that government experts, such as the FAA, should set safety standards for the industry.

DO CONSUMERS KNOW BEST?

This argument seems plausible, but it ignores two key points. First, how is the *government* to know the efficient level of safety? Even if the FAA knows the costs of all possible safety measures, it still does not have enough information to set efficient safety standards because it does not know the value that people place on safety. Without such information, the FAA has no way to assess the benefits of additional safety and hence no means of knowing whether those benefits are greater or less than the added costs.

Second, people want to reach their destinations safely. Even if they cannot observe whether an airline hires good pilots or bad pilots, they can see whether that airline's planes land safely or crash. If it is *safety* that is important to consumers—and not the obscure, hard-to-measure *reasons* for that safety—the fact that consumers cannot easily measure metal fatigue in jet engines may be totally irrelevant to the process of achieving the efficient level of safety.

Interestingly, evidence shows that consumers are indeed cognizant of the safety performance of airlines and that they "punish" airlines that perform in an unsafe manner. Researchers have found that when an airline is at fault in a fatal plane crash, consumers appear to downgrade their safety rating of the airline (i.e., they revise upward their estimates of the likelihood of future fatal crashes). As a result, the offending airline suffers substantial adverse financial consequences over and above the costs of losing the plane and being sued on behalf of the victims. These findings suggest a striking degree of safety awareness on the part of supposedly ignorant consumers.

What About Terrorism?

Of course, this discussion leaves open the issue of how to handle safety threats posed by terrorists and other miscreants. For example, much of the information that goes into assessing terrorist threats is classified as secret, and its revelation to airlines or consumers might compromise key sources of the data. Hence, there could be an advantage to having the government try to approximate the efficient safety outcome by mandating certain screening provisions without revealing exactly why they are being chosen. Similarly, because airlines are connected in networks (so that people and baggage move from one airline to another in the course of a trip), achieving the efficient level of safety might require a common set of screening rules for all airlines. Even so, this does not inform us whether the government should impose those rules or the airlines should come to a voluntary joint agreement on them.

We began this chapter with the commonplace observation that airlines are safer than cars. Yet many people still worry for their safety every time they get on an airplane. Are they being irrational? Well, one-third of all fatalities in car crashes are caused by drunk drivers, one-third are due to excessive speed, and one-half are among people not wearing seatbelts. (Presumably, some people are doing two or even all three of these at once.) So a sober, seatbelt-wearing driver who obeys the speed limit might well think her chances are better on the ground than with an unknown pilot at the controls. It is presumably this reasoning that quite sensibly makes people nervous whenever they find themselves approaching an airport.

DISCUSSION QUESTIONS

1. Is it possible to be too safe? Explain what you mean by "too safe."

2. Suppose it is possible to observe (or measure) four attributes of airlines: (i) the size of their planes (measured in passenger-carrying capacity), (ii) the experience levels of their pilots, (iii) the age of their planes, and (iv) the length of the typical route they fly. Which airlines would be likely to have the fewest fatal accidents? Which would be expected to have the most?

3. Is safety likely to be a "normal" good (i.e., something people want to consume more of as they get richer)? Use your answer to this question to predict likely safety records of airlines based in North America and Europe, compared to those based in South America and Africa. Then go to www.airsafe.com to see if your prediction is confirmed or refuted by the facts.

4. Many automobile manufacturers routinely advertise the safety of their cars, yet airlines generally do not mention safety in their advertising. Can you suggest an explanation for this difference?

5. Many economists would argue that private companies are likely to be more efficient than the government at operating airlines. Yet many economists would also argue that there is a valid reason for the government to regulate the safety of those same airlines. Can you explain why the government might be good at ensuring safety, even though it might not be good at operating the airlines?

6. Professional football teams sometimes charter airplanes to take them to their away games. Would you feel safer on a United Airlines plane that had been chartered by the Washington Redskins than on a regularly scheduled United Airlines flight?

CHAPTER 4

The Mystery of Wealth

Why are the citizens of some nations rich while the inhabitants of others are poor? Your initial answer might be, "because of differences in the **natural resource endowments** of the nations." It is true that ample endowments of energy, timber, and fertile land all help raise wealth. But natural resources can be only a very small part of the answer, as witnessed by many counterexamples. Switzerland and Luxembourg, for example, are nearly devoid of key natural resources, yet the real incomes of citizens of those countries are among the world's highest. Similarly, Hong Kong, which consists of a few square miles of rock and hillside, is one of the economic miracles of modern times, while in Russia, a land amply endowed with vast quantities of virtually every important resource, most people remain mired in economic misery.

A number of studies have begun to unravel the mystery of **economic growth.** Repeatedly, they have found that it is the fundamental political and legal **institutions** of society that are conducive to growth. Of these, political stability, secure private property rights, and legal systems based on the **rule of law** are among the most important. Such institutions encourage people to make long-term investments in improving land and in all forms of **physical capital** and **human capital.** These investments raise the **capital stock,** which in turn provides for more growth long into the future. Also, the cumulative effects of this growth over time eventually yield much higher standards of living.

THE IMPORTANCE OF LEGAL SYSTEMS

Consider first the contrasting effects of different legal systems on economic growth. Many legal systems around the world today are based on

Table 4–1   Differing Legal Systems

Common Law Nations	Civil Law Nations
Australia	Brazil
Canada	Egypt
India	France
Israel	Greece
New Zealand	Italy
United Kingdom	Mexico
United States	Sweden

one of two models: the English **common law system** and the French **civil law system.** Common law systems reflect a conscious decision in favor of a limited role for government and emphasize the importance of the judiciary in constraining the power of the executive and legislative branches of government. In contrast, civil law systems favor the creation of a strong centralized government in which the legislature and the executive branches have the power to grant preferential treatment to special interests. Table 4–1 shows a sampling of common law and civil law countries.

Research reveals that the security of **property rights** is much stronger in common law systems, such as those observed in Britain and its former colonies, including the United States. In nations such as France and its former colonies, the civil law systems are much more likely to yield unpredictable changes in the rules of the game—the structure of **property and contract rights.** This unpredictability makes people reluctant to make long-term fixed investments, which ultimately slows the economic growth of these nations and lowers the standard of living for their citizens.

The reasoning is simple. If you know that the police will not help you protect your rights to a home or a car, you are less likely to acquire those assets. Similarly, if you cannot easily enforce business or employment contracts that you make, you are less likely to make those contracts—and hence less likely to produce as many goods or services. If you cannot plan for the future because you don't know what the rules of the game will be in ten years or perhaps even one year from now, you are less likely to make the productive long-term investments that take years to pay off. And if you cannot be assured of the rewards from developing successful new goods and services, innovation will be stifled (see Chapter 2). Common law systems seem to do a better job at enforcing contracts and securing property rights and so would be expected to promote economic activity now and economic growth over time.

THE ECONOMIC IMPACT OF INSTITUTIONS

Research into the economic performance of nations around the world from 1960 to the 1990s found that economic growth was one-third higher in the common law nations, with their strong property rights, than in civil law nations. Over the more than three decades covered, the standard of living—measured by real **per capita income**—increased more than 20 percent in common law nations compared to civil law nations. If such a pattern persisted over the span of a century, it would produce a staggering 80 percent real per capita income difference in favor of nations with secure property rights.

Other research has taken a much broader view, both across time and across institutions, in assessing economic growth. Institutions, such as political stability, protection against violence or theft, security of contracts, and freedom from regulatory burdens, all contribute to sustained economic growth. Indeed, it is key institutions such as these, rather than natural resource endowments, that explain long-term differences in economic growth and thus present-day differences in levels of real income. To illustrate the powerful effect of institutions, consider the contrast between Mexico, with per capita real income of about $18,000 today, and the United States, with per capita real income of about $56,000. Had Mexico developed with the same political and legal institutions that the United States has enjoyed, per capita income in Mexico would today be equal to that in the United States.

THE ORIGINS OF INSTITUTIONS

Given the great importance of such institutions in determining long-term growth, one might ask another important question: How have countries acquired the political and legal institutions they have today? The answer has to do with disease, of all things. An examination of more than seventy former European colonies reveals that a variety of strategies were pursued. In Australia, New Zealand, and North America, the colonists found geography and climates that were conducive to good health. Permanent settlement was attractive, so colonists created institutions to protect private property and curb the power of the state. When Europeans arrived in Africa and South America, however, they encountered tropical diseases, such as malaria and yellow fever, that produced high mortality rates. This discouraged permanent settlement and encouraged a mentality focused on extracting metals, cash crops, and other resources. As a result, there were few **incentives** to promote democratic institutions or stable long-term property rights systems.

The differing initial institutions helped shape economic growth over the years and, because of the broad persistence of those institutions, continue to shape the political and legal character and the standard of living in these nations today.

INSTITUTIONAL CHANGE TODAY

Recent events also illustrate that the effects of political and legal institutions can be drastically accelerated—in either direction. Consider China, which in 1979 began to change its institutions in two key ways. First, China began to experiment with private property rights for a few of its citizens, under narrow circumstances. Second, the Chinese government began to clear away obstacles to foreign investment, making China a more secure place for Western companies to do business. Although the institutional changes have been modest, their combined effects have been substantial. Over the years since, economic growth in China has accelerated, averaging almost 7 percent per year. If that doesn't sound like much, keep in mind that it has been enough over that period to raise real per capita income in China by a factor of 10.

For an example of the potential *destructive* impact of institutional change, we need to look no further than Zimbabwe. When that country won its independence from Britain in 1980, it was one of the most prosperous nations in Africa. Soon after taking power as Zimbabwe's first (and so far only) president, Robert Mugabe began disassembling that nation's rule of law, tearing apart the institutions that had helped it grow rich. He reduced the security of property rights in land and eventually confiscated those rights altogether. The Mugabe government also gradually took control of the prices of most goods and services in the nation, and confiscated large stocks of food and much of anything of value that might be exported out of or imported into Zimbabwe. In short, anything that is produced or saved became subject to confiscation, so the incentives to do either are—to put it mildly—reduced.

As a result, between 1980 and 1996, real per capita income in Zimbabwe fell by one-third, and since 1996, it has fallen by an additional third. Eighty percent of the workforce is unemployed, investment is nonexistent, and the annual inflation rate reached an astonishing 231 million percent. (In 2009, Zimbabwe gave up on having its own currency, and began using several foreign currencies as **legal tender,** including the American dollar.) The fruit of decades of labor and capital investment has been destroyed because the institutions that made that progress possible have been eliminated. It is a lesson we ignore at our peril.

DISCUSSION QUESTIONS

1. Go to a source, such as the CIA *World Factbook* or the World Bank, and collect per capita income and population data for each of the nations listed in Table 4–1. Compare the average per capita income of the common law countries with the average per capita income of the civil law countries. Based on the discussion in the chapter, identify at least two other factors that you think are important to take into account when assessing whether the differences you observe are likely to be the result of the systems of the countries.

2. Most international attempts to aid people living in low-income nations have come in one of two forms: (i) gifts of consumer goods (such as food) and (ii) assistance in constructing or obtaining capital goods (such as tractors, dams, or roads). Based on what you have learned in this chapter, how likely are such efforts to *permanently* raise the standard of living in such countries? Explain.

3. Both Louisiana and Quebec have systems of local law (state and provincial, respectively) that are heavily influenced by their common French heritage, which includes civil law. What do you predict is true about per capita income in Louisiana compared to the other U.S. states, and per capita income in Quebec compared to the other Canadian provinces? Is this prediction confirmed by the facts (which can be readily ascertained with a few quick Web searches)? Identify at least two other factors that you think are important to take into account when assessing whether the differences you observe are likely due to the influence of civil law institutions.

4. Consider two countries, A and B, that have identical *physical* endowments of a key natural resource. In country A, any profits made from extracting that resource are subject to confiscation by the government, while in country B, there is no such risk. How does the risk of expropriation affect the *economic* endowment of the two nations? In which nation are people richer?

5. In light of your answer to question 4, how do you explain that in some countries there is widespread political support for government policies that expropriate resources from some groups for the purpose of handing them out to other groups?

6. If the crucial factor determining a country's low standard of living is the adverse set of legal and cultural institutions it possesses, can you offer suggestions for how the other nations of the world might help in permanently raising that country's standard of living?

CHAPTER 5

The Economics
of Exclusion

What do California surfers and Maine lobstermen have in common?
Hint: It's more than just salt water. In fact, both groups have devised
ingenious systems to conserve natural resources. Not only do these systems not require any help from the government but they actually do
their work *despite* government rules that would otherwise cause those
resources to be squandered.

COMMON PROPERTY

If you've ever seen a picture of the Washington Monument, you've seen
an example of a **common property resource,** that is, a resource jointly
owned by a group of individuals who cannot (for legal or physical reasons) divide the resource into pieces and dispose of them separately.
Every owner (in this instance, every citizen of the United States) simultaneously owns the entire structure. Similarly, most highways and streets
are also common property, owned by the citizens of the relevant jurisdic-
tion, who, despite their ownership, may not sell any piece of the roadway.
    Common property resources do not have to be owned by a gov-
ernment. Indeed, many are not. For example, the members of a neighborhood swimming pool association each own common property (the
swimming pool and accompanying land and buildings), but the membership in the association is limited to those people willing to pay for the
right to be members, and thus is closed to those who won't pay.

ACCESS: OPEN OR CLOSED?

There is a crucial distinction between the situations just mentioned and
other examples of common property resources. Both the Washington

Monument and the swimming pool association are said to be **closed access** common property. In the example of the Washington Monument, even if you are a citizen and thus an owner, you cannot simply access the monument any time you like. Instead, you must first obtain a ticket that specifies the day and time slot when you are allowed to enter the facility. Although there is no charge for the ticket, you are excluded from the monument unless you have one. Similarly, the association swimming pool has closed access: Only owners and their guests are lawfully allowed to use it. No matter how hot and humid the day, and despite the great relief you would get from a quick dip, if you are not an owner or an authorized guest, you are excluded from the pool.

Now consider streets, roads, and highways. Nearly all of these (in the United States and elsewhere) are said to be **open access.** That is, day or night, anyone who wishes to is legally free to use them. You need not pay a fee to drive on the road, nor even have a ticket. This is true even if you are not an owner of the road (because, for example, you are a citizen of another nation). That is, unlike the example of closed access property, no one legally may be excluded from open access property. (Toll roads are closed access—you may not use them without paying a monetary toll. We'll note later in this chapter why some roads are operated this way.)

The Problem with Open Access

The good news about open access resources is that everyone may lawfully use them at their own convenience, without directly paying for access. Not even a "free" ticket is required. But this is also the *bad* news about open access resources. Consider the example of the Washington Monument. Once it officially opened on October 9, 1888, anyone could ride the elevator or climb stairs to the top any time they wanted, during its hours of operation. Yet the monument, which was immensely popular from the outset, steadily attracted more and more visitors, and the crowds created **congestion.** Long lines formed to get inside, and once there, visitors faced extended waits to use the elevator. Even though one could walk up the 897 stairs that led to the top, these were jammed with people going up and down, making the transit a slow, miserable process. The more people that packed in, the more unpleasant it became for every other visitor. Plenty of people were *visiting* the monument, but few were *enjoying* it.

This sort of congestion plagues all popular open access resources. In the case of urban highways, for example, the congestion comes in the form of huge and frequent traffic jams. These traffic jams not only make drivers miserable and waste their time (and gasoline) but also result in *less* traffic actually flowing over the highway, because people are moving so slowly. Plenty of people are *on* the road, but almost no one obtains what they actually want—speedy travel to their intended destination.

SURF GANGS

Areas along the California coast known as "surf breaks" are locations where waves are particularly conducive to high-quality surfing. California law defines the coast as open access up to the high-tide mark. This makes surf breaks a classic open access resource, subject to congestion due to excessive entry by individuals hoping to enjoy the resource. People can (and in many places do) crowd into surf breaks in such numbers that they markedly degrade the surfing experience for everyone. In the language of economics, the heavily congested surf breaks are said to be overexploited: The total enjoyment of surfers is actually *less* than it would be if some surfers were excluded from the breaks.

Longtime regular surfers, known as "locals" (or surf gangs), have battled back against the overcrowding at many surf breaks. They seek to limit the total number of surfers at a site and to regulate the use of waves by people who surf there. In both instances, the objective is to reduce the congestion and overexploitation of the valuable resource (high-quality waves).

Surf gangs employ two specific practices. First, they establish unwritten but unmistakable rules of etiquette for each surf break. These rules, enforced by members of the local surf gang, help establish who gets to ride which wave at a site. This reduces collisions and enhances the surfing experience. These rules are just like the rules of the road on a highway, except they are established and enforced by private individuals rather than by a government.

The second practice of the surf gangs is known as "localism." Quite simply, people who are not established surfers at a particular break are not allowed to surf in the best areas of the break. Enforcement of this practice (as well as the etiquette rules) is undertaken via unpleasant verbal assaults and sometimes even physical hostility. In this way the surf breaks are converted from open access resources to closed access.

THE BENEFITS OF CLOSED ACCESS

The actions of the surf gangs create benefits and enhance **economic efficiency** in two ways. First, by limiting the number of surfers on the break and having rules of etiquette, crowding and collisions are reduced, thereby enhancing the quality of the surfing experience. Second, many locations have hidden hazards, such as underwater rocks or dangerous currents, and local knowledge can reduce the harm caused by them.

Understanding how to read the water at a particular location can lead to better surfing. The value of the time investment it takes to learn about such specific factors can be sharply reduced or wiped out by congestion. When excessive entry by nonlocals is prevented, local surfers are encouraged to undertake the effort to learn and master local conditions, creating knowledge that can be passed on to others. The result is greater safety and overall enjoyment of the surfing experience.

It is worth noting that surf gangs are not always successful in their efforts. When breaks are close to densely populated areas, nonlocals can simply show up in overwhelming numbers, making it impossible for the locals to prevent congestion or enforce etiquette. In these situations, overexploitation of the resource takes place, and the result is a low-quality surfing experience for all.

Lobster Gangs

On the opposite coast of America, lobster fishermen in Maine organize themselves into harbor (or lobster) gangs to prevent the overexploitation of the lobster fishery. Until 1997, under Maine law the lobster fishery was open access. As a practical matter, commercial fishing for lobster was open to anyone who wished to set out traps.

Many people liked the freedom offered by open access, but it led to excessive fishing, threatening the very existence of the Maine lobster. Hence, all along the Maine coast, local fishermen organized themselves into gangs, which established and enforced rules regarding who could fish commercially for lobster in each harbor area and how the commercial fishing could take place (such as setting permissible locations for traps). Intruders from outside a gang were initially warned with a distinctive knot tied in the line connecting the trap to the floating buoy that marked its location. If the warning failed, the line was cut (causing the loss of the $80 trap, line, and buoy), or the trap was hauled to the surface by a gang member and permanently disabled.

Technically such actions by the gangs are in violation of Maine law. But the *effect* of the gangs has been to preserve and even enhance the population of Maine lobsters. Without the lobster gangs—without exclusion—indiscriminant commercial fishing by all comers under the open access regime would have decimated lobster populations.[1]

---

1 Since 1997, Maine has limited the number of commercial lobstermen with a license system, and also set limits on the number of traps that each person may set out. Both actions have helped close access to the fishery and thus complemented the work of the lobster gangs in protecting the population of Maine lobsters.

THE GANGS AND THE MONUMENT

When the National Park Service (NPS) decided to close access to the Washington Monument by requiring tickets, it was acting completely within the law. The actions of the surf gangs and lobster gangs technically are outside the law. Nevertheless, the actions of the NPS and the gangs protected and enhanced resources, the value of which was being destroyed by the open access to them.

Under open access, a visit to the Washington Monument eventually became a tedious, often unpleasant, experience for visitors. Closed access under the ticket system has dramatically improved the quality of a visit to the monument. Moreover, because the system evens out the flow of visitors over the course of the day, it actually became possible for the NPS to admit *more* total visitors to the site each year.

Under open access, even the best surf breaks yield a low-quality surfing experience because the extreme overcrowding leads to collisions, near-misses, and long waits to get a small segment of a surfable wave. The closed access and etiquette imposed by the surf gangs have dramatically improved not only the locals' surfing experience but also their safety, because surfers have an enhanced incentive to learn about local hazards and transmit that knowledge to their peers.

Under open access, the Maine lobster fishery was threatened with depletion, perhaps even destruction (see Chapter 26 to learn more about the global threat posed by open access to fisheries). In closing access, the harbor gangs of Maine have protected the resource by reducing fishing pressure, helping the lobster population grow to record levels.

NO PAIN, NO GAIN

Of course, in each instance, there are some people who are made worse off and, thus, are unhappy. People who fail to carefully plan their visits to the monument are often disappointed because they either cannot get a ticket or cannot gain entry at a time best for them. Similarly, surfers visiting breaks policed by local surf gangs find that they are relegated to the inferior portions of the break. And in Maine, outsiders may attempt to fish only at the peril of losing their fishing gear.

As a practical matter, it seems almost impossible to ensure that no one will be made worse off when an open access resource is converted to a closed access resource. Consider tolls for roads or bridges, useful in reducing vehicular congestion and increasing traffic flow. Some users are likely to have preferred slow travel and no toll to speedy travel with a toll. Some people will even choose not to pay the toll and thus be relegated to a route that for them is inferior even to the original highly congested route. Both groups clearly lose due to the toll.

Even so, limiting access to congested or overexploited resources has been shown repeatedly to improve the well-being of the vast majority of individuals and increase human wealth, in the broadest sense of that term. Indeed, when the open access resource is a natural resource (such as a fishery), limiting access—exclusion—is often the *only* way we can preserve the very thing that our attempts to enjoy are threatening to destroy. In a world of scarcity, this is a fact that simply cannot be avoided.[2]

DISCUSSION QUESTIONS

1. Is access to the house or apartment in which you live open or closed? If it is currently a closed access resource, how would it likely be treated differently if it were converted to an open access resource— one that anyone could use at any time in any way she chose? Explain.

2. Explain the sense in which your classroom is an example of a closed access resource. Discuss what would happen to the quality of your education if access to the room were open—in the sense that anyone could come in during class time and, say, have a rave.

3. Referring back to the last question, raves and education are both goods. That is, people typically prefer more of each to less. Do you think it is proper that people may not hold raves in the room when your class meets? Can you suggest a general principle that could guide university administrators as to when access to your room should be closed rather than open? Would the rule you suggest make *some* people worse off? If so, who?

4. Some nominally closed resources are effectively open access. For example, to gain entry to Yellowstone National Park by automobile, one must pay a fee of $25. But during the popular summer months, at this price, far more people want to drive into the park than can be readily accommodated by its roads. The result is terrible road congestion, added air pollution, and frayed tempers. In fact, the park is then (very nearly) an open access resource, heavily visited by many but not fully appreciated by any, at least

---

2 The late Elinor Ostrom won the 2009 Nobel Prize in Economic Sciences for her analysis of common property management by traditional societies. The methods these societies use look a great deal like those employed by surf and lobster gangs.

during the peak season. The National Park Service could trans-form Yellowstone into a closed access resource simply by raising the entry fee. Explain who would gain and who would lose if this were done. Why do you think the Park Service has thus far refused to raise the entry fee? Explain.

5. It is generally acknowledged that more people would like to attend the Super Bowl each year than in fact attend. (Presumably, many people stay away due to the high cost of the tickets, which are priced at many hundreds of dollars apiece.) Suppose a law were passed specifying that people who wished to attend need not even have a ticket, much less pay for one? How would attendance at the game change? What would determine who got into the stadium? Who would gain and who would lose due to the law?

6. Almost all privately owned resources are closed access. Many (perhaps most) government-owned or -controlled resources are open access. Can you suggest any explanations for this observation? Explain.

PART TWO

Supply and Demand

CHAPTER 6

Sex, Booze, and Drugs

Before 1914, cocaine was legal in this country. Today it is not. Alcoholic beverages are legal in the United States today. From 1920 to 1933, they were not. Prostitution is legal in Nevada today. In the other forty-nine states, it is not.[1] All these goods—sex, booze, and drugs—have at least one feature in common: The consumption of each brings together a willing seller with a willing buyer, creating an act of mutually beneficial exchange (at least in the opinion of the parties involved). Partly because of this feature, attempts to proscribe the consumption of these goods have met with less than spectacular success and have yielded some peculiar patterns of production, distribution, and usage. Let's see why.

SUPPLY-SIDE ENFORCEMENT

When the government seeks to prevent voluntary exchange, it must generally decide whether to go after the seller or the buyer. In most cases (and certainly where sex, booze, and drugs are concerned), the government targets sellers, because this is where the authorities get the most benefit from their enforcement dollars. A cocaine or heroin dealer, even a small retail pusher, often supplies many dozens of users each day, as did speakeasies (illegal saloons) during Prohibition; a streetwalker may service three to ten "tricks" per night. By incarcerating the supplier, the police can prevent several, or even several hundred, transactions from

---

1 These statements are not entirely correct. Even today, cocaine may be obtained legally by prescription from a physician. Prostitution in Nevada is legal only in counties that have chosen to permit it. Finally, some counties in the United States remain "dry," prohibiting the sale of beer, wine, and distilled spirits.

taking place, which is usually much more cost-effective than going after the buyers one by one. It is not that the police ignore the consumers of illegal goods. Indeed, sting operations, in which the police pose as illicit sellers, often make the headlines. Nevertheless, most enforcement efforts focus on the supply side, and so shall we.

Law enforcement activities directed against the suppliers of illegal goods increase the suppliers' operating costs. The risks of fines, jail sentences, and possibly even violence become part of the costs of doing business and must be taken into account by existing and potential suppliers. Some entrepreneurs will leave the business, turning their talents to other activities. Others will resort to clandestine (and costly) means to hide their operations from the police. Still others will restrict the circle of buyers with whom they are willing to deal to minimize the chances that a customer is a cop. Across the board, the costs of operation are higher, and at any given price, less of the product will be available. There is a reduction in supply, and the result is a higher price for the good.

This increase in price is, in a sense, exactly what the enforcement officials are after, for the consumers of sex, booze, and drugs behave according to the **law of demand:** The higher the price of a good, the lower the amount consumed. So the immediate impact of the enforcement efforts against sellers is to reduce the consumption of the illegal good. There are, however, some other effects.

VIOLENCE EMERGES

First, because the good in question is illegal, people who have a **comparative advantage** in conducting illegal activities will be attracted to the business of supplying (and perhaps demanding) the good. Some who have an existing criminal record may be relatively unconcerned about adding to it. Others may have developed skills in evading detection and prosecution while engaged in other criminal activities. Simply put, when an activity is made illegal, people who are good at being criminals are attracted to that activity.

Illegal contracts are usually not enforceable through legal channels. (Even if they were, few suppliers of illegal goods would be foolish enough to complain to the police about not being paid for their products.) Thus, buyers and sellers of illegal goods must frequently resort to private methods of contract enforcement, which often entails violence.[2]

---

2 Fundamentally, violence—such as involuntary incarceration—also plays a key role in the government's enforcement of legal contracts. We often do not think of it as violence, of course, because it is usually cushioned by constitutional safeguards and procedural rules.

Hence, people who are relatively good at violence are attracted to illegal activities and have greater **incentives** to employ their talents. This is one reason why the murder rate in America rose to record levels during Prohibition and then dropped sharply when liquor was again made legal. It also helps explain why the number of drug-related murders soared during the 1980s and why drive-by shootings became commonplace in many drug-infested cities. The Thompson submachine gun of the 1930s and the MAC-10 machine gun of the 1980s were just low-cost means of contract enforcement.

USAGE CHANGES

The attempts of law enforcement officials to drive sellers of illegal goods out of business have another effect. Based on recent U.S. whole-sale prices, $300,000 worth of pure heroin weighs less than ten pounds, while $300,000 worth of marijuana from Mexico weighs about three hundred pounds. As any drug smuggler can tell you, hiding ten pounds of contraband is a lot easier than hiding three hundred pounds. Thus, to avoid detection and prosecution, suppliers of the illegal good have an incentive to deal in the more valuable versions, which for drugs and booze mean the more potent versions. Bootleggers during Prohibition concentrated on hard liquor rather than on beer and wine. Even today, moonshine typically has roughly twice the alcohol content of legal hard liquor such as bourbon, scotch, or vodka. After narcotics became illegal in this country in 1914, importers switched from the milder opium to its more valuable and more potent derivative, heroin.

The move to the more potent versions of illegal commodities is enhanced by enforcement activities directed against users. Not only do users, like suppliers, find it easier (cheaper) to hide the more potent versions, but there is also a change in relative prices due to user penalties. Typically, the law has lower penalties for using an illegal substance than for distributing it. Within each category (use or sale), however, there is commonly the same penalty regardless of value per unit. For example, during Prohibition, a bottle of wine and a bottle of more expensive, more potent hard liquor were equally illegal. Today, the possession of one gram of heroin brings the same penalty, regardless of its purity. Given the physical quantities, there is a fixed cost (the legal penalty) associated with being caught, regardless of value per unit (and thus potency) of the substance. Hence, the structure of legal penalties raises the relative price of less potent versions, encouraging users to substitute more potent versions—heroin instead of opium, hashish instead of marijuana, and hard liquor instead of beer.

Penalties against users also encourage a change in the nature of usage. Before 1914, cocaine was legal in this country and was used openly as a mild stimulant, much as people today use caffeine. (Cocaine was even an ingredient in the original formulation of Coca-Cola.) This type of usage—small, regular doses over long time intervals—becomes relatively more expensive when the substance is made illegal. Extensive usage (small doses spread over time) is more likely to be detected by the authorities than intensive usage (a large dose consumed at once), simply because possession time is longer and the drug must be accessed more frequently. Thus, when a substance is made illegal, there is an incentive for consumers to switch toward more intensive usage. Rather than ingesting cocaine orally in the form of a highly diluted liquid solution, as was commonly done before 1914, people switched to snorting or injecting it. During Prohibition, people dispensed with cocktails before dinner each night; instead, on the less frequent occasions when they drank, they more often drank to get drunk. The same phenomenon is observed today. People under the age of twenty-one consume alcoholic beverages less frequently than people over the age of twenty-one. But when they do drink, they are more likely to drink to get drunk. Binge drinking becomes the norm.

INFORMATION COSTS RISE

Not surprisingly, the suppliers of illegal commodities are reluctant to advertise their wares openly; the police are as capable of reading billboards and watching television as potential customers are. Suppliers are also reluctant to establish easily recognized identities and regular places and hours of business because to do so raises the chance of being caught by the police. Information about the price and quality of products being sold goes underground, often with unfortunate effects for consumers.

With legal goods, consumers have several means of obtaining information. They can learn from friends, advertisements, and personal experience. When goods are legal, they can be trademarked for identification. The trademark cannot legally be copied, and the courts protect it. Given such easily identified brands, consumers can be made aware of the quality and price of each one. If their experience does not meet expectations, they can assure themselves of no further contact with the unsatisfactory product by never buying that brand again.

When a general class of products becomes illegal, there are fewer ways to obtain information. Brand names are no longer protected by law, so falsification of well-known brands ensues. When products do not meet expectations, it is more difficult (costly) for consumers to punish suppliers. Frequently, the result is degradation of and uncertainty about product quality. The consequences for consumers of the illegal goods are often unpleasant and sometimes fatal.

DANGEROUS SEX

Consider prostitution. In Nevada counties where prostitution is legal, the prostitutes are required to register with the local authorities, and they generally conduct their business in well-established bordellos. These establishments advertise openly and rely heavily on repeat business. Health officials test the prostitutes weekly for venereal disease and monthly for HIV (the virus that causes AIDS). Contrast this with other areas of the country, where prostitution is illegal. Suppliers are generally streetwalkers, because a fixed, physical location is too easy for the police to detect and raid. They change locations frequently to reduce harassment by police. Repeat business is reported to be minimal. Frequently, customers have never seen the prostitute before and never will again.

The difference in outcomes is striking. In Nevada, the spread of venereal disease by legal prostitutes is estimated to be almost nonexistent. To date, none of the registered prostitutes in Nevada has tested positive for HIV. By contrast, in some major cities outside of Nevada, the incidence of venereal disease among streetwalkers is estimated to be near 100 percent, while the incidence of HIV can reach the double digits. Due to the lack of reliable information in markets for illegal goods, customers frequently do not know exactly what they are getting. As a result, they sometimes get more than they bargained for.

DEADLY DRUGS AND BAD BOOZE

Consider alcohol and drugs. Today, alcoholic beverages are heavily advertised to establish their brand names and are carried by reputable dealers. Customers can readily punish suppliers for any deviation from the expected potency or quality by withdrawing their business, telling their friends, or even bringing a lawsuit. Similar circumstances prevailed before 1914 in this country for the hundreds of products containing opium or cocaine.

During Prohibition, consumers of alcohol often did not know exactly what they were buying or where to find the supplier the next day if they were dissatisfied. Fly-by-night operators sometimes adulterated liquor with far more lethal methyl alcohol. In tiny concentrations, this made watered-down booze taste like it had more kick, but in only slightly higher concentrations, the methyl alcohol blinded or even killed the unsuspecting consumer. Even in "reputable" speakeasies (those likely to be in business at the same location the next day), bottles bearing the labels of high-priced foreign whiskeys were refilled repeatedly with locally (and illegally) produced rotgut until their labels wore off.

The adulterated booze, combined with the incentive to consume intensively, was deadly. The death rate from acute alcohol poisoning (due to overdose) was more than thirty times higher than it is today. In 1927 alone, 12,000 people died from acute alcohol poisoning, and many thousands more were blinded or killed by contaminated booze.

During the 1990s, the use of prescription opioid painkillers (such as Oxycodone) began to rise, as doctors sought more effective means of relieving pain among an aging generation of baby boomers. Along with this came higher rates of prescription drug abuse. When a federal crackdown forced manufacturers of powerful painkillers to make them resistant to abuse, the abusers quickly switched to illegal but easy-to-obtain heroin and its much more powerful synthetic cousin, fentanyl (the drug that killed the pop star Prince).

Today cheap-to-make fentanyl is used as a cutting agent to heighten the effects of other illegal drugs, including heroin, and to increase the potency of counterfeit look-alikes of prescription medicines such as Percocet and Xanax. The problem is that fentanyl is fifty times more potent than heroin, and an amount as small as three grains of sugar can be lethal for an adult. Drug overdoses now kill about 48,000 people a year in the United States. About 19,000 of these are attributed to prescription painkillers, with another 11,000 tied to heroin. But fentanyl is so deadly and has become so widespread as an adulterant in illegal drugs that it may actually be responsible for many of the overdoses attributed to other drugs. Clearly, caveat emptor ("let the buyer beware") is a warning to be taken seriously if one is consuming an illegal product.

INFORMATION AND THE INTERNET

The importance of (the lack of) information in markets for illegal goods is highlighted by the growing role of the Internet in driving one of these markets—that for sexual services. Over the last twenty years, a number of Internet sites have evolved around the world on which prostitutes advertise the services and prices they offer. Customers can even post reviews, much as they might do on TripAdvisor for restaurants or hotels. Other sites enable suppliers to exchange information about their clients—not names, of course, but whether they are prone to violence or fail to pay for services rendered. There are even sites that enable buyer and seller to share verified results from sexual-health tests.

There is growing evidence that these sites have had salutary effects on both sides of the market. Suppliers have been able to move off the streets, because a public display of their bodies is no longer the only way to advertise. And because word about violent customers now spreads more rapidly, Internet-based suppliers seem to suffer less violence than their streetwalking counterparts. On the demand side, customers are much more likely to get what they hoped for, rather than what they wanted to avoid. And in some cases, buyer and seller have been able to eliminate the middleman—the madam or pimp who previously took a share of the fees.

Parallel developments have occurred in those states where marijuana has been made legal for medical purposes, and especially in the states where it is now lawful for all adults to consume. Customer reviews of various strains are available on the Internet, and suppliers advertise their wares as they would other goods. Product quality has risen, and the legal and physical risks facing both buyers and sellers have fallen sharply. Total consumption of marijuana in these locales has risen, but consumption among underage individuals has not—presumably because suppliers don't want to lose their licenses by making unlawful sales.

Success Is Limited

We noted at the beginning of this chapter that one of the effects of making a good illegal is to raise its price. One might well ask, "by how much?" During the early 1990s, the federal government was spending about $2 billion per year in its efforts to stop the importation of cocaine from Colombia. One study concluded that these efforts had hiked the price of cocaine by 4 percent relative to what it would have been, had the federal government done nothing to interdict cocaine imports. The study estimated that the cost of raising the price of cocaine an additional 2 percent would be $1 billion per year. More recently, Nobel Laureate Gary Becker and his colleagues have estimated that America's war on drugs costs at least $100 billion per year. And the results? The prices of heroin and cocaine are at record-low levels.

Several years ago, most states and the federal government began restricting sales of cold medicines containing pseudoephedrine, because that ingredient was widely used for making the illegal stimulant methamphetamine in home laboratories. The restrictions succeeded in reducing home production of "meth." They also led to a huge increase in imports of a far more potent version of meth from Mexico. Overall, it is estimated that neither consumption of nor addiction to methamphetamine was reduced by the restrictions. But overdoses from the drug rose sharply because of the greater purity of the imports. Moreover, the "shake-and-bake" method of domestic production that arose after the crackdown on cold medicines had an unintended and often fatal consequence. The mixing process often goes wrong, and when it does, the ensuing explosion causes horrific and sometimes fatal burns of the head and upper torso. Many emergency rooms and hospital burn centers were overwhelmed by these casualties.

Consider also the government's efforts to eliminate the consumption of alcohol during the 1920s and 1930s. They failed so badly that the Eighteenth Amendment, which put Prohibition in place, was the first (and so far the only) constitutional amendment ever to be repealed. As for prostitution, it is reputed to be "the oldest profession" and, by all accounts, continues to flourish today.

The government's inability to halt the consumption of sex, booze, or drugs does not mean that its efforts have failed. Indeed, the impact of these efforts is manifested in their consequences, ranging from overdose deaths to disease-ridden prostitutes. The message instead is that when the government attempts to prevent mutually beneficial exchange, even its best efforts are unlikely to meet with spectacular success.

DISCUSSION QUESTIONS

1. From an economic perspective, is it possible for laws restricting dangerous or destructive activity to be *too* strict? Explain. (*Hint:* Revisit Chapter 3.)

2. In recent years, about twenty states have passed so-called medical marijuana laws. Typically, these laws permit individuals to lawfully purchase marijuana from licensed stores, provided they have a letter from their doctor recommending its use. In a number of these states, the price of medical marijuana is observed to be higher than that of the pot sold illegally just down the street. Use the reasoning in this chapter to explain (i) why people would be willing to pay a higher price for the medical marijuana, and (ii) why it might be misleading to compare the observed price of the medical variety with the observed price of the illegal weed.

3. The federal government currently taxes alcohol on the basis of the 100-proof gallon. (Alcohol that is 100 proof is 50 percent pure ethyl alcohol; most hard liquor sold is 80 proof, or 40 percent ethyl alcohol, whereas wine is usually about 24 proof, and most beer is 6–10 proof.) How would alcohol consumption patterns change if the government taxed alcohol strictly on the basis of volume rather than also taking its potency into account?

4. During Prohibition, some speakeasy operators paid bribes to ensure that the police did not raid them. Would you expect the quality of the liquor served in such speakeasies to be higher or lower than in those that did not pay bribes? Would you expect to find differences (e.g., in income levels) between the customers patronizing the two types of speakeasies?

5. The markets for prostitution in Nevada and New Jersey have two important differences: (i) prostitutes in New Jersey face higher costs because of government efforts to prosecute them and (ii) customers in New Jersey face higher risks of contracting diseases from prostitutes because the illegal nature of the business makes reliable information about product quality much more costly to obtain. Given these facts, in which state would you expect the price of prostitution services to be higher? Which state would have the higher amount of services consumed (adjusted for population differences)? Explain your answer.

6. According to the Surgeon General of the United States, nicotine is the most addictive drug known to humanity, and cigarette smoking kills perhaps 300,000–400,000 people per year in the United States. Why then isn't tobacco illegal in America?

CHAPTER 7

The Economics
of Obesity

The data are hard to deny. The World Health Organization estimates that as many as 1.3 billion adults are overweight, while an additional 600 million are **clinically obese**. In the United States, the numbers are even more alarming: Two-thirds of adults are either overweight or obese, and half of those who are obese suffer from chronic health conditions, such as diabetes and high blood pressure. The latest study by the Global BMI Mortality Collaboration confirms that being overweight or obese is also associated with an increase in "all-cause mortality." In other words, if you have a **body mass index (BMI)** above 25, you have a higher chance of premature death.[1]

How Did We Get Here?

For most of humankind's history, malnutrition has been a major cause of death—people got too little to eat, not too much. In the first sixty years of the twentieth century, however, as incomes rose and the price of food declined, weights began to rise. In America, the average adult male put on about sixteen pounds, with the average female gaining slightly less. That initial weight gain was considered a benefit, because at the beginning of the twentieth century, many Americans were malnourished. But in the following sixty years up to the present day, the average

---

1 To determine your personal BMI score, multiply 703 by your weight in pounds and then divide that figure by the square of your height in inches. BMI scores between 25 and 30 indicate that a person is overweight and a BMI score of more than 30 indicates obesity.

male has put on almost thirty additional pounds and the average female has added almost twenty-five pounds. That type of dramatic weight gain has never been observed before in the history of any nation. There are many explanations for this alarming health phenomenon. Some say it's too much junk food, while others say it's a lack of knowledge of proper nutrition or too much time sitting around binge-watching *Game of Thrones*.

CAN'T WE BLAME OUR SEDENTARY LIFESTYLES?

In addition to junk food, lack of knowledge about nutrition, and too much TV time, some argue that Americans have gained weight because of a change in how we work. In essence, America went from a society in which we worked with our hands and bodies to one in which we simply sit at a desk and, at best, type on a computer keyboard or touch the keys on a smartphone or tablet device.[2]

It is indeed true that physical activity in the United States has declined, particularly in the world of work, as Americans left jobs in agriculture and manufacturing to earn more using brains rather than brawn. Americans also spend less time physically doing household chores. And as a substitute for work and chores, they are looking at screens. But these trends started well before the 1970s, so sedentary lifestyles cannot be the sole explanation of why Americans have gained so much weight since 1970. To understand the weight-gain phenomenon of recent years, we have to look at the root cause—increased caloric intake.

IT'S ALL ABOUT CALORIES

At the beginning of the 1970s, the average daily calories consumed by those living in the United States was about 2,000. Since then, the U.S. Department of Agriculture estimates that average calories consumed increased by 25 percent to more than 2,500 calories per day. Moreover, we didn't do this by adding protein, fruits, and vegetables. Instead, we piled on more oils and fats in processed foods, flour, cereals, and breads. These categories jumped from 37 percent of our diet in 1970

---

2 As voice recognition software and artificial intelligence continue to improve, perhaps soon the only muscles used at work will be those that control speech.

to 46 percent today. The average American now consumes an extra 550 calories of added fats, oils, and sugars every day of every year, which includes cheese instead of milk and plenty of refined grains rather than whole grains. The result of the combination of more calories and more food types that are easily converted to fat is inevitable—higher average weights.

CHEAP FOOD + LAW OF DEMAND = WEIGHT GAIN

Why are we chowing down all these extra (and mostly "empty") calories? Part of the answer is innovation. The tractor replaced horses and mules on American farms, and improved pesticides, fertilizers, and genetically modified plants (see Chapter 21) have all increased crop yields and pushed down the price of food. As we know from the **law of demand,** as an item gets cheaper, people want to consume more of it.

Federal government programs that subsidize the production of corn, wheat, rice, soybeans, and other crops have amplified this process by increasing the **supply** of food. As a consequence, because these subsidized crops are cheaper than they would be otherwise, they end up being converted into refined grains and high-calorie juices, as well as soft drinks loaded with corn syrup sweeteners. Moreover, the cheap corn is fed to livestock, which then yield high-fat meat.

Diets full of subsidized food tend to contain few fruits and vegetables and an abundance of carbohydrates and high-fat meats. Because exposure to these unhealthful foods begins in childhood, people develop poor eating habits that last a lifetime, and have lifetime consequences. When comparing Americans who eat the greatest amount of subsidized food with those who eat the least, the former group has a 37 percent higher risk of being obese and a 41 percent greater risk of having elevated belly fat. On both counts—obesity and excess belly fat—these individuals are at increased risk of health problems and premature death.

It is also worth noting that people living in poverty tend to be more sensitive to lower prices, so they end up eating relatively more of the subsidized (unhealthful) foods. Those with less education also eat more of these foods, because they are less likely to be aware of the adverse health consequences. Both the poor and the poorly educated tend to have worse than average health during their lives, and to have shorter than average lifespans. There are many causes for poor health and premature death, but unhealthful eating is surely one of them.

The (Full) Price Matters

We have already noted that when price goes down, the quantity demanded goes up, and that the market price of food (**inflation corrected,** of course) has been falling. But there is another concept that is relevant here: the **full price** of food. This includes both the market price and the value of the time that goes into preparing and consuming it—valuable time that could have been spent doing something else.

In the 1960s and before, food was prepared in the home by family members and eaten there. Today, we can buy prepared, pre-packaged food that we pop in the microwave. We can go to a drive-thru window in a fast food restaurant on our way to school, work, or home. In other words, the **time cost** of eating has, for those who want a quick meal, been reduced from hours to minutes. This has played a key role in reducing the full price of food in the modern era.

These developments have been spurred by two major economic changes, which began in the 1950s and accelerated in the 1970s. First, the automobile became the primary mode of transportation in the United States, making it cheap and easy to go out to eat, and especially to enjoy fast food. Second, the **labor force participation rate** of women has more than doubled, and along with this, women have moved out of traditional low-paying jobs (such as teaching) and into high-paying professions once dominated by males, including medicine, law, and the upper levels of management. Men and women have thus looked to timesaving ways to put food on the table, and the food industry has responded accordingly with more frozen, already-prepared, or microwavable meal alternatives.

The combination of lower market prices for food and lower time costs of preparing and eating it has yielded a huge reduction in the **full cost** of food. This has provided many benefits for consumers, but it has also led them to pack on the pounds.

Menu Mandates—A Solution for Supersizing?

In the face of growing numbers of overweight and obese Americans, some people have argued that the problem can be reduced by letting consumers know the exact calorie count of everything they are putting in their mouths. That thought was the motivation behind Section 4205 of the Patient Protection and Affordable Care Act of 2010 (see Chapter 19). This component of the Affordable Care Act (ACA) went beyond the established nutritional labeling for packaged and canned products that we see in our supermarkets. It did so by mandating that standard menu items in restaurants, vending machines, and elsewhere contain nutritional labeling that reveals calorie contents.

Nationwide, Section 4205 affects more than 300,000 establishments (and their subsidiaries). These include chain restaurants, movie theaters, vending machines, and salad and hot bars in grocery stores. Because of this federal law, when we go to Starbucks, for instance, every mouthwatering pastry has a calorie-content label.

Before this federal law, some cities, including New York City, had already instituted so-called **menu mandates** such as are included in the ACA. Back in 2008, for example, New York City administrators argued that such mandates would reduce average weights by 7.5 pounds, by cutting 106 calories out of the average fast-food transaction. Did New Yorkers' weights really drop because of the city's menu mandates? Not according to a wide-ranging study from the Behavioral Risk Factor Surveillance System, which examined thirty cities with mandates, including New York City. Immediately after the passage of each menu mandate, consumers did seem to take note and cut back on their calories, especially among the young and the less educated. Within short order, however, people stopped paying attention and calorie counts went back up. For all groups studied, the mandates had an impact on average weight of approximately . . . *zero*. There is little reason to believe that the ACA mandates will fare any better.

THE ROLE OF SMOKING

There is one final point to our story, which illustrates that even the best of intentions sometimes yields adverse unintended consequences. Over the same period that Americans have been packing on the pounds, the taxes on cigarettes have risen sharply, even while the number of places where it is lawful to smoke has shrunk significantly. On both counts, the full cost of smoking (price per pack, plus the hassle) has been rising, and one consequence is that smoking has declined in the United States. It is well known that people have a tendency to eat more when they stop smoking, and this very fact seems to be showing up in the national statistics on excess poundage.

Where the full costs of smoking have risen the greatest, so too has the incidence of obesity. In effect, people are being induced to substitute eating for smoking. Despite the adverse health effects of the resulting weight gains, the *net* health trade-offs here are likely positive, given the highly lethal effects of smoking. Still, this development reminds us that although people's behavior can easily be understood by examining the incentives they face, sometimes it is difficult to determine ahead of time what the full range of incentives will be.

DISCUSSION QUESTIONS

1. Obesity and smoking are both linked to numerous adverse health consequences, including heart disease, cancer, and strokes, among others. The Affordable Care Act permits health insurance companies to charge people higher premiums if they smoke or are obese. But the law forbids the companies from charging higher premiums or denying coverage to people who have suffered strokes or have heart disease or cancer. Can you suggest a rational argument why the law might be structured this way?

2. Who benefits the most from menu mandates—caloric labeling of food in restaurants and vending machines—and why? Are there any costs associated with menu mandates? If so, what are they?

3. If you compare the actual physical size of a dress in 1950 that was labeled size 6 with a dress labeled size 6 today, you will notice a difference. What do you think that difference is? Why have dress manufacturers changed their size-labeling system? Similarly, if you look at the sizes of men's clothes in stores catering to Millennials, as opposed to those catering to Baby Boomers, you will find that an item labeled "Large" means something very different. Is the lack of uniform sizing across stores and over time a form of customer deception? Could you argue (as an economist, of course) that clothing manufacturers should not be allowed to change their size-labeling system to fit the circumstances? Explain.

4. We all undertake risks throughout our lives. When we pass a car on a two-lane highway, we implicitly know that we are increasing the risk of an auto accident, yet we do it anyway. When we drive faster at any time while driving, more often than not, we implicitly increase the risk of suffering greater bodily harm if an accident occurs. When our actions cause us to put on pounds, we are increasing our risk of numerous illnesses and perhaps even premature death. Is there a difference between incurring increased risk by our voluntary driving behavior and incurring increased risk by our voluntary eating and physical activities? Answer this same question with respect to both smoking and excessive alcoholic drinking.

5. The U.S. Department of Agriculture publishes nutritional guidelines, and the Affordable Care Act mandates calorie counts on menus. Yet the federal government also subsidizes the production of foods that end up causing Americans to violate those guidelines and consume calories that contribute to the national obesity epidemic. How do you explain this seeming inconsistency? (Hint: Who benefits from agricultural subsidies and how might they react to decreases in such subsidies?)

6. The inflation- and quality-corrected prices of just about every technological device have fallen dramatically. The prices have gone down and the quality has gone up for flat-screen TVs, smartphones, tablets, and gaming computers, among others. Few will argue that we are worse off because of falling prices of technological goods. Why do we not use the same reasoning when we discuss the large decline in the price of food?

CHAPTER 8

Kidneys for Sale

This year, about 8,000 Americans will die waiting for an organ transplant. They will not die because physicians are unable to transplant organs or because their health insurance does not cover the cost of the transplant. They will die because since 1984, it has been against federal law to pay for human organs.[1] It is lawful to pay a man for his sperm, a woman for her eggs, and members of either gender for their blood. It is even lawful to donate an organ or to receive one as a gift. And it is certainly legal to pay the surgeons who perform the transplants. It is even lawful for hospitals to make a profit on organ transplants performed in their operating rooms. But it is against the law for you to sell a cornea, a kidney, or a lobe of your liver. It is even unlawful for your loved ones to be paid for any organs harvested after your death. Thus 8,000 people die every year, waiting in vain for someone to donate an organ to them.

AN OVERVIEW OF ORGAN TRANSPLANTS

The transplantation of human body parts is not new. The first cornea was successfully transplanted in Austria in 1905. The first successful kidney transplant (between identical twins) was conducted in Boston in 1954. Since then, successful transplants of the pancreas, liver, intestine, heart, lung, hand, and even face have been performed. Indeed, there are now thirty-seven different organs and types of human tissues that can be

---

1 Rep. Al Gore (D., Tenn.) introduced this legislation. He subsequently was elected vice president of the United States (1993–2001).

transplanted. None of this is cheap. In the United States, a kidney transplant costs about $260,000 on average, a liver transplant runs $580,000, and a heart transplant costs an average of $1,000,000. None of these figures include payment for the organ itself because such payments are illegal in the United States and in most other countries.

These astronomical sums are obviously out of the reach of most people. In fact, however, transplants done in the United States are generally not paid for directly by the recipients. For a person under the age of 65 with health insurance, private insurance pays for the transplant. For anyone 65 or older, the federal Medicare system pays for the transplant. For people under 65 with neither private insurance nor the wealth to pay by themselves, transplants are paid for by the Medicaid system, which is financed jointly by the federal government and the states.

There are services that arrange for international transplants—performed, for example, in India or China—at prices about one-half the level available in the United States. People who avail themselves of such transplants are often referred to as "transplant tourists." Neither private insurance plans nor Medicare or Medicaid will pay for international transplants, which are generally chosen only by relatively affluent people who are unwilling to wait—or to die waiting.

THE CASE OF KIDNEYS

Now, to begin our inquiry into the economics of organ transplants, let's consider the case of kidneys. We start here because the technical features of the transplant process have become relatively routine and because each of us is born with two kidneys but can manage quite well with only one. In fact, thanks to the technique known as dialysis, humans can actually survive for several years without functioning kidneys. In 2015, over 100,000 people were awaiting kidney transplants in the United States. In the same year, 11,000 Americans received transplants from deceased strangers. Another 6,000 received a transplant from a living donor (recall that "extra" kidney we each have), usually a close friend or relative. Tragically, more than 8,000 of the people waiting for a kidney either died or were dropped from the list because they had become too sick to qualify for a transplant. Another 4,000 suffered the same fate waiting for a liver, heart, lung, or other critical organ.

Could they be saved if it were as lawful to pay for kidneys as it is to pay for the surgeons who transplant them? Or would a market for kidneys ultimately become a black market, relying on "donated" organs removed from unwilling victims by unscrupulous brokers motivated by cash rather than kindness? This is precisely the nexus of the debate over whether we should permit people (or the relatives of just-deceased donors) to be remunerated for lifesaving organ donations.

First things first: Surely we cannot object to a market for organs because the act of donating a kidney or the lobe of a liver is potentially hazardous to the donor. After all, we currently permit people to undergo such risks under the current system with *no* monetary compensation. If it is safe enough to allow friends or family to donate without payment, why is it too risky for someone to give up a kidney or part of her liver in return for money?

The Case of Iran

There are, of course, many other contentious issues. To start exploring them, let's look first at a nation where it *is* legal to pay people for human organs: Iran, which just happens to have the highest living-donor rate in the world, at twenty-three donations per million people. Monetary compensation for organs in Iran has been lawful since 1988, and in the ensuing decade, Iran eliminated the *entire* backlog of kidney transplant patients, something no other nation has achieved.

Under the Iranian system, a person awaiting a kidney must first seek a suitable, willing donor in his or her family. If none is forthcoming, the person must wait up to six months for a suitable deceased donor. At this point, the potential recipient can apply to the national transplant association for a kidney from a willing donor who is paid for the kidney. The donor receives from the government $1350 plus a year of fully paid health insurance and a payment of $4,000–$5,000 from the recipient (or a charity, if the recipient is poor). There are still purely altruistic donors in Iran, as well as cadaveric donations from the recently deceased. But it is the payment for organs that has permitted essentially all who seek kidney donations in Iran to get them, and the Iranian system has done so *without* leading to "back alley" donations or to people who are unable to afford a transplant because of the high cost of the organs themselves. Meanwhile, the system has saved the lives of many thousands of Iranians.[2]

---

2 Late in 2016, New Zealand decided to allow payments to live donors of kidneys, although the compensation is limited to any loss in wages suffered due to the donation. (Donating a kidney is a major operation and recovery time can be significant.) As yet, there are not enough data to determine whether the new system has been beneficial.

The Fear of Involuntary Donations

Many people worry about a system of payment for human transplants because of the possibility that it would yield *involuntary* donors. That is, if there is a market for organs, some unscrupulous brokers might be tempted by profits to knock people over the head and harvest their organs for sale at the highest price. Yet it is generally agreed that the Iranian system has worked for almost thirty years without a hint of any such activities. Perhaps this should not be too surprising, given the medical techniques developed to ensure that the tissue match between organ and recipient is close enough to make transplants feasible. These and other DNA tests can now quickly ascertain with substantial certainty that "organ A" came from voluntary "donor A" rather than from involuntary "donor B."

Indeed, apart from gruesome works of fiction, most of the horror stories about the hazards of allowing markets for human organs are stories about behavior caused by the *lack* of a market for organs. In China, for example, many transplant tourists have received organs taken from the bodies of the thousands of prisoners who are executed there every year. China insists that prisoners' organs are used only with their "consent," a claim that many human rights groups dispute. Of course, on one point all agree: There have been no payments to the prisoners or their surviving relatives. The organs are simply taken. China has announced that it will halt prisoner transplants. But because more than *half* of all transplants in China have used organs from prisoners, many observers are skeptical.

In both the United States and Britain, there have been highly publicized cases of what amount to "body snatching"—removal of organs and other body parts from the recently deceased. Some of these cases involved body parts used in research, while other body parts were intended for sale at a profit. In each of these cases, removal was done without the prior consent of the deceased or the postmortem consent of relatives. But this amounts to theft. It is singularly horrifying, but we must remember that it is theft. Consider another form of stealing: Every year many thousands of senior citizens are defrauded of their hard-earned retirement funds by unscrupulous individuals who masquerade as "financial advisers." Should we make it illegal for anyone to pay for investment advice—or should we devote our efforts to prosecuting and incarcerating the perpetrators of such crimes?

In Pakistan and the Philippines, there were small-scale markets for transplant organs until recently, although Pakistan has now banned the trade in human organs, and transplants for non-Filipinos have been outlawed in their nation. In both countries, there were anecdotes of donors who sold kidneys for $2,000–$3,000 (about a year's worth of per capita income in either nation), but who later came to regret the transaction because of adverse long-term health effects. This would be a potential issue even with unpaid donors, and in any nation, such as the United States, donors in a market for organs would surely receive at least as much medical and psychological counseling as volunteer donors receive now. In Iran, where payments are permitted, long-term health outcomes for donors are reported to be at least as good as outcomes for the rest of the population.

The Costs and Benefits of Paying for Organs

Now, what about the expense of allowing payments for donated organs? Would this break the budgets of Medicare or Medicaid or empty the coffers of the private insurance companies that pay for the bulk of transplants? In the case of kidneys, we have enough information from elsewhere to say the answer is probably not, although the outcomes may be very different for private and public insurers. In Iran, where per capita income is about $12,000 per year, payments to donors smaller than this amount have been sufficient to clear the market for kidneys. In Pakistan and the Philippines, payments equivalent to a year's worth of per capita income were enough to support a substantial transplant tourist market in both countries.

At more than $50,000 per year, average per capita income in the United States is clearly much higher than in any of these nations, suggesting that payments for kidneys would also have to be much larger to induce a substantial increase in the number of donations. Nevertheless, an extensive cost-benefit analysis of paying for kidney donation finds not only benefits for donors and recipients but also *decreases* in the total medical costs associated with kidney disease.

Donors and their families clearly would gain monetary wealth from a payments system. And this gain would be net of follow-up medical costs for living donors, which would be paid for by the government under the system. Recipients of organs would benefit from longer lives, because life expectancy on dialysis is lower than life expectancy with a donor organ. Quality of life would also be much greater for recipients, because they would no longer be connected to dialysis machines for up to twenty-four hours a week.

It is true that allowing payments for human organs would almost surely increase the number of transplants each year—indeed, this is the very point. Payments would bring forth more organs, and this would in turn reduce deaths among people waiting for transplants. One might think that the added transplants would place a huge financial burden on taxpayers and insurance companies. In fact, taxpayers now save money every time a kidney transplant takes place, because dialysis costs are so high. These savings would increase with donor payments, because people would spend far less time on dialysis. Private insurance companies would fare less well, because they tend to pay a larger proportion of organ transplant costs (and a smaller proportion of dialysis costs) than do taxpayers. Overall, the savings to taxpayers exceed the extra private insurer costs—but that might not be much consolation to the owners of the insurance companies.

Now, paying for organs would cause a reduction in the number of altruistic donations. But the analysis just presented takes this fully into account by assuming payment for *all* donations, including those from both living and deceased individuals. When we contemplate the fact that thousands of people would have their lives extended and improved, it is difficult to understand why anyone would oppose paying for organ donations.

EXPLOITATION OF THE DISADVANTAGED?

Some observers have argued that despite the seeming advantages of an organ payment system, there is one compelling reason for continuing the prohibition on payments. These observers argue that a payment system would exploit poor and disadvantaged individuals. The reasoning here is that economically disadvantaged individuals would be most likely to donate organs in return for compensation. Because an organ donation entails both immediate and future elevated medical risks for the donor, it is claimed that the disadvantaged could actually be made worse off by allowing payments for their organs.

It is difficult to put much credence in this argument. After all, the payments would be strictly voluntary, and the organ donation process already involves intensive counseling to ensure that potential donors understand the risks. Moreover, donors generally receive extensive follow-up care at no cost to themselves. Under the current system of altruistic donations, we allow people to take these risks with *no* compensation; why is it too risky to permit payments? The reasoning seems much like saying that the economically disadvantaged should be prevented from working as police or fire fighters, because these workers are paid for accepting elevated on-the-job risks.

Indeed, the exploitation claim really has things exactly *backwards*. The present system, in which donor payments are legally prohibited, has resulted in a huge shortage of transplant kidneys that seriously harms especially the disadvantaged. These individuals are considerably over-represented on organ waiting lists because they have much higher rates of end-stage kidney disease. Compensation for donors would greatly increase the availability of transplant kidneys, making all transplant candidates, especially the disadvantaged, much better off.

WHO IS REALLY BEING CALLOUS?

All these calculations seem a callous way to view a human life. By the standards of medical care today, however, allowing payments for human organs is almost surely a safe and remarkably cheap way to alleviate needless suffering and save thousands of lives every year. Once this is clear, aren't the truly callous people those who would deprive human beings of that opportunity?

DISCUSSION QUESTIONS

1. The financial burden of organ transplants tends to be borne more heavily by private insurance companies, while the financial burden of dialysis is borne more heavily by the taxpayer (through funding for Medicare and Medicaid). Instituting payments for kidney donors would likely save each taxpayer $100 per year or less (due to reduced dialysis), but could cost major health insurers hundreds of millions of dollars each (due to increased transplants). On balance, total costs would fall. Even so, is it possible that private insurers might be able to block the introduction of payments for kidney donors? (*Hint:* How does the concentration of costs among a few insurers affect their willingness to oppose payments? Compare this to the incentives of taxpayers, who would each save only a small amount if we went to a payment system.)

2. Per capita income varies substantially across the country. If there were a free market in which payment for kidneys was permitted within the United States, would you expect there to be different prices in different parts of the country? In which areas of the country would you expect the most organs to be offered for donation? Keeping in mind that insurance, either private or public, pays for essentially all transplants, would these same areas also be the chief "exporting" areas? Explain.

3. Why might the owners of the private insurance companies that pay for most organ transplants (but don't pay for most dialysis) be in

favor of a system that prohibits paying for a donated organ? Should the taxpayers of the United States, who ultimately cover the cost of Medicare and Medicaid transplants, but also pay for most dialysis costs, similarly be opposed to paying for donated organs?

4. If payment for organs drives up the financial costs of transplants compared to the costs of dialysis, is it possible that private insurance companies, and even Medicare and Medicaid, might respond by changing their standards for transplants? Could the standards change in different directions (tighter for one, looser for the other)? If the standards were to change, who would gain and who would lose compared to the current system?

5. The average waiting time on transplant lists is about five years for kidneys (although this is expected to rise sharply due to the rising incidence of diabetes, a major cause of kidney damage). Many of these people waiting must undergo dialysis, at a cost of $90,000 per year for the dialysis, plus another $30,000 per year for related medical expenses. These costs are paid for by in part by private insurance, but mostly by Medicare or Medicaid. Suppose that if payment for organs were permitted, the transplant waiting time was shortened by four years, and that for the average patient, the result was forty-eight months less on dialysis. At what price for a kidney would a system of paying for organs be a "break-even" proposition for insurers? Show all calculations and explain your reasoning.

6. The United States currently has an "opt-in" system for organ donations from the deceased: People must explicitly choose postmortem donation ahead of time (as when they obtain their driver's licenses). Many other nations have "opt-out" systems: A desire to donate postmortem is presumed to exist unless an individual explicitly chooses ahead of time *not* to permit donation. How—if at all—would a shift to an opt-out system likely change the supply of cadaveric (postmortem) donations?

CHAPTER 9

Are We Running Out of Water?

If you believe the headlines, humans are about to die of thirst. A few examples should be enough to convince you:

"A World of Thirst" (*U.S. News & World Report*)

"Water Shortages May Lead to War" (*Financial Times*)

"Drying Up" (*The Economist*)

"Water Shortages Could Leave World in Dire Straits" (*USA Today*)

The world, it seems, is running out of water.

How can this be true? After all, about 71 percent of the earth's surface is covered with water. Lake Michigan alone contains twice as much water as the world's population uses in a year. Even more to the point, the earth is a closed system. Using water does not destroy water. Whether we drink it, flush it, irrigate with it, or even let it evaporate, it comes back to us eventually, just as pure as the raindrops of a spring shower. In fact, every three weeks, enough rain falls to satisfy the water uses of the entire world's population for a year. So what, exactly, is the problem?

THE ULTIMATE RENEWABLE RESOURCE

Water is the ultimate renewable resource: The act of using it begins the process that returns it to us. But—and this is the crux of the matter—water is also *scarce*. That is, having the amount of clean water we want, where we want it, and when we want it there is not free. We must sacrifice other resources to accomplish this. Moreover, as the level of economic activity grows, the demand for water grows, and so the costs of consuming water also grow.

In this sense, water is no different from any other **scarce good.** If we want more of it, we must sacrifice more of other things to achieve that goal. What makes water seem different is that unlike, say, broccoli, if we do entirely without it, disastrous things happen in a relatively short period of time. If water becomes sufficiently scarce, people may start doing some pretty unpleasant things to each other to ensure that they, rather than their neighbors or enemies, are the ones who end up with it. Before we see if this is really something we should worry about, we had better start by learning a little more about water.

WATER, WATER EVERYWHERE

Of the enormous amount of water on the earth's surface, about 97.2 percent is ocean water, which is too saline under normal circumstances to drink or use for irrigation. Another 2.15 percent is polar ice, which is certainly not a very convenient source. Of the remaining 0.65 percent, about 0.62 percent is underground in aquifers and similar geological structures. This groundwater takes hundreds of years to recharge and so is not really a sustainable source of freshwater over the relevant time span. That leaves us with rain.

Fortunately, it rains a lot, and despite the headlines, on a *worldwide* basis, the amount of rainfall doesn't vary much from year to year. About two-thirds of the rain falls on the world's oceans, where almost no one lives. Even so, and even taking into account evaporation and the fact that much of the rain over land quickly runs off into the oceans before it can be captured, there is still a lot of usable rainfall every year. Indeed, there is enough to yield 5,700 liters per person every day—about six times as much as the average person actually consumes in all uses.

Of course, Mother Nature is not particularly evenhanded in the distribution of this usable rainfall. For example, China gets only 5 percent of it, despite having 20 percent of the world's population. Brazil, Canada, and Russia, which together contain 6 percent of the world's population, receive 29 percent of the usable rainfall. Although the United States does pretty well on average, picking up 5 percent of the rain and having about 5 percent of the world's population, there are plenty of differences within our borders. Massive amounts of rain fall in southeastern Alaska and on the mountain slopes of Hawaii, while very little falls in Southern California. But the fact that people routinely choose to locate themselves in places where it does not rain highlights one of the fundamental points of this chapter: Water is an **economic good,** and the distribution and consumption of water are fundamentally economic problems, ones that can be solved in markets, just as other economic problems (such as the provision of food, shelter, and clothing) are solved in markets. To focus clearly on this point, let's examine some of the myths that have grown up around water in recent years:

Myth 1: The planet is drying up. As we have suggested earlier, there is nothing to worry about here. The cheapest (and completely sustainable) source of clean freshwater is rainfall, and roughly 113,000 cubic kilometers (3 quadrillion gallons) of the stuff falls every year on land areas around the world, year in and year out. Although small amounts of this are temporarily stored in plants and animals while they are alive, all of it eventually recharges groundwater or evaporates, forms clouds, and precipitates—all 113,000 cubic kilometers, year after year. Sometimes, more is in Brazil and less in Sudan, and sometimes more of it inconveniently runs off in floods. Nevertheless, because the earth is a closed system, all of that water stays with us.

Myth 2: We can save water by flushing less and using less in agriculture. Remember the closed system? That applies to toilets and alfalfa, too. Flushing the toilet does not send the water to the moon. It just sends it through the sewer system to a water treatment plant and eventually into aquifers under the ground or back down on our heads in the form of raindrops. So-called low-flow toilets (and shower-heads) have no effect on the amount of water in existence. (Because they may slightly reduce the amount of water running through water and sewer systems, they may conserve a bit on the amount of other resources used in these systems. There are, however, offsets. Such devices are routinely more costly to produce than regular toilets or showerheads, and they occupy people's time—because of double flushes and longer showers. On balance, besides not "saving" water, there is thus no evidence that such devices conserve resources at all.)

Even agriculture, notorious for consuming an enormous amount of water around the world, does not destroy the stuff. Most of the water used in agriculture evaporates or runs off into rivers or soaks into underground aquifers. A small amount is temporarily stored in the crops, but this, soon enough, is consumed by animals or humans and simply returns to the same system that delivers 113,000 cubic kilometers of water onto our heads every year. There is no doubt this use of water in agriculture is costly because it could be used elsewhere. Moreover, agricultural use of water is generally subsidized by taxpayers. Making farmers pay full market value for water would reduce agricultural use and raise our collective wealth by improving the allocation of resources, but it would not alter the amount of water available.

Having said this, agricultural use of water does present two important economic issues. First, as we just noted, government policies around the world routinely cause water for agriculture to be heavily subsidized. Farmers often pay as little as $10 to $20 per acre-foot (about 325,000 gallons) for water that costs anywhere from $500 to $1,000 per acre-foot to provide to them. Because of this huge subsidy, farmers are no doubt richer, but the losses to society are much greater, meaning that our overall wealth is lower. (For an explanation of why we get such subsidies despite this, see Chapter 27.)

Second, we not only subsidize water use for agriculture, but also routinely forbid farmers to sell or lease their water to other users, especially nonagricultural users. This is a particular problem in the relatively arid American West, where farmers effectively own most of the rights to surface and groundwater but must "use it or lose it"—if they don't put it to beneficial use on their crops, they lose their rights to it. Often this water would be much more productively "used" if it were left in the streams to help support the spawning and other essential life activities of downstream species, such as trout or salmon. Laws are slowly changing to recognize environmental uses as being "beneficial" uses, but existing restrictions on the use of water still yield lower overall wealth for us.

Myth 3: Water is different from other goods. Many people seem to think that because it is essential to life, water is somehow different from other goods—or at least that it should be treated differently in some very specific ways. Let's first get rid of the notion that water doesn't obey the laws of demand and supply. In fact, although the demand for water in some uses is relatively **inelastic,** consumption of water in *all* uses responds as predicted by the **law of demand**—when the price of water goes up, people use less of it. In fact, the demand for water behaves very much like the demand for gasoline. A 10 percent rise in the price of either good induces consumers to use about 3 to 6 percent less of the good in question. Thus, although the demand for water (or for gasoline) is relatively inelastic, there is no doubt that people change their consumption patterns when price changes.

Similarly, although getting water from where it is to where people would like it to be is costly, the **law of supply** still holds true—when the price of water rises, suppliers of water provide more of it to consumers. Sometimes this process is as simple as diverting a stream or capturing rainfall. Sometimes it is as complicated as using reverse osmosis to convert seawater into freshwater. Nevertheless, even if the production technique is as esoteric as recycling urine into fresh, drinkable water (as is done on the International Space Station), the fact remains that when water becomes more valuable, people are incredibly ingenious in finding ways to make sure it is available.

Myth 4: Price controls on water protect low-income consumers. Some people claim that water should *not* be treated like other goods, specifically arguing that both the price of water received by suppliers and the price paid by consumers should be kept down by government decree. This, it is said, will protect people, especially those who are poor, from high water prices and will prevent suppliers from earning "excessive" profits. After all, some 1.1 billion people around the world currently do not have ready access to clean water, which makes an inviting target for anyone who might become a monopoly supplier to substantial numbers of these people.

It is true that government can reduce the profits of the suppliers of water (or anything else) by limiting the prices they charge. In reality, however, this does not protect consumers, particularly not the poorest consumers. Price controls on water *reduce* the amount supplied and, especially for the poor, generally make consumers worse off. They end up with less water than if prices were allowed to reach equilibrium levels, and they are forced to undergo nonprice rationing schemes (ranging from limited hours of service to no clean water at all). In fact, if we examine places around the world where the poor have little or no access to clean water, we find that government efforts to supposedly "protect" people from water suppliers are in fact a key reason for this lack of access.

In Brazil, for example, government limits on private water rates forced a major international water project company to cease operations there, reducing the supply of clean water. In India, the widespread insistence by many local governments that water be provided free of charge has effectively stalled most efforts to improve water distribution in that country. In China, government price controls have discouraged water utilities from developing new water supplies and from upgrading water distribution systems. As we see in detail in Chapters 8 and 10, government controls on prices make goods *more* scarce, not less, and it is generally the disadvantaged members of society who suffer the most as a result.

Myth 5: The ocean is too salty to drink. As a practical matter, prolonged consumption of salt water by species not specifically adapted for it is highly deleterious. But the technology for desalination of seawater is advancing rapidly and the cost of desalination is falling just as rapidly—more than 95 percent over the past twenty years. In relatively arid parts of the earth (including Southern California), desalination has become price-competitive with other sources of supply, and large-scale desalination plants are in operation around the world.

The process yields highly concentrated brine as a by-product. To avoid damage to ocean species sensitive to excess salinity, this brine must be handled carefully (diluted or dispersed widely) when it is returned to the sea. Nevertheless, this is simply a matter of routine care. Moreover, if local conditions make wide dispersal impractical or expensive, the brine can be evaporated, and the resulting solid materials then either used or disposed of in ordinary landfills. The upshot is that with continued technological progress in desalination, water from the ocean will likely become cheaper than collecting rainfall in large portions of the world. Far from running out of water, people everywhere will then find themselves able to secure it as easily as, well, turning on the tap.

Discussion Questions

1. How much water do people "need"? Is your answer the same if *you* have to pay *their* water bills?

2. Evaluate the following: "Although taxpayers foot the bill for federal water sold to farmers at subsidized prices, they also eat the crops grown with that water. Because the crops are cheaper due to the subsidized water, taxpayers get back exactly what they put in, and so there is no waste from having subsidized water for farmers." Would you give the author of this quote an A or an F in economics? Explain.

3. During the droughts that periodically plague California, farmers in that state are able to purchase subsidized water to irrigate their crops, while at the same time many California homeowners have to pay large fines if they water their lawns. Can you suggest an explanation for this difference in the treatment of two different groups of citizens in the state of California?

4. If allocating water through nonprice measures generally harms society, can you suggest why governments often do this?

5. Consider two otherwise identical communities; call them P and N. Suppose that in P, all homes, apartments, and businesses have meters that record the usage of water. In addition, the users of the water must pay more when they use more water. Thus, water is priced like most other goods. In community N, there are no meters and the local supplier of water charges everyone in the community a fixed amount per person, per month for their water service. Thus, using another gallon costs the user nothing. In which community will per

capita water usage be higher? Explain, using the relevant principles of economics.

6. Referring back to the facts of the previous question: Suppose you knew that in one community water is supplied by a privately owned company, while in the other community water is supplied by the local government. In which community do you predict that water is supplied by the privately owned company? Explain.

CHAPTER 10

Bankrupt Landlords, from Sea to Shining Sea

Take a tour of Santa Monica, a beachfront enclave of Los Angeles, and you will find a city of bizarre contrasts. Pick a street at random, and you may find run-down rental units sitting in disrepair next to multimillion-dollar homes. Try another street, and you may see an abandoned apartment building adjacent to a luxury car dealership or trendy shops selling high-fashion clothing to Hollywood stars. Sound strange? Not in Santa Monica—known locally as the People's Republic of Santa Monica—where stringent rent-control laws once routinely forced property owners to leave their buildings empty and decaying rather than even bothering to sell them.

Three thousand miles to the east, rent-control laws in New York City—known locally as the Big Apple—have forced landlords to abandon housing units because the laws imposed huge financial losses on owners. Largely as a result of such abandonments, the city government of New York at one point owned thousands of derelict housing units— empty, except for rats and small-time cocaine dealers. Meanwhile, in part because the controls also discourage new construction, average rents on uncontrolled apartments are around $3,400 per month.

From coast to coast, stories like these are commonplace in the two hundred or so American cities and towns practicing some form of **rent control**—a system in which the local government tells building owners how much they can charge for rent. In each of these cities, the stories are the same: poorly maintained rental units, abandoned apartment buildings, tenants trapped by housing gridlock in apartments no longer suitable for them, rent-control bureaucracies, and even homeless families that can find no one who will rent to them. In each of these cities, the reason for the stories is the same: legal limits on the rent people may pay for a place to live.

A Brief History of Rent Controls

Our story begins in 1943, when the federal government imposed rent control as a temporary wartime measure. Although the federal program ended a few years after the war, New York City continued the controls on its own. Under New York's controls, a landlord generally could not raise rents on apartments as long as the tenants continued to renew their leases. Rent controls in Santa Monica are more recent. They were spurred by the inflation of the 1970s, which, combined with California's rapid population growth, pushed housing prices and rents to record levels. In 1979, the city of Santa Monica (where 80 percent of the residents were renters) ordered that rents be rolled back to the levels of the year before and stipulated that future rents could go up by only two-thirds as much as any increase in the overall price level. In both New York and Santa Monica, the objective of rent controls has been to keep rents below the levels that would be observed in freely competitive markets. Achieving this goal required that these cities impose extensive regulations to prevent both landlord and tenant from evading the controls—regulations that are costly to enforce and that distort the normal operation of the market.

It is worth noting that the rent-control systems in New York and Santa Monica are slowly yielding to decontrol. For a number of years, many apartments in New York have been subject to only "rent stabilization" regulations, which are somewhat less stringent than absolute rent controls. In addition, New York apartments renting for over $2,700 per month are deregulated when a lease ends. In Santa Monica, the state of California eventually mandated that rent for newly vacant apartments could increase. Even so, in both cities, much of the rental market is dominated by some form of rent controls. Accordingly, in this chapter we focus on the consequences of those controls.

The Adverse Effects of Rent Controls

In general, the unfettered movement of rental prices in a freely competitive housing market performs three vital functions: (i) it allocates existing scarce housing among competing claimants; (ii) it promotes the efficient maintenance of existing housing and stimulates the production of new housing, where appropriate; and (iii) it rations usage of housing by demanders, thereby preventing waste of scarce housing. Rent control prevents rental prices from effectively performing these functions. Let's see how.

Rent control discourages the construction of new rental units. Developers and mortgage lenders are reluctant to get involved in building new rental properties because controls artificially depress the most important long-run determinant of profitability—rents. Thus, in one recent year, 14,000 new housing units were built in Dallas, a city with a 7 percent rental vacancy rate but no rent-control statute. In that same year, only 4,000 units were built in San Francisco, a city with a 2 percent vacancy rate but stringent rent-control laws. In New York City, the only rental units being built are either exempt from controls or heavily subsidized by the government. Private construction of new apartments in Santa Monica also dried up under controls, even though new office space and commercial developments—both exempt from rent control—were built at a record pace.

Rent control leads to the deterioration of the existing supply of rental housing. When rental prices are held below free market levels, property owners cannot recover the costs of maintenance, repairs, and capital improvements. Thus, such activities are sharply curtailed. Eventually, taxes, utilities, and the expenses of the most rudimentary repairs—such as replacing broken windows—can exceed the depressed rental receipts. Under rent controls in Santa Monica, the city insisted that owners wishing to convert empty apartment buildings to other uses had to build new rental units to replace the units they no longer rented. At a cost of up to $300,000 per apartment, it is little wonder that few owners were willing to bear the burden, choosing instead to leave the buildings empty and graffiti-scarred.

Rent control impedes the process of rationing scarce housing. Tenants are understandably reluctant to give up controlled apartments, so one consequence of rent controls is that tenant mobility is sharply reduced. Even when a family's demand for living space changes—due, for example, to a new baby or a teenager's departure for college—there can be substantial costs in giving up a rent-controlled unit. In New York City, some landlords charge "key money" (a large up-front cash payment) before a new tenant is allowed to move in. The high cost of moving means that large families often stay in cramped quarters while small families or even single persons reside in large apartments. In New York, this phenomenon of nonmobility came to be known as *housing gridlock*. It is estimated that more than 20 percent of renters in New York City live in apartments that are bigger or smaller than they would otherwise occupy. In Santa Monica, some homeowners rented out portions of their houses found themselves trapped by their tenants, whom they could not evict even if they wanted to sell their homes and move to a retirement community.

EFFORTS TO EVADE CONTROLS

The distortions produced by rent control lead to efforts by both landlords and tenants to evade the rules. This in turn leads to the growth of cumbersome government bureaucracies whose job is to enforce the controls. In New York City, where rents can be raised when tenancy changes hands, landlords have an incentive to make life unpleasant for tenants or to evict them on the slightest pretense. The city has responded by making evictions extremely difficult and costly for landlords. Even if a tenant blatantly and repeatedly violates the terms of a lease, the tenant cannot be evicted if the violations are corrected within a "reasonable" time period. If the violations are not corrected eviction requires a tedious and expensive judicial proceeding. For their part, tenants routinely try to sublet all or part of their rent-controlled apartments at prices substantially above the rent they pay the owner. Because both the city and the landlords try to prohibit subletting, the parties often end up in the city's housing courts, an entire judicial system developed chiefly to deal with disputes over rent-controlled apartments.

Strict controls on monthly rents force landlords to use other means to discriminate among prospective tenants. Simply to ensure that the rent check comes every month, many landlords rent only to well-heeled professionals. As one commentator put it, "There is no disputing that Santa Monica became younger and richer under rent control." The same pattern occurred under the rent-control laws of Berkeley, California, and Cambridge, Massachusetts.

BUREAUCRACIES FLOURISH

There is little doubt the bureaucracies that evolve to administer rent-control laws are cumbersome and expensive. Between 1988 and 1993, New York City spent $5.1 billion rehabilitating housing confiscated from private landlords. Even today, the overflow and appeals from the city's housing courts clog the rest of New York's judicial system, impeding the prosecution of violent criminals and drug dealers. In Santa Monica, the Rent Control Board began with an annual budget of $745,000. Today a staff of 20 reports to the five-member Rent Control Board, whose $5 million budget is about the same as that of the City's Fire Department. Funding for the Board comes from landlords, who are required to pay an annual assessment of $175 per unit. Also, even though state law now mandates that apartment rents in Santa Monica can be increased when a new tenant moves in, the new rent is then controlled by the city for the duration of the tenancy. The Rent Control Board conveniently maintains a Web site (http://www.smgov.net/rent-control/) where one can go to learn the maximum allowable rent on any of the 28,000 rent-controlled residences (about 70 percent of the total supply) in Santa Monica.

THE LOSERS FROM RENT CONTROLS

Ironically, the big losers from rent control—in addition to landlords—are often low-income individuals, especially single mothers. Indeed, many observers believe that one significant cause of homelessness in cities such as New York and Los Angeles is rent control. Poor individuals often cannot assure the discriminating landlord that their rent will be paid on time—or paid at all—each month. Because controlled rents are generally well below free market levels, there is little incentive for apartment owners to take a chance on low-income individuals as tenants. This is especially true if the prospective tenant's chief source of income is a welfare check. Indeed, a significant number of tenants appearing in New York's housing courts are low-income mothers who, due to emergency expenses or delayed welfare checks, have missed rent payments.

Often their appeals end in evictions and residence in temporary public shelters or on the streets. Before the state-mandated easing of controls, some apartment owners in Santa Monica, who used to rent one- and two-room units to welfare recipients and other low-income individuals, simply abandoned their buildings, leaving them vacant rather than trying to collect artificially depressed rents that failed to cover operating costs. The disgusted owner of one empty and decaying eighteen-unit building had a friend spray-paint his feelings on the wall: "I want to tear this mess down, but Big Brother won't let me." Perhaps because the owner had escaped from a concentration camp in search of freedom in the United States, the friend added a personalized touch: a drawing of a large hammer and sickle, symbol of the former Soviet Union.

DAMAGE AROUND THE WORLD

The ravages of rent controls are not confined to the United States. In Mumbai, India, rents are still set at the levels that prevailed back in 1940. A two-bedroom apartment near the center of the city may have a controlled rent of as little as $8.50 per month. (Nearby, free market rents for an apartment of the same size can be as much as $3,000 per month.) Not surprisingly, landlords have let their rent-controlled buildings decay, and collapsing apartments have become a regular feature of life in this city of twenty-two million people. Over the past decade, almost one hundred people have been killed in the collapse of rent-controlled buildings. The city government estimates that a hundred or more apartment buildings are currently on the verge of collapse.

Even communist nations are not exempt from rent controls. Long after the last American troops left Vietnam, that nation's foreign minister, Nguyen Co Thach, declared that a "romantic conception of socialism" had destroyed his country's economy after the Vietnam War. Thach stated that rent control had artificially encouraged demand and discouraged supply and that all of the housing in Hanoi had fallen into disrepair as a result. Thach concluded by noting, "The Americans couldn't destroy Hanoi, but we have destroyed our city by very low rents. We realized it was stupid and that we must change policy."

Apparently, this same thinking was what induced the state of California to compel changes in Santa Monica's rent-control ordinance. The result was an almost immediate jump in rents on newly vacant apartments, as well as a noticeable rise in the vacancy rate—exactly the results we would expect. Interestingly enough, however, prospective new tenants were less enthusiastic about the newly available apartments than many landlords had expected. The reason? Twenty years of rent controls had produced many years of reduced upkeep and hence apartments that were less than pristine. As one renter noted, "The trouble is, most of this area … [is] basically falling apart." Another complained, "I don't want to move into a place that's depressing, with old brown carpet that smells like chicken soup." The easing of rent controls has changed both the ambience and the aroma of Santa Monica apartments—but only because the market is better able to perform its functions.

DISCUSSION QUESTIONS

1. Why do you think governments frequently attempt to control apartment rents but not house prices?

2. What determines the size of the key-money payments that landlords demand (and tenants offer) for the right to lease a rent-controlled apartment?

3. Who, other than the owners of rental units, loses as a result of rent controls? Who gains from rent controls? What effect would the imposition of rent controls have on the market price of an existing single-family house? What effect would rent controls have on the value of vacant land?

4. Why do the owners of rental units reduce their maintenance expenditures on the units when rent controls are imposed? Does their decision have anything to do with whether they can afford those expenditures?

5. Because rent controls reduce the rental price below the market clearing price, the quantity of rental units on the market must decline. What does this imply *must* happen to the full cost of renting an apartment including "key money," harassment by the landlord, and so forth? Explain.

6. How does the percentage of voters who are renters (as opposed to owners) affect the incentives for politicians to propose rent controls? Does this incentive depend on the likelihood that renters are less likely to vote in local elections than owners of apartments and houses? Why do you suppose renters are less likely to vote in local elections? Explain.

PART THREE

Labor Markets

CHAPTER 11

Das Kapital in the Twenty-First Century

In 1867, German intellectual Karl Marx wrote *Das Kapital*, the full title of which in English is *Capital: Critique of Political Economy*. A central theme of this work was that in a **capitalist system,** the motivating force was the exploitation of labor. In his view, workers were never paid the full value of their services, which left what he called a surplus value from which employers obtain their profits. Marx predicted that "The worker becomes all the poorer the more wealth he produces . . . ."

Sounds pretty grim, doesn't it? So how have things turned out since Marx made his predictions? Well, the average standard of living since 1867 has risen the most in—you guessed it—capitalist economies. But maybe averages are fooling us. At least that is what some anticapitalists argue.

The Rich Get Richer and the Poor Get Poorer?

In recent years, there has been an increased interest in the topic of **income inequality.** Are Karl Marx's predictions finally coming true? Some politicians in America, many politicians in Europe, and at least a few economists believe so. Before we tackle the actual statistics on inequality in the United States, let's first look at the modern-day version of the reasoning in *Das Kapital*.

The core claim of those who argue that Marx's predictions are (finally) coming true goes something like this. People who invest in **capital**—plant, equipment, research and development, and the like—obtain a return on their investment that exceeds the rate of economic growth. The result, it is argued, is an ever-increasing inequality of **wealth** and

income. Supposedly, then, capitalism inevitably results in wealth concentrated in fewer and fewer hands. To prevent this, it is claimed, we
must raise the **marginal tax rate**—on income, on wealth, indeed on
most anything and everything that might possibly be taxable.

THE EBB AND FLOW OF INEQUALITY

If we look back over the decades since World War II, or indeed over the
past two centuries, there has been remarkably little substantive change
in the inequality of either income or wealth. Why, then, is there rising
concern over inequality today? It is because the inequality of both wealth
and income appear to have risen substantially since about 1980. Thus, it
is claimed, unless there is government intervention in this process, the
distribution of income and wealth will continue to become less equal.

Thirty or even forty years is a blink of time in the sweep of world,
or even American, history. One could easily select other periods of such
length from the past and reach very different conclusions about the trend
in inequality. The reason is simple: The ebb and flow of prosperity and
depression, innovation and stagnation, and war and peace routinely
change economic outcomes unevenly and unpredictably for people at
all points in the economic stratum.

Thus, three questions arise. First, just what *has* happened to measures of economic inequality over the past few decades? Second, how
much should we rely on these measures? And third, should we be concerned at the prospect of more economic inequality?

INCOME INEQUALITY IS RISING

As a major report by the Congressional Budget Office (CBO) makes
clear, government transfer payments (most importantly Social Security
and heavily subsidized Medicare benefits) are an important source of
income for many low- and middle-income individuals. These programs
have had a significant impact in reducing one form of inequality that
used to be prevalent in America. Until about 1960 or so, older Americans
typically had the lowest incomes and highest poverty rates of all age
groups. But as the CBO (and other researchers) demonstrate, people over
sixty-five have the *lowest* poverty rate of all age groups today, importantly because of Social Security and Medicare.

Based on the CBO and other readily available data, a number of
economists have now re-examined the changing distribution of income
over the past few decades. They have found two striking facts. First,
people at all income levels have experienced rising incomes. As is

conventionally done, the researchers divided people up into income "quintiles," ranked from top to bottom, with 20 percent of the population in each group. For every single quintile, average inflation-adjusted incomes have risen over this period. Income has risen the fastest in the top quintile over this period, and within this top group, incomes rose the fastest at the very top. But it is also worthy of note that people in the *bottom* quintile have experienced the second fastest rate of growth of income. It is in the middle of the income distribution where, although income has grown, it has done so sluggishly.

The conclusion from this research is that **real income** is rising across the income spectrum. The rich are getting richer, but so too are the poor. They are just not getting richer as quickly as the people at the top of the economic spectrum.

INCOME MOBILITY

In thinking about the distribution of income, it is important to remember that in America, most people exhibit a great deal of **income mobility**— individuals move around within the income distribution over time. The most important source of income mobility is the "life-cycle" pattern of earnings: Incomes are lowest for people when they are young, rising to a maximum at about age fifty-five, and then declining slowly until retirement. Earnings at the end of one's career are generally well above those at the beginning. Thus, a snapshot of the current distribution of earnings will find most individuals on the way up, toward a higher position in the income distribution. People who have low earnings now are likely, on average, to have higher earnings in the future.

Lady Luck is another source of income mobility. At any point in time, the income of high-income people is likely to be abnormally high (relative to their average income) due to recent good fortune—they may have just won the lottery or received a long-awaited bonus. Conversely, the incomes of people who currently have low incomes are likely to be abnormally low due to recent bad luck, perhaps because they are laid up after an automobile accident or have become temporarily unemployed. Over time, the effects of Lady Luck tend to average out across the population. Accordingly, people with high incomes today will tend to have lower incomes in the future, while people with low incomes today will tend to have higher future incomes.

The effects of the forces that produce income mobility are strikingly revealed in studies examining the incomes of individuals over time. Over any given decade, almost half of the people in the bottom quintile will move to a higher quintile. Similarly, almost half of the people in the top quintile will have moved to a lower quintile. Just as importantly, in recent decades, there has been *no* tendency for the amount of income mobility in America to diminish. As Raj Chetty and his co-authors have concluded, "the rungs on the income ladder have grown farther apart," but "children's chances of climbing from lower to high rungs have not changed."

MIS-MEASUREMENT

Most attempts to examine the U.S. distribution of both income and wealth begin with federal income tax returns. Because the federal government taxes income, it goes to great lengths to measure it accurately. But what is accurate for tax purposes may turn out to be misleading for other purposes—and this is especially true for recent decades.

Over the last thirty-five years or so, there have been changes in U.S. tax rules so dramatic that the income tax data can easily produce misleading conclusions about what has been happening to inequality. The key changes in the tax laws fall into three broad areas:

Tax reporting—Tax laws were changed to require more reporting of income from capital by wealthy individuals and less reporting of income from capital by lower- and middle-income individuals. Any failure to account for these changes in reporting will overstate the growth of income and wealth at the top and understate it at the bottom.

Switching from corporate to individual tax returns—In 1980 the top individual tax rate was 70 percent, while the corporate tax rate was only half this. Hence, the wealthy created corporations to move their measured incomes off their individual tax returns. By 1988, the top individual tax rate had been cut to 28 percent, so the wealthy began dissolving their corporations and reporting their income on their individual tax returns. These developments caused vast sums of income to be labeled as individual income, whereas before such income had been labeled as corporate income. This made the individual incomes of the wealthy appear to be rising far faster than they actually were.

Tax rates and capital gains—Taxes on **capital gains** (which arise when an asset is sold) were slashed in 1997 and again in 2003. Many individuals, particularly wealthier ones, took advantage of these tax cuts by selling some assets to convert them into other assets. The tax records make it look like these sales were generating huge increases in income and wealth at the top of the economic spectrum, when in fact people were mostly just rebalancing their portfolios because it had become cheaper to do so.

Is Economic Equality Important?

Although the most commonly used numbers thus overstate the growth in inequality in America over the last several decades, income and wealth do seem to be less equally distributed than in, say, 1980. But we must put this fact in the context of another fact we noted earlier: The overall standard of living is rising in America, at the top, the middle, and the bottom of the economic spectrum. Given this, does it matter that the rich are getting richer faster than the rest of us are getting richer?

Envy, of course, is one reason we might object, although most of us would not like to admit that we are guilty of this example of one of the "seven deadly sins." There might also be a moral reason why everyone should get richer at the same rate, although economics can offer little insight on this rationale. Politics is another reason we might be concerned. After all, the wealthy have more resources that can be used to influence the outcomes of elections. But in America, at least, wealth has never been concentrated just among liberals or just among conservatives. Democrats and Republicans have both prospered, even in the rarified world of billionaires. Moreover, as long as the government does not restrict political contributions, then wealthy people across all political persuasions are free to invest in issues and candidates as they like. Competition is beneficial in the marketplace, and there is no reason to think it is otherwise in the political spectrum.

The Sources of Inequality

From an economic perspective, perhaps the most important reason we want to understand the facts of economic inequality is to help us understand the *sources* of inequality. In broad terms, there is no doubt that income and wealth are predominantly determined by the value of what people produce. This is easy to see in sports and entertainment—the superstars get rich while the second-stringers, has-beens, and never-weres struggle to make a living. But it is just as true in *all* walks of life: People are paid predominantly on the basis of what they produce.

But notice our use of the word *predominantly*, for it is certainly the case that factors other than productivity come into play. For example, wealthy people tend to leave more assets to their heirs than do lower-income individuals, which helps the children of the rich to be richer than otherwise. But asset inheritance accounts for only a very small part of the observed distribution of wealth. Moreover, heirs of the wealthy have shown a remarkable ability to spend their inheritances fast enough that their own heirs can expect relatively little to be left.

More important than inheritance is the possibility that the "rules of the game" might be skewed to favor the rich and disfavor the poor. Under these circumstances, rewards would not be distributed wholly in accord with production, and, thus, economic incentives would deviate from those that yield the highest possible level of output. That is, *total* real income and wealth in society would be lower. This scenario—the prospect that the rich might use the government to manipulate the rules in their favor—seems to be the one that is most troubling for many observers. But if this is so, then a "solution" that consists of higher taxes on the rich hardly makes sense. After all, if the rich can manipulate the government so expertly, then they will surely manipulate it to spend those extra tax proceeds on programs that benefit *them*, not the poor.

The key question, it might be argued, is not who is richer than whom or why either is wealthy. The question instead is why so many low-income individuals *don't* exhibit the upward income mobility that has been a hallmark of American history. As we noted above, about half of the people in the bottom quintile move upward within a decade. But this implies that about half *don't*. Understanding why this is so seems vastly more significant than worrying about whether someone's yacht is too big. America rose to greatness on the basis of opportunity for all, and maintaining that greatness requires that the promise of opportunity be real. So, despite the flaws of much of the data and many of the arguments, if the discussion of inequality gets us to focus on this issue, it has been a success.

DISCUSSION QUESTIONS

1. Does envy of those who are rich depend on the source of that wealth? For example, consider two people who are both equally rich. One of them worked eighty hours a week year after year to accumulate her wealth, while the other won the lottery. Would the envy felt by others toward each of these people differ?

2. When the capital gains tax rate was reduced from 28 to 20 percent in 1997 and especially when it was cut again to 15 percent in 2003, many people believed that these reductions would be temporary. How did this belief affect the incentives to sell assets when the tax rates were cut, compared to a situation in which taxes were cut

permanently? How would the belief that the cuts were temporary alter the choice between selling assets that had experienced large capital gains versus those that had experienced only small capital gains?

3. In 1984, individual balances in private retirement plans were $865 billion. By thirty years later, they had risen to almost $25 trillion. In general, balances in private retirement plans are not included in the statistics that show rising income or wealth inequality. How might such an oversight affect our conclusions about inequality?

4. Today, usually at little or no cost, you can Skype your friends and family, no matter where they are located. Are you both psychologically and economically richer? Why or why not? Similarly, you can follow the lives of the rich and famous via their Twitter feeds, their blogs, or their Facebook pages. Are you better or worse off because you have this option?

5. If you play poker with a group of friends, you are playing what is called a zero-sum game. What you win, they lose and vice versa. The sum of the funds that you start with together does not change. All that changes is who owns more or less of that sum at the end of your poker game. Many commentators (and politicians, too) believe that wealth creation is a zero-sum game. Is this a correct analogy? Why or why not?

6. Some observers have proposed higher income and wealth taxes on the wealthy. Given that one's wealth generally depends primarily on how much output one produces, how do these taxes affect the incentives of people who are the most productive? Assume that the proceeds from the taxes are given out to the poor. How does this affect *their* incentives? Overall, what do you predict will happen to the total income and wealth of society as a result of higher taxes such as these?

CHAPTER 12

(Why) Are Women Paid Less?

Since the middle of the twentieth century, there has been a revolution in the job market. Women have entered the paid workforce in unprecedented numbers. In 1950, only about one-third of working-age women were in the paid workforce. Today, about 57 percent are. Over the same period, the male **labor force participation rate** has fallen from 86 percent to 69 percent, so women now account for almost half of the paid workforce in America. There also has been an overwhelming change in the nature of paid work done by women. Fifty years ago, professional careers for women outside of nursing or teaching were unusual. Today, women comprise roughly half of the newly minted attorneys and physicians starting work each year. Over the same period, there has been a transformation of wages, too. In 1950, median earnings of women were only two-thirds those of men. Today, women earn 80 percent of what men are paid.

Reread that last sentence. On average, for every dollar a man earns, a woman gets paid 80 cents. Can this possibly be true? Consider this fact: Nearly 70 percent of employers' costs are accounted for by labor. An employer who hired only women at 80 cents on the dollar could cut labor costs by 20 percent relative to an employer who hired only men. This would yield added profits of about 14 percent of sales—which would more than *triple* the **profit** earned by the typical firm. If women are paid 20 percent less than men, how could any employer possibly afford to hire anyone *but* women?

Is It Discrimination?

At this point you may be saying to yourself, "Surely, there are differences between men and women other than their sex that can help account for this 'gender gap' in earnings." You would be correct. Earnings are a reflection of experience, education, marital status, and age, for example. But even when economists control for all of these individual characteristics—using nationwide data, such as from the U.S. Census Bureau or the Bureau of Labor Statistics—unexplained differences between the pay of men and women persist. Men with the same measured individual characteristics are paid at least 10 percent more than women, and some studies find a difference twice that size.

The widespread opinion of many observers is that the unexplained gap between the pay of men and women is chiefly the result of discrimination against women. The reasoning is simple. Most business owners and senior managers are men, and, given a choice between hiring a man or a woman, the "old-boy network" operates in favor of the man. According to this view, women can get the job only if they agree to accept lower wages.

Consider this fact, however: For over fifty years, it has been illegal to discriminate in the workforce on the basis of race or gender. Two major federal agencies, the Equal Employment Opportunity Commission and the Office of Federal Contract Compliance, are wholly or largely devoted to ensuring that this antidiscrimination mandate is enforced. As interpreted by the courts, the law now says that if the statistical *appearance* of lower wages for women (or minorities) is present in a workplace, the employer is *presumed* guilty of discrimination and must prove otherwise. No one thinks that federal agencies do a perfect job at enforcing the law here or elsewhere, but it is hard to believe that a persistent 20 percent pay difference could escape the notice of even the most nearsighted federal bureaucrat.

A hint of what might be going on begins to emerge when economists study the payroll records of individual firms, using actual employee information that is specific and detailed regarding the location of the firm, type of work, employee responsibilities, and other factors. These analyses reveal that the so-called wage gap between men and women is much smaller—typically no more than 5 percent—and often there is no gap at all. The sharp contrast between firm-level data and economy-wide data suggests that something may be at work here besides (or in addition to) outright gender discrimination.

THE IMPORTANCE OF CHILDREN

That something is actually three things. First, women's pay is extremely sensitive to whether or not they have children. In Britain, for example, where this issue has been studied intensively, the average pay earned by a woman begins to fall shortly before the birth of her first child and continues to drop until the child becomes a teenager. Although earnings begin to revive once the first child passes the age of twenty or so, they never fully recover. The earnings drop associated with motherhood is close to one-third, and only one-third of that drop is regained after the nest is empty. American data suggest that the same pattern is present on this side of the Atlantic.

The parenthood-pay declines suffered by women stem from a variety of sources. Some are put on the "mommy track," with reduced responsibilities and hours of work. Others move to different employers around the time their first child is born, taking jobs that allow more flexible work schedules but offer correspondingly lower pay as well. Overall, a woman with average skills who has a child at age twenty-four can expect to receive nearly $1 million less compensation over her career compared to one who remains childless. It is worth emphasizing that no similar effect is observed with men. In fact, there is some evidence that men with children are actually paid *more* than men without children. These findings strongly suggest a fact that will come as no surprise to most people. Despite the widespread entry of women into the labor force, they retain the primary responsibility for child care at home, and their careers suffer as a result.

Occupational Selection

The second factor at work in explaining male–female wage differences is occupational selection. Compared to women, men tend to concentrate in paid employment that is dangerous or unpleasant. Commercial fishing, construction, law enforcement, firefighting, truck driving, and mining, to name but a few, are occupations that are much more dangerous than average and are dominated by men. As a result, men represent 92 percent of all occupational fatalities. Hazardous jobs offer what is known as a **compensating differential,** extra pay for assuming the differential risk of death or injury on the job. In equilibrium, these extra wages do no more than offset the extra hazards. So even though measured earnings *look* high relative to the educational and other requirements of the jobs, appearances are deceiving. After adjusting for risk, the value of that pay is really no greater than that for less hazardous employment—but the appearance of higher pay contributes to the measured gender gap.

Women's measured pay is also held down by two other elements of their occupational choices. First, they tend to work in industries that are much less subject to job losses and unemployment than are men. In the latest recession, for example, 6 million men lost their jobs, but only 2.7 million women did so, and the unemployment rate among women is consistently below that of men, in good times and bad. Thus, an implicit component of compensation for women is job security. Second, women tend to select college majors—such as sociology, psychology, and education—that feed into lower paying occupations. Men, by contrast, are more likely to pick engineering or computer science, where earnings are much higher.

Hours of Work

The third key factor influencing pay is hours of work. Men are more than twice as likely as women to work in excess of fifty hours per week in paid employment. Overall, the average paid workweek for men is about 15 percent longer than it is for women. Men are also more likely than women to be in full-time, rather than part-time, paid employment, and the wage differences here can be huge. Working an average of forty-four hours per week versus thirty-four hours per week, for example, yields more than twice the pay, regardless of gender. This substantial gender gap in hours of paid work is due in part to the "mommy track" phenomenon, but the question that remains is: Does this constitute discrimination on the part of employers, or is it the result of choices by women?

Although we cannot answer that question definitively, there is reason to believe that some differences in occupational choice (and thus in pay) are due to discrimination. For example, the highest-paying blue-collar jobs are typically union jobs, and industrial and crafts unions have had a long history of opposition to women as members. Or consider medicine. Women are becoming much more numerous in specialties, such as dermatology and radiology, where schedules tend to be more flexible, hours of work can be limited, and part-time practice is feasible. But many physicians would argue that the underrepresentation of women in the high-paying surgical specialties is partly the result of discrimination against women, rather than reflecting the occupational choices preferred by women. If this argument is correct, then even if women in a given specialty are paid the same as men in that specialty, the exclusion of women from high-paying slots will lower their average wages and make them worse off.

Dental Discrimination?

If you are inclined to dismiss the explanations offered for the differences in pay between men and women, it may be useful to consider dentists. Women dentists earn only 74 cents for each dollar earned by male dentists—a number even worse than observed for the population as a whole.

Yet dentists are overwhelmingly self-employed, either as solo practitioners or as members of partnerships they have created. Are women dentists discriminating against themselves? Are female patients, when they utilize male dentists, foolishly turning their backs on a 26 percent discount offered by women dentists? Neither of these explanations seems plausible. Yet if we reject the notion of pay differentials based on hours of work and experience, we are left with these.

The extent of gender discrimination in the workplace is unlikely to be definitively settled any time soon. Measured earnings differences, even those that account for experience, education, and other factors, clearly overstate the true pay gap between equally qualified men and women. Just as surely, however, given the heavier parenting demands typically made on women, even when they receive equal pay, it is not for equal work.

DISCUSSION QUESTIONS

1. Suppose an employer offers a base wage of $20 per hour for the first forty hours of work each week and overtime pay of $30 per hour for any hours beyond forty per week; the employer allows workers to choose their own hours of work. Suppose employee A chooses to work thirty-six hours per week and employee B chooses to work forty-two hours per week. Compute the average weekly earnings for employees A and B and the "earnings gap" (in percentage terms) between them. In your view, does this observed earnings gap constitute discrimination? Justify your conclusion.

2. A recent British study found that married men earned more than unmarried men, but only if their wives did *not* have full-time paid employment. Suggest an explanation for this finding. (*Hint:* In which case is a man more likely to share in the household responsibilities, including child care?)

3. Women who own their own businesses earn net profits that are only half as large as the net profits earned by men who own their own businesses. First, consider why women would be willing to accept lower profits. Could this reflect poorer options for women as employees? Alternatively, could it reflect other attributes of self-employment that women might find more advantageous than men do? Then, think about why women earn lower profits. Is this evidence of discrimination? If so, by whom? If not, what else might account for the lower profits?

4. Why do you think we have laws that prohibit discrimination in pay based on gender or race but permit employers to discriminate in pay based on education or experience?

5. Suppose you own a company. If you hire ten men, each of them at $70,000 per year, your firm will be able to sell $1,000,000 in output this year, and you will be able to earn $50,000 in profits, an amount that is normal for a firm of your size in your industry. (Your firm's other costs, such as for rent and advertising, will be $250,000 this year.) Now assume that you could hire ten women for $56,000 each, instead of hiring the men. What would your total profits be if you hired the women and they were just as productive as the more expensive men? Show all calculations.

6. Refer back to the last question. Based on the discussion in the chapter, what would you want to know about these women to satisfy yourself that they will be at least as productive as the men? List the key factors and explain briefly.

CHAPTER 13

The Effects of the Minimum Wage

Ask workers if they would like a raise, and the answer will surely be a resounding yes. But ask them if they would like to be fired or have their hours of work reduced, and they would undoubtedly tell you no. The effects of the minimum wage are centered on exactly these points.

Proponents of the **minimum wage**—the lowest hourly wage firms may legally pay their workers—argue that low-income workers are underpaid and therefore unable to support themselves or their families. The minimum wage, they say, raises earnings at the bottom of the wage distribution, with little disruption to workers or businesses. Opponents claim that most low-wage workers don't have families to support. The minimum wage, they say, merely enriches a few at the far greater expense of many others, who can't get jobs. Most important, opponents argue, many individuals at the bottom of the economic ladder lack the skills needed for employers to hire them at the federal minimum. Willing to work but unable to find jobs, these people never learn the basic job skills needed to move up the economic ladder to higher-paying jobs. The issues are clear—but what are the facts?

BACKGROUND

The federal minimum wage was instituted in 1938 as a provision of the Fair Labor Standards Act. It was originally set at 25 cents per hour, about 40 percent of the average manufacturing wage at the time. Over the next forty years, the legal minimum was raised periodically, roughly in accord with the movement of market wages throughout the economy. Typically, its level has averaged between 40 and 50 percent of average manufacturing wages. In response to the high inflation of the late 1970s, the minimum wage was hiked seven times between 1974 and 1981, reaching $3.35 per hour—about 42 percent of manufacturing wages. President Ronald Reagan vowed to keep a lid on the minimum wage, and by the time he left office, the minimum's unchanged level left it at 31 percent of average wages. Legislation passed in 1989 raised the minimum to $3.80 in 1990 and $4.25 in 1991. Five years later, Congress raised it in two steps to $5.15 per hour. Over the period 2007–2009, the minimum was hiked in three steps to its current level of $7.25 per hour.

About 1.3 million workers earn the minimum wage. Another 1.7 million are paid even less because the law doesn't cover them. Supporters of the minimum wage claim that it prevents exploitation of employees and helps people earn enough to support their families and themselves. Even so, at $7.25 per hour, a full-time worker earns only about 60 percent of what the government considers enough to keep a family of four out of poverty. In fact, to get a family of four with one wage earner up to the poverty line, the minimum wage would have to be more than $12.00 per hour.

Yet opponents of the minimum wage argue that such calculations are irrelevant. For example, 98 percent of married people earn *above* the minimum wage, and single people paid the minimum earn enough to put them 20 percent above the poverty cutoff. Overall, almost one-quarter of minimum wage workers are teenagers, most of whom have no financial obligations, except perhaps clothing and automobile-related expenditures. Thus, opponents argue that the minimum wage chiefly benefits upper-middle-class teens who are least in need of assistance at the same time that it costs the jobs of thousands of disadvantaged minority youths.

Does Low-Wage Mean Low-Income?

Much of the discussion of the minimum wage glosses over the very real distinction between "low wage" and "low income." If we go back to 1939, just after the federal minimum wage was established, we find that 85 percent of low-wage workers were in poor families. Hence, the original minimum wage did a good job of targeting the poor. Fast-forward to the present, and only 18 percent of low-wage workers are now in poor families.

There are several reasons why there is only a weak link between low wage and low income today. First, due to the rising incidence of multiple-earner families, many low-wage workers are in higher-income families. Second, some workers in poor families earn more than the minimum hourly wage but, voluntarily or otherwise, don't work enough hours to get out of poverty. Finally, about half of poor families have no workers at all. The net effect of these factors is that only 18 percent of the benefits of a higher minimum wage would go to the poor—and 32 percent would go to families earning more than triple the poverty line.

RECENT EVIDENCE

The debate over the minimum wage intensified a few years ago when research suggested that a change in the New Jersey minimum wage had no adverse short-run impact on employment. Further research by other scholars focusing on Canada reveals more clearly what actually happens when the minimum wage is hiked. In Canada, there are important differences in minimum wages both over time and across different provinces. These differences enabled researchers to distinguish between the short- and long-run effects of changes in minimum wages. The short-run effects are indeed negligible, as implied by the New Jersey study. But the Canadian research shows that in the long run, the adverse effects of a higher minimum wage are quite substantial. In the short run, it is true that firms do not cut their workforce by much in response to a higher minimum. But over time, the increased costs from paying a higher minimum wage force smaller firms out of business, and it is here that the drop in employment shows up clearly.

The Canadian results are consistent with the overwhelming bulk of U.S. evidence on this issue, which points to a negative impact of the minimum wage on employment. After all, the number of workers demanded, like the quantity demanded for all goods, responds to price: The higher the price, the lower the number desired. There remains, however, debate over how many jobs are lost due to the minimum wage. For example, when the minimum wage was raised from $3.35 to $4.25, credible estimates of the number of potential jobs lost ranged to 400,000.

When the minimum was hiked to $5.15, researchers suggested that at least 200,000 jobs were at stake. More recently, economists have estimated that the latest increase in the federal minimum wage to $7.25 from $6.55 caused 300,000 people to lose their jobs. With a workforce of over 155 million persons, numbers like these may not sound very large. But most of the people who don't have jobs as a result of the minimum wage are teenagers. They comprise less than 5 percent of the workforce but bear almost all the burden of foregone employment alternatives.

THE BIG LOSERS

Significantly, the youths most likely to lose work due to the minimum wage are disadvantaged teenagers, chiefly minorities. On average, these teens enter the workforce with the fewest job skills and the greatest need for on-the-job training. Until and unless these disadvantaged teenagers can acquire these skills, they are the most likely to be unemployed as a result of the minimum wage—and thus least likely to have the opportunity to move up the economic ladder. With a teen unemployment rate of about 15 percent (triple the overall rate) and unemployment among black youngsters around 30 percent, critics argue that the minimum wage is a major impediment to long-term labor market success for minority youth.

Indeed, the minimum wage has an aspect that its supporters are not inclined to discuss: It can make employers more likely to discriminate on the basis of gender or race. When wages are set by market forces, employers who would discriminate face a reduced, and thus more expensive, pool of workers. But when the government mandates an above-market wage, the result is a surplus of low-skilled workers. It thus becomes easier and cheaper to discriminate. As former U.S. Treasury secretary Lawrence Summers noted, the minimum wage "removes the economic penalty to the employer. He can choose the one who's white with blond hair."

Critics of the minimum wage also note that it makes firms less willing to train workers who lack basic skills. Instead, companies may choose to hire only experienced workers whose abilities justify the higher wage. Firms are also likely to become less generous with fringe benefits in an effort to hold down labor costs. The prospect of more discrimination, less job training for low-skilled workers, and fewer fringe benefits for entry-level workers leaves many observers uncomfortable. As the economist Jacob Mincer noted, the minimum wage means "a loss of opportunity" for the hard-core unemployed.

FIGHT FOR $15

Despite these adverse effects of the minimum wage, many people argue that all workers should be paid a wage on which they can "afford to live." In fact, some states and localities mandate that minimum wages (sometimes called "living wages") be well above the federal minimum, reaching $15 per hour in some places. There is even a nationwide movement, called "Fight for $15," which organizes efforts to raise state and local minimum wages. This movement is funded almost wholly by labor unions, whose members generally are paid far above the minimum wage. Interestingly, where the fight for a higher minimum has been successful at the state or local level, these same unions have insisted that their members should be *exempt* from the law—that is, *not* paid at the new higher rate. Not surprisingly, some critics of minimum wages have thus argued that the interest of unions is not in improving the welfare of low-wage workers. Instead, the critics say, unions are hoping to raise the cost of the non-union labor, which competes with and is a direct substitute for union labor.

Between 2014 and 2017 more than half the states raised their minimum wages, as did many cities. Only a few locations have implemented or scheduled minimums as high as $15. So far, the biggest hikes have occurred in locations such as New York and California, where market wages are relatively high. Hence, the adverse employment effects of many of the new state or local minimums have been relatively modest—so far. But if a major minimum wage increase were imposed at the national level, the negative effects would likely be substantial, especially in the low-wage rural South and among unskilled workers. As noted financier Warren Buffett put it: "I may wish to have all jobs pay at least $15 an hour. But that minimum would almost certainly reduce employment in a major way, crushing many workers possessing only basic skills."

Nothing Is Easy

When politicians decide to raise the minimum wage, it is only after heated battles often lasting months. Given the stakes involved—an improved standard of living for some and a loss of job opportunities for others—it is not surprising that discussions of the minimum wage soon turn to controversy. As one former high-level U.S. Department of Labor official said, "When it comes to the minimum wage, there are no easy positions to take. Either you are in favor of more jobs, less discrimination, and more on-the-job training, or you support better wages for workers. Whatever stance you choose, you are bound to get clobbered by the opposition." When Congress and the president face this issue, one or both usually feel the same way.

Discussion Questions

1. Are teenagers better off when a higher minimum wage enables some to earn higher wages but causes others to lose their jobs?

2. Are there methods other than a higher minimum wage that could raise the incomes of low-wage workers without reducing employment among minority youngsters?

3. Why do you think organized labor groups, such as unions, are supporters of a higher minimum wage, even though all of their members earn much more than the minimum wage?

4. Is it possible that a higher minimum wage could ever *increase* employment?

5. Even without a minimum wage, the unemployment rate would almost surely be higher among teenagers than among adults. Suggest at least two reasons why this is so.

6. Why is it that teenagers (rather than members of any other age group) are most likely to lose their jobs (or get turned down for employment) when the minimum wage is raised?

CHAPTER 14

The (Dis)incentives of Higher Taxes

Politicians always seem to be looking for additional ways to raise tax revenues. Most often, politicians talk (and even act) as if their taxing decisions have no effect on the quantity supplied or the quantity demanded of whatever good or service they wish to tax. Indeed, there is a saying among economists that politicians believe all demand curves and supply curves are **perfectly inelastic.** In such a world, higher taxes would have no effect on either quantity demanded or quantity supplied. What a wonderful world that would be—for politicians.

THE LUXURY TAX

In the real world, however, changes in taxes cause changes in **relative prices,** and individuals in their roles as consumers, savers, investors, and workers react to these relative price changes. Consider a truly telling example: the luxury tax enacted by Congress in 1991. Members of Congress were looking for additional revenues to reduce the federal budget deficit. What better way to raise these hoped-for revenues than with new taxes on the purchases of high-priced luxury items, such as big boats, expensive cars, furs, planes, and jewelry? After all, rich people don't really care how much they pay, right? So Congress passed a 10 percent luxury surcharge tax on boats priced over $200,000 in today's terms, cars over $60,000, aircraft over $500,000, and furs and jewelry over $20,000.

The federal government estimated that it would rake in $18 billion in extra revenues over the following five-year period. Yet just a few years later, the luxury tax was quietly eliminated. Why? Because the actual take for the federal government was almost *nothing*.

Rich people, strange as it may seem, react to relative price changes, too. For high-priced new boats, for example, they had alternatives. Some bought used luxury boats instead of new ones. Others decided not to trade in their older luxury boats for new ones. Still others bought their new boats in other countries and never brought them back to the United States to be taxed. The moral of the story for politicians is that the laws of supply and demand apply to everyone, rich and poor, young and old, whatever their description might be.

STATIC VERSUS DYNAMIC ANALYSIS

The discrepancy between the fantasyland of politics and the reality of human behavior can be traced in part to the fact that politicians routinely engage in **static analysis.** They assume that people's behavior is static (unchanging), no matter how the constraints they face—such as taxes—might change. If the politicians who had pushed for the luxury tax had used **dynamic analysis,** they would have correctly anticipated that consumers (even rich ones) were going to change their buying decisions when faced with the new taxes.

Dynamic analysis takes into account that the impact of the tax *rate* on tax *revenue* actually collected depends crucially on the **elasticity** of the relevant demand or supply curves. That is, even a high *rate* (measured in tax per item or as a percentage of the value of the item) can yield relatively little *revenue* (total dollars collected) if consumers are highly responsive to the tax-inclusive price of the good. For example, in the case of the luxury tax, the **elasticity of demand** for new, high-end boats was relatively high: When the tax per boat went up, the quantity demanded fell so far that tax collections were negligible.

INCOME TAXES AND LABOR SUPPLY

Now let's shift from the demand side of this taxing issue to the supply side. Does quantity supplied react to changing relative prices? Yes, but you might not know it from listening to politicians. The first modern federal personal income tax was imposed in 1916. The highest rate was 15 percent. Eventually, the top federal personal marginal income tax rate reached an astounding 91 percent during the years 1951–1964. This marginal tax rate was cut to 70 percent in 1965. In 1980, it was lowered to 50 percent. For much of the 1980s and into the present, the highest federal marginal income tax rate has ranged from 31 percent to about 40 percent.

Often politicians (and even some members of the general public) believe that the income tax rates paid by America's richest individuals do not matter to them because they are so rich that even after paying taxes, they are still very rich. The underlying "theory" behind such a belief is that the supply of labor is completely unresponsive to the after-tax price received by the providers of labor. Stated another way, if you were to draw the **supply curve** of labor, it would be a nearly vertical line for each individual at some fixed number of work hours per year. Supposedly, then, the **elasticity of supply** of labor is low—indeed, just about zero.

To be sure, you might know somebody who loves work so much that she will work with the same intensity and for the same number of hours per year no matter what the income tax rate is. But changes occur at the margin in economics (meaning in the real world). If there are *some* individuals who respond to higher federal marginal tax rates by working less, then the overall supply curve of labor is going to be upward-sloping even for the ultrarich—just like all other supply curves for goods and services.

The Evidence Is Clear

The data seem to confirm our economic predictions. In 1980, the top marginal income tax rate was 70 percent. The highest 1 percent of income-earning Americans paid 17 percent of all federal personal income taxes in that year. In 2009, when the top tax rate was 35 percent, the richest 1 percent paid more than double that share. How can this be explained? The answer is relatively straightforward: Lower marginal income tax rates create an incentive for people to work more and harder because the rewards of doing so are greater. Also, in their role as risk-taking entrepreneurs, individuals are almost always going to be willing to take bigger risks if they know that success will yield greater after-tax increases in their incomes.

Data from Europe suggest that exactly the same incentives are at work across a broad spectrum of income earners. Researchers have found that a tax increase of just over 12 percentage points induces the average adult in Europe to reduce work effort by over 120 hours per year—the equivalent of almost four weeks of work. Such a tax change also causes a sharp reduction in the number of people who work at all and prompts many others to join the underground economy. Overall, then, higher tax rates cause lower output and lower employment and also induce marked increases in efforts devoted to tax evasion.

Incentives Apply to Everyone

It is also true that what we have been talking about applies even among people who are at the very bottom of the income distribution. In many countries today, and in many circumstances in the United States, poorer individuals receive benefits from the government. These benefits can be in the form of food stamps, subsidized housing, subsidized health care or health insurance, and direct cash payments (often referred to as *welfare*). Those who receive such government benefits typically pay no income taxes on these benefits. In the United States, they may even receive an **earned income tax credit,** which is a type of **negative tax** or **tax credit.**

If such individuals were to accept a job (or a higher-paying job, if they are already employed), two things will normally occur. First, they will lose some or all of their government benefits. Second, they may have to start paying federal (and perhaps state) personal income taxes. They understand that the loss of a benefit is the equivalent of being taxed more. And when they also have to pay explicit taxes, they know that the result is effectively double taxation.

A Lesson from Ireland

Just as at the top end of the income ladder, the quantity of labor supplied by people at the lower end is affected by changes in the marginal income tax rates they face. If taking a good job and getting off the welfare rolls means losing benefits plus paying income taxes, the person on welfare has less incentive to accept a job. A good case in point is Ireland, which for most of the past twenty-five years was the fastest-growing economy in Europe. In the late 1980s, its economy was a disaster, one of the poorest among European countries. One of the problems was that individuals on welfare faced an effective (implicit) marginal income tax rate of about 120 percent if they got off the dole and went back to work. Obviously, they weren't directly taxed at 120 percent, but with the actual income tax that did apply, combined with the loss in welfare benefits, the *implicit* marginal tax rate was indeed 120 percent. Stated differently, their available spendable income would drop by about 20 percent if they went back to work! Needless to say, large numbers of poorer Irish stayed on the welfare roles until the program was completely overhauled.

Interestingly enough, this overhaul of the incentives facing low-income individuals was accompanied by an overhaul of the tax rates (and thus incentives) facing high-income corporations, with much the same results. In the 1990s, the Irish slashed the corporate profits tax to 12.5 percent, the lowest in Europe and only about one-third as high as the U.S. rate of 35 percent. Beginning in 2004, the Irish government also began offering a 20 percent tax credit for company spending on research and development, offering high-tech firms an opportunity to cut their taxes by starting up and expanding operations in Ireland. Almost immediately, Ireland became a magnet for new investment and for successful companies that didn't want to hand over one-third or more of their profits to the tax collector.

The combination of lower corporate tax rates and tax breaks on research and development induced hundreds of multinational corporations to begin operations in Ireland. They brought with them hundreds of thousands of new jobs (and this to a nation of only four million residents), and Ireland quickly became number one among the European Union's fifteen original members in being home to companies that conduct research and development. And tax revenues of the Irish government? Well, despite the drastic cut in tax rates, tax revenues actually soared to levels never seen before. Indeed, measured as a share of gross domestic product, Ireland soon collected 50 percent more tax revenues out of corporate profits than America did, despite Ireland's lower tax rate.

The lesson of our story is simple. It is true that "nothing in life is certain but death and taxes." But it is equally true that higher tax rates don't always mean higher tax revenues. This is a lesson that politicians can ignore only at their own peril.

DISCUSSION QUESTIONS

1. Suppose the government spends more this year than it collects in taxes, borrowing the difference. Assuming that the government will repay its debts, what does this imply about what must happen to taxes in the *future*? How might people adjust their behavior to account for this predicted change in taxes?

2. Consider three scenarios. In each, your neighbor offers to pay $500 if you will clear brush out of his backyard this week.

   Scenario 1: If you decline the offer, you can collect $200 in unemployment benefits this week. If you accept the offer, you get to keep the entire $500 without having to pay taxes on it.

   Scenario 2: If you decline the offer, you can collect $100 in unemployment benefits this week. If you accept the offer, you must pay $100 in income taxes out of your earnings from work.

   Scenario 3: If you decline the offer, you collect no unemployment benefits. If you accept the offer, you must pay $200 in income taxes out of your earnings from work.

   What is the net monetary gain from working in each of these three scenarios? How, if at all, do your incentives change between scenarios? Explain briefly.

3. If you found yourself in the 91 percent federal personal income tax bracket in 1951, how great would have been your incentive to find legal loopholes to reduce your federal tax liabilities? If you found yourself in the lowest federal personal income tax bracket of, say, 15 percent, would your incentive to find loopholes to reduce your tax bill be the same? Explain.

4. Explain how the incentive effects of each of the following hypothetical taxes would cause people to change their behavior. Be sure to explain what people are likely to do *less* of and what they are likely to do *more* of in response to each tax:

   (a) A $1,000,000-per-story tax on all office buildings more than two stories tall

   (b) A $2,000-per-car tax on all red (and only red) cars

   (c) A $100-per-book tax on all new college textbooks

5. Suppose federal marginal personal income tax rates will rise significantly over the next ten years. Explain the ways in which individuals at all levels of income can react over time, not just immediately after taxes are raised. How will the size of the response differ, say, a year after the rise in tax rates compared to a week after the increase? Is it possible that some people will actually change their behavior *before* the higher tax rates go into effect? Explain.

6. How does a country's tax structure affect who decides to immigrate into the nation or emigrate out of the nation? Contrast, for example, nations A and B. Assume that nation A applies a 20 percent tax on every dollar of income earned by an individual. Nation B applies a 10 percent tax on the first $40,000 per year of income and a 40 percent tax on all income above $40,000 per year earned by an individual. Start by computing the tax bill in each country that must be paid by a person earning $40,000 per year and the tax bill that must be paid by a person earning $100,000 per year. Then consider the more general issue: If the language, culture, and climate of the two nations are similar, and if a person can choose to live on one side or the other of a river separating the two nations, who is more likely to choose to live in A and who is more likely to choose to live in B? To what extent does your reasoning apply if an ocean, rather than a river, separates the two countries? Does it apply if the language, culture, or climate in the two nations differs? Explain.

PART FOUR

Market Structures

CHAPTER 15

The Platform Economy

In 1967, the very first Super Bowl pitted the Kansas City Chiefs against the Green Bay Packers, who won. If you had bought a ticket for that game, the face value would have ranged from $6 to $12—or, in 2017 dollars, $45 to $90. Today, however, Super Bowl tickets have face values that can range from $850 to $1,800 for the "cheap seats" to $3,000 for club seats. But even at those prices, you would have a hard time buying a ticket. Simply put, there is an **excess quantity demanded** for Super Bowl tickets at their face value prices. Not surprisingly, as a result, many people who attend the game pay even higher prices for those coveted tickets. In fact, some fans have shelled out as much as $25,000 for a prime Super Bowl ticket!

Fortunately, the majority of Super Bowl tickets—and tickets to about any other event, sporting or otherwise—sell for less than $25,000. Back in 1967 if you wanted a hard-to-obtain event ticket, you could drive to a physical location or make a phone call. Most likely today, though, you would go online because there is an extensive resale market for such tickets. The buying and selling of tickets online is just one part of our growing **platform economy.** As you will see in this chapter, the proliferation of so-called platforms, based on the power of the Internet, already plays an important role in the economy and will channel our economic and social lives to an increasing degree in the future.

PLATFORMS AND TWO-SIDED MARKETS

If you decide you want to attend the next Super Bowl, your best bet is to enter the phrase "Super Bowl tickets" into your Web browser.

Search results will reveal a number of sites that offer Super Bowl tickets for sale. These online sites are **intermediary firms,** which link a group of resellers—those who already have Super Bowl tickets and want to resell them at a higher price than they paid—with buyers. This is a **two-sided market**—meaning an intermediary firm provides the services necessary to connect (1) a group of sellers and (2) a group of buyers.

Today, the intermediary firm is called a **platform firm** because it provides the platform (in this example, the Web site and all of the programming and digital storage behind it) for the two groups that wish to be linked together.

How Online Platform Firms Become Dominant

Platforms are becoming increasingly important throughout the economy. Consider the online platform for selling tickets to the Super Bowl, Broadway plays, major league baseball games, and music concerts. There are about 125 such platform firms (online resellers). Now, let's say you won a pair of Super Bowl tickets in a radio contest. Which platform firm would you choose if you wanted to resell those tickets? To get the best price in reselling your tickets, you would want a platform firm that has the widest audience of potential buyers. Sometimes firms obtain the widest audience simply by being the first firm to offer the platform. In other cases, dominance is achieved by offering the most favorable **quality-adjusted prices.**

In the case of online ticket resellers, the top firm is StubHub, which has 50 percent of the online-ticket reseller market. The second biggest reseller is Ticketmaster with 12 percent of the market. The remaining 38 percent of the market consists of more than one hundred other ticket resellers. (Interestingly, Ticketmaster initially became dominant in this industry because it was among the earliest platforms. StubHub came to dominance by offering better quality-adjusted prices.)

The market structure for online ticket reselling is called an **oligopoly,** in which a small number of producers or sellers share a market. Because the top two firms (StubHub and Ticketmaster), account for more than 60 percent of the ticket-reselling market, there is said to be high **industry concentration.** In addition, with StubHub's 50 percent share of the online-ticket-reseller market, this industry structure is also called a **dominant-firm oligopoly.** A dominant firm—here, StubHub—determines industry pricing. In this industry structure example, the price is the percentage commission paid by those offering tickets for resale on each platform. Today, that commission is usually 15 percent.

How Fringe Online Platform Firms Can Compete

Do you want to see *The Lion King* musical in your hometown? If so, you do not have to rely on just StubHub or Ticketmaster. You can go to other online ticket reselling sites, including viator.com, showticketbooth.com, boxofficeticketsales.com, viagogo.com, and FindTicketsFast.com.

If you choose SeatGeek.com, for instance, you can use its smartphone app to obtain tickets for sporting events and concerts and instantly see where you will be seated at the venue. If you are a reseller, all you do is drag a PDF of your ticket onto your SeatGeek account page. That service then captures all of the relevant event details for display to potential purchasers. SeatGeek also tells you what current offering prices are so you know what price to set. Finally, that platform firm handles payments using a system in which you do not have to give up your bank account details. By using its innovative mobile phone app, SeatGeek has found a niche in competing against its industry's more dominant firms.

Network Effects and Social Media

Not long ago, you could find quite a few social media sites similar to Facebook, including MySpace, Friendster, Xanga, and Classmates. Today, however, Facebook dominates the social media market like no other platform firm. Facebook is considered a platform firm because it satisfies the linking function within a two-sided market. On one side of this market are the consumers—those who want a Facebook account of their own, as well as access to other Facebook profiles. On the other side, of course, are the advertisers and others who want access to the approximately 1.8 billion users' (consumers') information contained in Facebook's "big data."[1]

How did Facebook become so dominant? It took advantage of what is known as a **network effect.** This effect describes a consumer's willingness to use a product or service as being dependent on how many others are willing to use the same product or service. For example, when the telephone industry was brand new at the turn of the twentieth century, if you had a telephone, there were precious few others to whom you could make a call. Gradually, though, as more people paid for telephone service, the value of obtaining that service (and keeping it) increased,

---

1 If you are on Facebook, you no doubt think of yourself as being there to interact with your friends. But if you and others did not also purchase goods and services offered by advertisers, Facebook would not have the funds to develop and operate the platform.

because there were more people with whom to talk. The telephone industry experienced *positive* market feedback, or network, effect.

Today, the same positive network effect applies to Facebook. As more and more individuals signed up for its services, Facebook's value to each user increased, which in turn, encouraged even more people to sign up. That is why Facebook is the dominant social media player, with other smaller players—such as Twitter, WhatsApp, Snapchat, and Pinterest—in the same market. Thus, similar to the online ticket reseller industry, the social media market structure is also a dominant-firm oligopoly.

NETWORK EFFECTS AND ONLINE AUCTIONS SERVICES

Because of positive network effects, the platform economy involves an increasing number of concentrated industries. In addition to the online ticket reselling and social media markets, the online auction industry is concentrated. In this two-sided market, as a seller, you would not want to use an online auction service to sell an item if only a few hundred people were using the same platform to buy something. Similarly, buyers would not use an auction platform unless there were plenty of sellers.

As it turns out, the online auction industry today is dominated by Overstock and eBay. Together, they account for more than 80 percent of such sales, making the online auction market a concentrated industry. In addition, like StubHub, eBay has more than 50 percent of the total market, making the online auction industry another dominant-firm oligopoly.

NETWORK EFFECTS AND ONLINE DATING SERVICES

In the old days, traditional matchmaking services involved a human matchmaker working personally with clients who wanted to find a wife or husband. The matchmaker gathered and analyzed information about the clients and was paid to decide which clients should physically meet for a possible "match." Of course, today we have online dating services. Platform firms—such as elitesingles.com, christianmingle.com, eHarmony.com, Match.com, and Zoosk.com—are the modern matchmakers.

Clearly, as with many other parts of the platform economy, an online dating service with thousands or even millions of members is more attractive than one with only a few hundred. There is a caveat here, though. If you are only interested in meeting people who live near you, you are not very interested in the thousands of others on that dating site who live elsewhere. So, if you live in a rural area, you may be loyal to the relatively small farmersonly.com, and willing to sacrifice a larger number of "matches" in return for matches you deem to be of higher quality.

Be that as it may, any online dating service that provides a larger number of potential dates offers a greater benefit to its users. Therefore, for a given match quality, firms with a larger clientele can either charge more for the service or charge more to advertisers who use their platforms. Positive market feedback allows for network effects, which tend to result in only a few dominant firms in the industry—specifically, with online dating, there are Match.com, Zoosk.com, and eHarmony.com. Usually, if you see an online dating service advertise on the national level, that platform firm has become dominant, or at the very least, has enough funding to try to become dominant.

BIG IDEAS, BIG PLATFORMS, BIG BUCKS

Do not doubt the power of the platform economy, which has given rise to some very successful platform firms. One of the today's major platform firm success stories is Uber—the world's most valuable startup and a leader in the race to transform the future of transportation. Launched in 2010, Uber attracted almost $20 billion in **venture capital.** Today, its implicit **market valuation** is more than $50 billion. No technology firm in history has raised more money from private investors before going public. Its online ridesharing service is so popular that the company name has become a verb: "Don't worry about me, I'll Uber home."

Uber now operates in more than 600 cities spread over 80 countries. More than 40 million people worldwide use its services. Uber does not own cars. It does not directly employ drivers. Indeed, it's just a platform in a two-sided market. On one side are individuals who have cars who want to offer their services. On the other side are individuals who need rides and want alternatives to taxis, buses, and subways. To be sure, Uber has competitors—such as Lyft in America, OLA in India, and Grab in Southeast Asia—but regardless, Uber stands out as the dominant platform firm in the ridesharing service industry.

Another highly valued platform firm is Airbnb, which is transforming another part of the service industry—temporary stays away from home. Like Uber, Airbnb has been met with serious political opposition to its services. Taxi firms have battled, via the political process, the invasion of Uber throughout the world. Some cities and countries have outlawed Uber. Others have tried to regulate it to death. Likewise, Airbnb has seen the same political response, supported by hotel owners, everywhere. Whenever there is a disruption in an industry, the first line of defense appears to be complaining to local politicians that such new competition is "unfair" (see Chapter 18). Despite the political attacks launched by competitors, these successful platform firms are proving that the platform economy can earn big bucks for big ideas.

THE PLATFORM ECONOMY JUST KEEPS GROWING

We could write a book on all aspects of the platform economy. In the music industry, for instance, Pandora, Spotify, and iTunes have upended the traditional way in which individuals listen to music. In the world of work, TaskRabbit, Handy, Amazon Home Services, and other platform firms are growing rapidly. These platform firms connect consumers who need work done around the house with those who seek to do such work. Gone are the days of just looking in the *Yellow Pages*.

In the world of finance, Kickstarter and Indiegogo, platform firms used for startup funding, are replacing the traditional intermediaries, such as **investment bankers.** In addition, you can obtain venture capital via AngelsList or use Rate Setter and Zopa for peer-to-peer lending without going through traditional banking sources.

Indeed, we are heading into a Brave New World, which was made possible first by computers, followed by the Internet. Then came cheap telecommunications, massive data storage centers, and ever-intelligent **algorithms** that are able to access and analyze big data. All of these developments set the stage for the platform economy that now permeates our everyday lives and workplaces. And the best is yet to come.

DISCUSSION QUESTIONS

1. In most cities in the world, it is necessary to purchase an expensive license—often called a *medallion*—to operate a taxi or a taxi company (see Chapter 18 for details). Would you expect the resale price of those medallions to rise or fall in the future, and why?

2. In a sense, all transactions in all markets are two-sided. What is the difference between traditional two-sided markets and modern platform-based, two-sided markets? (*Hint:* How does Amazon differ from your neighborhood Wal-Mart?)

3. If you were the owner of an online dating service, how would you differentiate your services from those of your competitors? How would such differentiations potentially create a greater demand for your online dating service? What would be your additional costs of providing those differentiations?

4. How is YouTube part of a two-sided market? What function does it perform? What are the two audiences that form each side of its two-sided market?

5. Consider the transactions between retailers and customers that involve debit or credit cards. Which firms act as platforms within this two-sided market involving retailers and cardholders? How do those platform firms get paid? (*Hint:* If you don't already know, a few minutes of online research will enable you to find out.)

6. Which platform firms are used by online businesses to interact with their customers? That is, which firms are the "platforms for the platforms"? How are those platform firms paid? (*Hint:* Again, a bit of online research will help you answer this.)

CHAPTER 16

Contracts, Combinations, and Conspiracies

The Sherman Act of 1890 outlaws any "contract, combination, . . . or conspiracy, in restraint of trade or commerce" in the United States. Translated from the legalese, this means that firms in America cannot lawfully join with competitors to form a **cartel** to raise prices above the competitive level.[1] Because successful cartels have the potential for great **profits,** there are strong **incentives** to form them. Usually, however, if the government discourages them, or even if it does not actively encourage them, cartels are difficult to keep together. This is because a cartel must meet four requirements for success:

1. *Share.* It must control a large share of actual and potential output, so that other producers of the good it sells will not be able to depress prices by expanding output significantly.

2. *Substitutes.* Consumers must regard alternatives to the cartel's product as relatively poor substitutes, and these substitutes must be few in number and relatively inelastic in supply. Such factors reduce the **elasticity of demand** facing the cartel, helping it raise prices.

3. *Stability.* There must be few outside factors disturbing **cost** or **demand** conditions in the industry, so that the cartel does not continually have to make new price and output decisions in response to changing conditions.

---

1 Despite this, many American agricultural producers are legally permitted to collectively agree to raise their prices on products ranging from almonds to oranges. They do so under the umbrella of "marketing orders," which are *de facto* cartels approved and enforced by the U.S. Department of Agriculture.

4. *Solidarity.* It must be relatively easy for the cartel to maintain solidarity by identifying and punishing members who cheat on the cartel agreement with price cuts.

All successful cartels have been able to meet these requirements to some extent. Conversely, a breakdown in one or more of these factors has been the downfall of each one that has failed. Most successful cartels are international. They are either effectively beyond (or exempt from) national laws forbidding them or encouraged by or made up of governments themselves.

THE OIL CARTEL

One of the most famous and most successful cartels has been the Organization of Petroleum Exporting Countries (OPEC). Formed in 1960, its members have included many major oil-producing countries, such as Algeria, Indonesia, Iran, Iraq, Kuwait, Libya, Nigeria, Saudi Arabia, and Venezuela. OPEC had little impact on the price of oil until the outbreak of the Middle East war in 1973 provided the impetus for cohesive action. Saudi Arabia, Kuwait, and several other Arab nations sharply reduced their production of oil. Because the **demand curve** for oil is downward sloping, this reduction in supply pushed oil prices—and thus the profits of OPEC members—up sharply. On January 1, 1973, one could buy Saudi Arabian crude oil for about $10 per barrel (in 2017 dollars). Within one year, the price of crude had risen to $35 per barrel. By the next year the price was $45, and by the end of the decade it was over $85 per barrel, with no end in sight.

Several forces combined to send oil prices in the opposite direction by the mid-1980s. At least partly in response to the high prices charged by OPEC, worldwide output of oil from other sources began to grow, led by rising production on Alaska's North Slope and by aggressive marketing of the oil flowing out of the Norwegian and British fields located in the North Sea. Eventually, this additional production significantly reduced the **market share** controlled by OPEC members and thus helped reduce their stranglehold on price.

The most important problem for OPEC, however, as for so many cartels, has been cheating on the cartel agreement by its members. Whenever there are numerous members of a cartel, there will always be some who are unhappy with the situation, perhaps because they think they are not getting enough of the profits. They cheat by charging a slightly lower price than the one stipulated by the cartel, a move that will result in a very large increase in the cheater's revenues (and thus profits).

The potential for cheating is a constant threat to a cartel's existence, and when enough of a cartel's members try to cheat, the cartel breaks up.

In the case of OPEC, war between the member nations of Iran and Iraq during the 1980s precipitated a major outbreak of cheating as those two nations expanded production beyond their **quotas,** using the extra sales to finance large military expenditures. Expressed in 2017 dollars, the price of crude oil plunged from $100 per barrel to less than $25 by 1986, when cheating on output quotas spread throughout the cartel. Saudi Arabia, the world's largest producer of crude, finally restored order when it threatened to double its output if other OPEC members did not adhere to their quotas. Crude oil prices hovered around $30 per barrel from then until early 2004, when they started a sharp climb due to rising world demand. After peaking at about $150 per barrel in 2008, prices subsequently dropped to $50 in response first to a worldwide recession and then to higher output from oil fracking operations in North America.

THE DIAMOND CARTEL

The difficulties faced by cartels are also illustrated in the diamond market. DeBeers, the famous diamond company, once controlled as much as 80 percent of the world's diamond supply, but now can claim only a 40 percent share. DeBeers itself produces about 25 percent of the world's diamond output and controls the marketing of another 15 percent through a cartel called the Diamond Trading Company (DTC). Under the direction of DeBeers, the DTC has long restricted the sale of rough-cut diamonds to keep their prices at levels that maximize the profits of its members. After many years of profitable success, however, the diamond cartel hit rough times in the 1980s and 1990s. Cartel profits spurred searches for new sources of supply, and major discoveries were made in Australia and Canada. Moreover, Russia, which accounts for about one-fourth of the world's output, defected from the DTC cartel to market its diamonds through a company known as ALROSA, the top DTC competitor. The combined effect of increased supplies and cartel defections pushed the inflation-adjusted price of top-quality diamonds down by 50 percent. Since 2000, the rapid growth of demand in China and elsewhere has helped drive prices back up to record levels.

THE CAVIAR CARTEL

The Russians have had troubles with their own historically successful cartel, the one that controls—or controlled—the supply of fine caviar. The principal source of some of the world's best caviar is the Volga

River delta, where Kazakhstan and Russia (both former members of the Soviet Union) share a border at the northern end of the Caspian Sea. Both the temperature and the salinity of the water in the delta make it the ideal spawning ground for sturgeon, the long-nosed prehistoric fish whose eggs have for centuries been prized as the world's finest caviar. Originally, the Russian royal families ran the show, eating what they wanted of the harvest and then controlling the remaining supplies to their advantage.

When the Russian Revolution disposed of the Romanov dynasty in 1917, the new communist regime quickly saw the potential profits achievable from cornering the market on caviar. Hence, for the next seventy-five years or so, a Soviet state-dominated cartel controlled the nation's caviar business from top to bottom. Although the Soviet sturgeon were considerate enough to produce an annual catch of some 2,000 tons of caviar, the communist cartel allowed only 150 tons out of the country. As a result, a state-supplied kilogram (2.2 pounds) of top-grade black caviar costing $5 or less on the Moscow black market commanded $1,000 or more in New York.

The demise of the Soviet Union spawned trouble, however, because **competition** reared its ugly head. As it turns out, the largest sturgeon fisheries fell under the jurisdictions of two different autonomous republics—Russia and Kazakhstan—each of which wanted to own and operate its own lucrative caviar business. Moreover, a variety of individuals, including enterprising Caspian Sea fishermen from these republics, staked private claims and, in some instances, set up their own **export** channels (behavior officially termed "black market piracy"). The effect of this capitalist behavior was a 20 percent drop in the official caviar export price during the first year of autonomy, plus an escalation of competition since then.

Caviar consumers were pleased at this turn of events, but old-line suppliers were not so happy. "We don't need this kind of competition," complained one. "All of these small rivals mean that prices will fall and the market will be ripped apart. This is a delicacy—we need to keep it elite." Recent years have seen a sharp upswing in world caviar prices, although not because Russia and Kazakhstan have managed to get competition under control. Instead, it turns out that pollution from leftover Soviet industry in the area has sharply reduced the region's sturgeon population. The resulting decline in the amount of harvestable caviar drove costs and prices up and profits even lower. Adding insult to injury, American firms have entered the caviar market in response to the higher prices. This has intensified the price–cost squeeze that the former Soviet republics are suffering, despite

Russian efforts to harvest caviar from fish farms. So, just as Soviet citizens found that communism wasn't all that it was cracked up to be, it appears some of them are now learning that capitalism may be more than they bargained for—but perhaps no less than Karl Marx warned them about.

THE COLLEGE SPORTS CARTEL

Oddly enough, despite the Sherman Act and other tough antitrust laws, one of the longest-running cartels can be found right here in the United States. The National Collegiate Athletic Association (NCAA), which operates under a special exemption from the antitrust laws, sets the rules not only for how intercollegiate sports competition takes place but also for how athletes are recruited and paid. And under NCAA rules, college athletes are not paid much. Indeed, as a practical matter, compensation for collegiate athletes is limited to the cost of room, board, books, and tuition at their university or college, an amount that typically ranges from $30,000 to $60,000 per year. This might sound like pretty good pay to you, and indeed, for a field hockey player or college wrestler, it probably is. But for the so-called revenue sports of college athletics, most notably football and basketball, such sums amount to a pittance compared to what these athletes would bring on the open market. This, of course, is exactly the point: Universities are joined together in the NCAA in part simply to keep down the costs of college athletics.

In the case of football, the underlying economic value of college players has been studied quite intensively, so we have a good idea of what top players are worth. A player who ends up getting drafted by a professional team is underpaid by $2 million over the course of his college career. And while lesser players are underpaid by lesser amounts, numbers like these make it clear that despite encouraging open competition on college playing fields, when it comes to competition in the marketplace, the NCAA is guilty of unsportsmanlike conduct.[2]

---

2 For many years, the NCAA also had agreements with the makers of sports-oriented video games that used the likenesses of college players. The twist: instead of the players being paid for this usage, the NCAA pocketed the fee. Eventually, the NCAA was sued for violating the antitrust laws, and after six years finally agreed to a monetary settlement for the players. The payout? A measly $1,200 apiece.

DISCUSSION QUESTIONS

1. Why are all cartels inherently unstable?

2. Would it be easier to form a cartel in a market with many producers or one with few producers?

3. What happens to the producers of caviar made from other types of fish eggs (such as salmon, whitefish, and trout) when the price of the finest sturgeon caviar changes? Would these firms ever have an incentive to help the governments of Russia and Kazakhstan reestablish the caviar cartel?

4. If the members of your class were to attempt to form a study-reduction cartel in which everyone agreed to study less, which individuals would have the most to gain from the cartel? Which ones would have the greatest incentive to cheat on the cartel?

5. The economy of India (with a population of one billion) has begun to industrialize, and per capita income there is rising. What impact will this growth have on the demand for oil and diamonds—and thus on their prices? Explain.

6. Suppose there is a decline in marginal costs for one member of a cartel. What impact will this have on the incentive of that firm to cheat on the cartel agreement? Explain.

CHAPTER 17

Coffee, Tea, or Tuition-Free?

A few years ago, the Internet retailing giant Amazon.com received some unwanted publicity when it was revealed that the company was charging customers different prices for the same movies. Amazon insisted that the price differences were random and amounted to an effort to simply test the market. But some customers complained that Amazon was using the practice to tailor prices to customer characteristics, charging more to people who were likely to be willing to pay more. The flap over Amazon's "market test" soon died out. But as time passes, Internet firms and other companies are finding it almost impossible to resist regularly charging customers different prices for everything from consumer electronics to razor blades. The reason is simple: By tracking people's buying habits, firms can get a pretty good idea of how to engage in **price discrimination** among their customers and thus increase their **profits.**

Shouldn't price discrimination be illegal? Actually, it *is* illegal, at least under some circumstances. Nevertheless, it is routinely practiced by businesses of all descriptions—and perhaps even by the college you attend. Interestingly, although price discrimination definitely benefits the firms (or colleges) that engage in it, you may benefit, too. Let's see how.

THE BASICS OF PRICE DISCRIMINATION

First things first: Price discrimination is defined as the existence of price differences for the same good that are not due to differences in the **marginal costs** of supplying the customers. Price discrimination can occur when (i) marginal costs are the same across customers but prices are different, or (ii) prices are the same despite differences in marginal costs.

An example of the former occurs when pharmacies or movie theaters charge lower prices to "senior citizens" than to other customers. An example of the latter can be found at "all-you-can-eat" buffets, where the price is the same for all diners, even though some eat much more food than others.

Three conditions must exist for a firm to engage in price discrimination. First, the firm must be, at least to some extent, a **price searcher**—it must be able to raise price above marginal cost without losing all of its sales to rivals. Second, there must be identifiable differences across customers in their willingness (or ability) to pay different prices for the same good. Third, the firm must be able to prevent customers who pay lower prices from reselling the good to customers who otherwise would be charged higher prices—or else customers eligible for the lowest price will buy on behalf of all customers.

The objective of price discrimination is, of course, higher profits for the firm that engages in it. To see how this might work, consider a firm selling to two identifiable groups of customers, say, retirees and working people. Also suppose that the retirees have lower incomes and so perhaps have a higher **price elasticity of demand** for the good—that is, they tend to be more sensitive to changes in price. In this situation, it may be possible for the firm to reallocate sales among customer groups, lowering prices slightly to retirees and raising them somewhat more to working people, thereby getting more revenue at the same costs and so earning higher profits. Of course, to accomplish this, the firm must be able to distinguish between the two groups. (For example, lower prices may be offered only to persons who can prove they are older and thus more likely to be retired.) The firm also must be able to prevent resale from low-price buyers to other customers. When pricing prescription medicines, pharmacies are aided by federal and state laws that forbid such resale. Movie theaters prevent resale by requiring that to get a lower price one must attend the movie personally. (This helps explain why movie rental companies such as Netflix are less likely than movie theaters to offer senior citizen discounts: It would be too easy for seniors to rent movies on behalf of younger people who wish to avoid the higher prices applicable to them.)

PRICE DISCRIMINATION BY AIRLINES

If you have ever traveled on an airplane, you are likely to have been a beneficiary of price discrimination (although your parents—or their employers—may have been victims of such discrimination if they fly on short-notice business trips). Before 1978, the fares charged by airlines in the United States were regulated by the federal government, so all air-lines offered the same government-approved fares; discounts were rare beyond late-night ("red-eye") or weekend flights.[1] Once deregulation occurred, airlines quickly discovered that there were large differences in the price elasticity of demand across customers. Business travelers typically had a lower price elasticity of demand and hence were willing to pay higher fares than leisure travelers. Fares charged to business trav-elers are now higher than they used to be, even though leisure fares are significantly lower than they were in the days of government regulation.

The precision and effectiveness with which the airlines engage in price discrimination have been rising steadily over time, thanks to a process known as "yield management." Combining sophisticated statistical techniques and massive historical databases, together with computerized up-to-the-minute bookings, the airlines can predict with almost pinpoint accuracy how many business customers will want seats on a given flight and how much they'll be willing to pay. As a result, says one industry insider, "high fares get higher and low fares get lower."

YIELD MANAGEMENT IN ACTION

The process begins months before a flight ever departs, as the airline divides the seats on a plane into as many as seven or more different fare classes, or categories. Initial fares on a flight are established for each of the categories, and the yield management computers begin the process of monitoring the reservations, comparing them to historical patterns. If advance bookings are slow, the airline will move seats to low-fare cat-egories. But if business travelers buy higher-priced, unrestricted tickets sooner than expected, the yield management computer removes seats from discount categories and holds them for last-minute business pas-sengers who are predicted to show up.

A host of techniques are used to optimize the blend between filling the seats on a plane and getting the highest fare for each seat. In the weeks leading up to a flight, the level of fares assigned to each category may be adjusted up or down based on the latest moves by competitors, and as the flight date approaches, lower-priced categories are likely to be closed out altogether. Moreover, some people seeking reservations may be told a given flight is "sold out" even though passengers using that flight as a connector to another of the airline's routes may find ample

---

1 Adjusted for inflation, average fares were also considerably higher than they are today, because the federal government agency responsible for regulating the airlines prevented them from competing on the basis of price.

seating—for a price, of course. The result of all this fine-tuning is that passengers on the same flight from, say, Chicago to Phoenix may pay round-trip fares that vary by a factor of 5—ranging, say, from $280 for the lowest-priced seats to $1,400 for the top fares.

You might think that all of these pricing tactics generate big profits—but you'd be wrong. Competition among airlines is so fierce that the profit on a one-hundred-passenger flight amounts to the price of a single ticket. Is it any wonder, then, that the companies are trying to get as much as they can for it?

PRICE DISCRIMINATION BY COLLEGES

Interestingly, the yield management techniques refined by the airlines are now being used by universities when they decide on financial aid packages offered to students. After all, given the nominal tuition at a university, a more generous financial aid offer can be thought of as a lower price, and students, like everyone else, behave according to the **law of demand.** Universities have found, for example, that they can offer less generous aid packages to students who apply for early admission because such students are more eager to attend. As one financial aid consultant notes, "Those who have the most interest in the school are going to be less price sensitive." In a similar vein, some colleges have found that people who come for campus interviews are more interested in attending. The response has been to offer slightly less generous aid packages to such students, even though the colleges routinely recommend that students come for interviews.

In addition to these regular features of price discrimination in financial aid offers, universities also monitor their enrollment figures each year, just as the airlines watch bookings by fare category. If a school is getting, say, too many premed students and not enough in the humanities, financial aid offers will be adjusted accordingly, with bigger than usual aid offers being made to the students the school is trying to attract. Schools that are noted for excellence in one area but are trying to maintain a balanced mix of majors have become particularly adept at the financial aid game. As the enrollment vice president for Carnegie Mellon University notes, without sophisticated adjustments to the blend of aid packages offered, "I'd have an institution full of engineers and computer scientists and I wouldn't have anybody in arts and design." Carnegie Mellon also recognizes the importance of competition in determining the prices it charges. After admitted students are notified of their aid offers in the spring, they are invited to fax the school any better offers they receive from other colleges. The university generally meets competing offers received by desirable students.

Price Discrimination by Drug Companies

Price discrimination can even be practiced on a worldwide scale. Most major pharmaceutical companies price discriminate based on the nationality of the people buying their drugs. Partly because incomes in other nations are lower than in the United States, people in other nations have higher elasticities of demand than American citizens. Consequently, pharmaceutical companies sell prescription drugs elsewhere at lower prices than they do in the United States. But one of these other nations is Canada, and American senior citizens have found that by getting on a bus (or even just visiting the Web site of a Canadian pharmacy), they can save a bundle on their prescriptions.[2] Although this practice is technically illegal, neither the United States nor Canada has stopped it.

Price discrimination certainly profits the firms that practice it, but there is an entirely different question—one that cannot be answered by economics—as to whether it is fair. Most student travelers who can stay over a Saturday night or make reservations a month in advance probably don't mind the lower fares made possible by price discrimination. But business travelers are far from pleased with the high fares they must pay to get where they want, when they want, usually on short notice. "They've got you, and they know it," says one executive. The flip side, of course, is that without the extra revenue generated by price discrimination, some companies or colleges would be hard-pressed to survive. Indeed, when asked about the equity of fine-tuning aid packages to willingness to attend rather than ability to pay, one financial aid official noted he had little choice in the matter: "I could make it very fair—and be out of business."

Discussion Questions

1. First-class passengers generally pay higher fares than coach passengers, even when they take advantage of advance-purchase discounts. Is this price discrimination? (*Hint:* Seats in first class are generally leather rather than fabric and are about 50 percent wider than coach seats. Also, there are more flight attendants per passenger in the first-class section.)

---

2 Another reason for lower prices in Canada is that it has a nationalized health-care system, meaning that the government buys drugs on behalf of all Canadians. This practice makes the Canadian government a **monopsonist** (literally, "single buyer"), with the power to force drug prices below what they otherwise would be.

2. Is it price discrimination when a professional football team charges, say, $350 per ticket for fifty-yard-line tickets in the lower deck and $100 per ticket for upper-deck tickets overlooking the end zone?

3. What factors other than income are likely to affect willingness to pay? How will differences in these factors among its customers affect the likelihood that a firm will engage in price discrimination?

4. Consider the following data from three different firms (1, 2, and 3) each selling to two different customers (A and B). Shown are the price per unit charged each customer and the marginal cost of producing each unit for the customer. (Thus, for example, Firm 1 has different marginal costs between customers and charges different prices.)

Which firms are engaged in price discrimination? Explain. Extra credit: For each firm, rank-order the elasticity of demand of the two customers.

	Customer A	Customer B
Firm 1		
Price ($)	100	150
Marginal cost ($)	100	150
Firm 2		
Price ($)	200	200
Marginal cost ($)	100	150
Firm 3		
Price ($)	150	200
Marginal cost ($)	100	100

5. Suppose a firm starts off with selling a uniform product to two different customers at the same price per unit for each. Now it decides to engage in price discrimination by raising the price to one customer and lowering the price to the other customer. Why doesn't the profit lost due to lowering the price for one customer eliminate all of the higher profits achieved by raising the price to the other customer?

6. Suppose a local beverage shop charges $6 for a six-pack of your favorite beverage and charges $15 for a case (containing four six-packs) of that same beverage? Is this price discrimination?

CHAPTER 18

Keeping the Competition Out

Most competitors hate **competition.** And who can blame them? After all, if a firm can keep the competition out, **profits** are sure to rise. How high they will rise obviously varies by industry, but the lowly taxicab market gives some indication of what is at stake.

TAXICAB MEDALLIONS

In New York City, the number of taxicabs is limited by law—limited, in fact, to one cab for every six hundred people, in a town where many people don't own cars. To legally operate a taxi in New York, one must own a taxi medallion, a city-issued metal shield affixed to the cab's hood. Although the number of taxi medallions in New York is determined by law, you are free to buy one from a current owner, assuming that you can come up with the prevailing market price, about $600,000. This price, we should note, does not include the taxi itself, although it does entitle you to the right to work long hours, subject to robbery, rude customers, and the erratic driving habits of other cabbies.

Lest you think New York taxi drivers are crazy to pay such sums, keep this in mind: Because the city keeps the competition out, the taxi business has been so lucrative that the medallions can be used as collateral to borrow at favorable interest rates, and any cabbie who wants to leave the business can quickly find a buyer for his or her medallion. In fact, the long-run **rate of return** on New York taxi medallions compares favorably with the long-run rate of return on stocks listed on the New York Stock Exchange.

There are just one or two small clouds on the horizon, however. As recently as 2014, the price of a New York taxi medallion was upwards of $1 million, quite a contrast to the current value. In that same year, taxis provided more than 90 percent of the rides per hire in New York, a number that recently was down to 60 percent—and falling. But before we examine developments of the last few years, let's first look at why keeping the competition out made taxi medallions special for so long.

How It Works

Keeping the competition out works quite simply. Reducing the number of firms in an industry decreases the **supply** of the good, thus driving up its price. Firms that remain thus enjoy both a higher price for their product and a larger **market share.** Consumers are the losers, however, as they suffer from higher prices and fewer alternative sources of supply from which to choose. The firms that are excluded also lose. Their owners are forced to go into lower-paying pursuits for which they are not as well suited. The higher profits enjoyed by the firms protected from competition thus come at the expense of consumers and excluded competitors. The net result is also an overall loss to society as a whole because the limit on competition reduces the total extent of mutually beneficial exchange.

Note that we said that the number of taxi medallions in New York is limited by the government. This is typical. Even though many government agencies (for example, the Federal Trade Commission and the Department of Justice at the federal level) are supposed to promote competition, getting the government involved is usually the most effective way to *stifle* competition. Consider telephones. It used to be that both long-distance and local telephone markets were regulated by the federal government. In 1984, the long-distance market was deregulated, and AT&T had to begin competing with other firms for customers. The result was a 40 percent drop in inflation-adjusted long-distance rates. Local telephone service continued to be regulated by the Federal Communications Commission (FCC), however, and over the same period of time, local phone rates *rose* 40 percent in real terms—chiefly because the FCC kept competition out of the local phone service market.

Occupational Licensing

Keeping the competition out seems to be growing in popularity across America. As the economy has moved from manufacturing to services, the number of people working in licensed professions has risen sharply.

Thirty years ago, there were about eighty occupations for which one or more state governments required a license. Today, there are over eleven hundred occupations that require a license in at least one state, ranging from secretaries in Georgia to wallpaper hangers in California. Roughly 30 percent of the U.S. labor force, about forty-eight million individuals, now belongs to a licensed profession. Officially, of course, this is all done to protect the consumer from unscrupulous or incompetent practitioners. In fact, such licensing requirements serve chiefly—if not solely—to keep the competition out and elevate the earnings of those who manage to get licensed.

Many of the decision makers who work for the government agencies that limit competition are lawyers, so it is not surprising that competition among lawyers is limited. For example, in every state but one (California), the number of law schools is capped by state law, thereby restricting entry into the profession and driving up earnings. Real estate agents are also well represented among the members of state legislatures, and so it may come as no surprise that they, too, have been successful in keeping the competition out. In addition to having to pass examinations to be licensed, real estate agents are prohibited—at their own request—from engaging in all sorts of competitive behavior. In a dozen states, agents are prohibited from discounting their prices even if they perform fewer than the usual number of services for their customers. In eight states, real estate agents are not permitted to perform fewer services than the local realty association specifies, even if the customer does not want those services. These crimps on competition make life both comfortable and profitable for real estate agents, but it's not such a good deal for home buyers and sellers. In the United States, the average real estate agent's commission is 5.1 percent of the sale price of the home; the average commission in other countries is 3.6 percent. Thus, by restricting competition, real estate agents in America are able to charge 40 percent more for their services.

SOME HAIRY COMPETITION

Sometimes the government gets involved in unlikely markets in its efforts to prevent the ravages of competition from taking their toll. Consider hair braiding. Some African Americans like to have their hair straightened in beauty shops, a procedure that requires a touch-up every four weeks, for an average monthly cost (excluding cutting and styling) of about $100. An alternative is to get one's hair braided at a braiding salon. There are now about ten thousand of these salons across the country. Braids need maintenance only once every ten weeks, cutting the cost to $50 per month.

The same low cost and convenience that make braiding salons attractive to consumers also make them threatening to the conventional beauty shops that straighten hair, especially in fashion-conscious California. Claiming that they are seeking to protect consumers, agents of the California Barbering and Cosmetology Board regularly raid the salons of unlicensed hair braiders. Not surprisingly, the hair braiders think the state is actually trying to protect state-licensed cosmetologists at beauty shops, who must spend $6,000 for sixteen hundred hours of training to get their licenses. Indeed, one of the braiders, Ali Rasheed, argues that the marketplace is better than state licensing boards at protecting consumers. "It's simple," he says. "If I mess up your hair, you don't come back. You spread the word. And very quickly I'd be out of business." Perhaps so, but it looks like the state of California doesn't want to give consumers that option.

Licensing is even tougher for would-be braiders in Utah. There, the "Barber, Cosmetology/Barber, Esthetics, Electrology and Nail Technology Licensing Board" requires them to pay $16,000 in tuition and undergo two thousand hours of training in cosmetology—even though none of the certified schools in Utah actually teach hair braiding. Around the nation, cosmetologists are required to obtain an average of 372 days of training. Required training for emergency medical technicians averages just 33 days. Can hair cutting, braiding, and coloring really be more important than saving lives? Some people think so. As the director of one barber school in Michigan put it, "I'm not saying we are as important as doctors, but we are the closest you can get."

GOVERNMENTS DON'T LIKE COMPETITION EITHER

Back in New York, we can see that even the government likes to protect itself from competition. New York City is well known for its massive public transit system, comprising both subways and bus lines. What is not so well known is that mass transit in New York City started off as a private enterprise. The first horsecars and elevated trains in the city were developed by private companies. Moreover, even though New York's first subway was partly financed by a loan from the city, it was otherwise a private operation, run profitably at a fare of a nickel (the equivalent of about a dollar today).

New York's politicians refused to allow fares to rise during the **inflation** of World War I, yielding financial losses for the private transit companies. Promising to show the private sector how to run a transit system efficiently while simultaneously offering to protect the public from the "dictatorship" of the transit firms, the city took over the subway, merged it with the bus line, and promptly started raising fares. Despite fare increases double the inflation rate, however, costs have risen even faster, so that today, even though the basic single fare is $3.00, the city *loses* about as much on each passenger because fares don't cover costs.

Competition Uber All?

The high prices brought on by taxicab regulations and inefficient mass transit systems have, in recent years, attracted some new competition. Start-ups such as Uber and Lyft now offer so-called "ride-sharing" services. With the Uber app installed on your smartphone, for example, you can see a map of Uber drivers available in your area and, for a mutually agreeable price, hire them to transport you to your destination. None of these drivers work for Uber itself, but the company certifies the drivers and takes 20 percent of the fares to cover its costs. It may come as no surprise to you that in the eighty or so nations where Uber has operations, taxi companies and mass transit systems have fought desperately to keep the competition out. So far, however, Uber and other firms like it are still expanding, lowering prices and improving the quality of customer service along the way.

It is Uber's entry into the New York City ride-for-hire market that has been chiefly responsible for those "clouds" on the New York taxi horizon we mentioned earlier. Uber drivers have taken a substantial chunk of business away from traditional taxis in the city. The competition from Uber has not just reduced the market value of New York taxi medallions by 40 percent. It has also made it *much* easier to get around New York. So, despite the best efforts of those who hate the competition, consumers so far seem to be getting the best of this one.

Discussion Questions

1. Consider two different ways of beating your competition. One way is to offer your customers lower prices and better service. The other is to get a law passed that raises your competitors' costs—for example, by imposing special operating requirements on them. Can you see any difference between these two methods, assuming that both succeed in keeping your competition out?

2. Although governments at all levels sometimes act to prevent some individuals from competing with others, the federal government is probably the most active in this role, state governments are less active, and local governments are the least active. Can you explain this pattern?

3. Is there any difference between prohibiting entry by a group of firms and levying a special tax on those firms?

4. Manicurists and pedicurists are required to be licensed in both California and Florida. In California, people practicing these occupations must take 400 hours of classroom training; in Florida, they must take only 240 hours of classroom training. *Ceteris paribus* (that is, holding other factors constant), in which state would you expect pedicures and manicures to be more expensive? Explain. How could you use per capita consumption of pedicures and manicures in the two states to help you decide whether the classroom-training requirement was chiefly designed to improve the quality of pedicures and manicures or to keep the competition out?

5. Although New York City's mass transit system is the largest in the country, it is not the only one that is heavily subsidized by taxpayers—in fact, as far as we know, *all* mass transit systems are heavily subsidized by taxpayers. Suggest at least one economic and one political reason why these systems are heavily subsidized.

6. Labor unions are a device for limiting competition, in this instance competition among workers. The union bargains on behalf of all members, presumably resulting in a higher wage for workers and higher costs for employers. Use this fact, combined with the fact that international trade has played an increasing role in the American economy over the last fifty years, to explain the observation that union membership has declined as a share of private sector employment over this period in the United States. Your explanation should be consistent with the fact that union membership has *not* declined as a share of *public* sector employment over this period.

PART FIVE

Political Economy

CHAPTER 19

Health Insurance for All . . . Or Maybe Not

The Affordable Care Act (ACA), sometimes referred to as Obamacare, was signed into law by President Obama in 2010. By the time Obama left office in January 2017, the law was in trouble—deep trouble. Insurance premiums under the ACA were skyrocketing and consumer choices were shrinking, as major insurers dropped out of the market across the country. Plans available under Obamacare had gotten so expensive that millions of healthy individuals were paying fines rather than buying the insurance. In hundreds of counties, including all counties in five states, there was no choice among insurers when purchasing an ACA plan—only one firm was left in the market.

Before we can understand the crisis of Obamacare and why President Trump vowed to repeal it, we'll need to first see how we got here. By the time you read this, Obamacare may have been replaced, but we'll talk in this chapter as though it is still with us.

INSURANCE COVERAGE

At the time of the ACA's passage, almost 50 million Americans were without healthcare insurance. There is no doubt the law has increased the number of Americans with health insurance. By 2017, about 20 million people had gained coverage due to the ACA. Roughly 40 percent of these people purchased private insurance policies through new government-operated exchanges (online markets). The other 60 percent became eligible for Medicaid, the federal–state health insurance program for low-income individuals. Nevertheless, this left almost thirty million adults uninsured, and most knowledgeable observers now predict that over the next decade the number of uninsured adults is unlikely to decrease much more.

Originally, the ACA was forecast to have a much greater impact on the number of uninsured people. After all, the law is quite specific. You are required to have health insurance, and if you don't have it, you are fined each year—a fine that, depending on your circumstances, is now either $695 or 2.5 percent of your income. The requirement to purchase insurance is called the **individual mandate.**

THE FAILURE OF THE MANDATE

The original purpose of the individual mandate was to ensure that younger, healthier individuals would buy medical insurance. When the insurance pool does not contain significant numbers of the young and the healthy, the high healthcare costs of older, sicker individuals can send insurance premiums skyrocketing. Moreover, because taxpayers are paying for Medicaid and subsidizing the private insurance obtained under the ACA, without the young and healthy, the burden on taxpayers is also rising.

To see how this works—or has failed to work under Obamacare—consider the fact that the average sixty-four-year-old consumes six times as much healthcare as the average twenty-one-year-old. Under open market conditions, the older individual would thus be expected to pay about six times as much for health insurance as the younger person—just as teens must pay more for their auto insurance, due to their high accident rates. But under Obamacare, insurers are not allowed to charge older customers more than three times as much as they bill the young. In our example, the law requires that the price to the young person be 75 percent *more* than her actual costs, while the older person would be charged 13 percent *less* than her costs. The sensible response of consumers is quite obvious. Older, costlier consumers sign up for insurance, while young people "just say no," declining to purchase the overpriced insurance. Even plenty of healthy people in their thirties, forties, and fifties have chosen to pay the fine rather than buy insurance. In 2016, eight million people paid fines rather than purchased insurance, leaving the insured population much sicker, and much more expensive.

YOU'RE SICK BUT HAVE NO HEALTH INSURANCE— NOT TO WORRY

The Affordable Care Act directs that you may not be turned down for health insurance due to a pre-existing ailment. The purpose of this rule was to ensure that people who had serious health problems could get insurance. But the rule has also had two other effects. First, people *without* serious problems are declining to buy insurance, knowing that when problems crop up, they are guaranteed insurance no matter how sick they are. This problem, known as **adverse selection,** drives up costs for everybody else—including both taxpayers and the relatively healthy insured population. Second, people with newly acquired insurance suddenly seem to develop health problems they never knew they had before, a phenomenon known as **moral hazard.** This, too, drives up costs for taxpayers and for others in the insured pool.

The combination of these forces began showing up quickly in the healthcare spending data. For example, during the first part of 2014, serious health problems were more than twice as prevalent among newly insured individuals, compared to those who had previously had insurance. Now, these high health costs were not totally a surprise. After all, one problem the law was designed to address was the inability of sick people to get insurance. But the *magnitude* of the high costs has exceeded all forecasts. With each passing year, costs have risen even faster. The jump in insurance rates from 2016 to 2017 exceeded 40 percent in five states, with rates rising nearly 150 percent in Arizona. Moreover, in all fifty states the number of firms offering insurance plans under the ACA has dropped sharply, because firms have found it too difficult to predict their costs. For example, the ACA was supposed to encourage people to obtain primary care physicians and to use them instead of emergency rooms for their health care. And while some of the newly insured are doing this, the fact is that emergency rooms visits are *up* sharply under Obamacare, the opposite of what was predicted by its backers.

The Hazards of Pre-existing Conditions

All insurers must concern themselves with potential adverse selection and moral hazard. But the challenges facing insurers operating under the ACA are amplified. This is because the law forbids insurers from denying coverage (or charging higher premiums) to people with costly to treat pre-existing medical conditions, such as diabetes or heart disease. You cannot purchase fire insurance on your house after a fire has started, just as you cannot buy auto insurance to cover the repairs from a previous accident. The health insurance market used to work the same way. If you had a known pre-existing medical condition, whether it was a broken arm or cancer, you could not buy health insurance to cover the costs of treating that condition. Under Obamacare, firms are *required* to sell you a policy that will cover those pre-existing ailments, and they must charge the same price to you that they charge to people without those conditions. This feature of the law has produced some innovative behavior.

Insurers are finding under the ACA that up to 20 percent of their costs are caused by people who purchase insurance and then immediately have a major medical procedure (such as a $40,000 hip replacement or $100,000 heart bypass operation). Then they drop the insurance as soon as the bills are paid.[1] In a slightly different twist, companies that perform kidney dialysis (see Chapter 8), are paying the insurance premiums for people with end-stage kidney disease to ensure that their dialysis (at a cost of $80,000 per year) will be covered. This is a great deal for these patients, of course, as well as for the dialysis providers. But because the premiums only cover about 5 percent of the cost of the treatment, the *other* people buying insurance are the ones who pay for the remaining 95 percent.

Many Hospitals Have Hit the Jackpot

Thus far, there is little doubt that the ACA has caused an increase in the demand for healthcare. Partly this is because many previously uninsurable people now have coverage. Plus, there are people who are now buying policies simply because they are eligible for government subsidies offered under the ACA to low-income individuals. Both groups are consuming more healthcare: more emergency room visits, more elective surgeries, more prescription drugs. And this additional healthcare has no doubt had substantial benefits for these consumers—which was, after all, the point of the law.

But there is another group of beneficiaries, the suppliers of healthcare services, most notably hospitals and pharmaceutical companies. *Uninsured* in-patient admissions have fallen at most hospitals throughout the United States, at the same time that *insured* admissions have risen even more, yielding a substantial net increase. Hospitals, therefore, benefit in two ways. They have more patients, and the revenue they collect per patient is higher than before. Pharmaceutical companies have also seen a sharp rise in demand for their products as new enrollees are taking advantage of their insurance coverage. Between 2010 (when the law

---

1 Under the ACA, people cannot simply purchase insurance any time they wish. But everyone is allowed to buy during the three months from November 1 to January 31, and many people qualify to purchase at other times during the year under special arrangements. For example, if you move across a state line (and in many cases just across a county line), you qualify to buy insurance immediately.

was passed) and 2017, the stock prices of healthcare companies rose by roughly 50 percent compared to the average of all stock prices, due to the upsurge in healthcare profits.

THE CONTINUATION OF A TWO-TIER
HEALTHCARE SYSTEM

One thing the ACA will not do is eliminate the two-tier healthcare system in the United States. Newly insured individuals fall into two broad groups—those who have purchased their own insurance policies on the exchanges and those whom the law has made newly eligible for Medicaid (the federal–state healthcare program for the poor). Although there are a variety of insurance plans available in the exchanges, their typical provisions are much more modest than employer-offered plans or even individual plans offered outside the exchanges. The amounts that people have to pay out of their own pocket for services ($6,000 to $10,000) are thus higher with exchange policies, and enrollees have sharply limited choices of doctors and especially hospitals. In short, none of these plans come close to the "Cadillac" plans commonly available to unionized employees, or even to the "Chevrolet" plans purchased outside the exchanges.

The situation is even worse for Medicaid enrollees. The federal and state governments place significant restrictions on what types of care Medicaid can provide and how much doctors and hospitals will be paid for this care. As a result, healthcare outcomes tend to be worse for Medicaid patients than for persons with their own health insurance. Moreover, because of the low reimbursement rates under Medicaid, about one-third of primary-care physicians and one-fourth of specialists have completely closed their practices to new Medicaid patients. The bottom line is that the newly insured are better off than they were, but the care they are getting is still significantly below average.

THE IMPACT ON THE PREVIOUSLY INSURED

Written into the ACA were many items that Congress and the president thought should be covered by all insurance plans, regardless of whether those plans were purchased through the exchanges. Thus, the law mandated that all policies offer maternity care, contraceptives, annual checkups, and so forth.

Almost 80 percent of individual plans in place when Obamacare became effective did not contain one or more of these provisions. Hence, insurers were required to *cancel* tens of millions of policies, which were no longer in compliance with federal law. Eventually people were able to purchase new coverage, but it typically cost more (sometimes much more) than their previous policies. In pushing for the law's passage back in 2010, the president had promised that "if you like your insurance, you can keep it." It was a promise not kept for many Americans.

THE RISE OF THE 49ERS

No, we are not talking about the football team. Rather, we are talking about companies that refuse to hire their fiftieth employee. Businesses with fewer than fifty employees are exempt from the most costly ACA requirements that larger employers incur under the healthcare law. Indeed, firms with fewer than fifty employees may lawfully offer no health insurance at all and avoid paying the penalties that apply to large companies that don't offer insurance. Thus, some firms have been reorganizing themselves, or simply firing employees, to get down to forty-nine or fewer employees. Others are shelving their company expansion strategies, which have now become uneconomical in light of the law's costly insurance requirements.

Firms with fifty or more employees do have options to avoid the law, however. They can make sure that many more of their employees are "29ers." That is, they can limit their employees to working twenty-nine or fewer hours a week because thirty hours or more per week is Obamacare's definition of full-time employment. Employers are not required to offer health insurance to part-time employees, so firms can save thousands of dollars per employee by utilizing this tactic. There are now about twenty-eight million part-time workers in America. Most would be working reduced hours even without the ACA, but observers generally agree that the health insurance law is contributing to the numbers.

THE BOTTOM LINE

The ACA has conferred substantial benefits on a narrow segment of the American population. Indeed, for people at the bottom of the income spectrum, it has been estimated that the law has added about 6 percent to their real income, by improving their healthcare or reducing their out-of-pocket healthcare costs. And for some of those people who were previously uninsurable, the law literally has been a lifesaver.

For many more individuals, the ACA has raised the cost of insurance and compelled some of them to pay for items of insurance coverage against their will. Some have had their policies cancelled and found the replacement policies offered them to be too expensive. Taxpayers' bills are rising also, both to pay for the expansion in Medicaid and to cover the subsidies on those policies sold on the insurance exchanges.

Overall, the law has contributed to an increase in the demand for healthcare, which has increased prices for healthcare services. The law has a number of provisions that are supposed to reduce healthcare costs by encouraging people to seek routine treatment before their health deteriorates. So far there is little evidence that people are doing this. Of course, Medicare and Medicaid (both enacted in the 1960s) were supposed to reduce costs in some of the same ways, but actually ended up drastically *raising* healthcare costs because of the sharp increase in demand for healthcare that they induced.

Not all of the uncertainties that have developed under the Affordable Care Act have resolved themselves, and they may not for quite some time. One thing does seem certain, however. Given the importance of healthcare to everyone and the high costs of consuming it, this is an issue that will not go away.

DISCUSSION QUESTIONS

1. Under what circumstances would you try to avoid purchasing health insurance?

2. Do the increased physician and hospital treatments for serious illnesses among those who are newly insured tell you anything about the price elasticity of demand for medical care? If so, what?

3. When an employer chooses to reduce the hours worked by many of its employees to fewer than thirty per week, what might be some of the negative consequences to the business? What damages might the affected employees suffer?

4. People over the age of sixty-five are eligible for Medicare, which offers subsidized healthcare—as long as the doctor involved agrees to accept the relatively lower fees paid by Medicare. Some people over sixty-five choose instead to pay out-of-pocket for so-called "concierge" physicians, who provide medical services on a cash or credit card-only basis. Can you explain why patients would turn their backs on Medicare and instead pay out of their own pockets?

5. In Britain, everyone has the right to healthcare provided by the National Health Service, paid for out of tax revenues. Nevertheless, two-thirds of British citizens earning more than $80,000 per year

currently purchase private health insurance. Why would these people opt to "pay twice" for healthcare services? (*Hint:* Think of Americans who pay to send their children to private schools.)

6. Under what circumstances would an employer be willing to pay an annual fine for not providing legally required employee health insurance?

CHAPTER 20

The Deception of Green Energy

If good intentions were all that were necessary to create "green" power, we would have so much of it today that we would not need to use coal, oil, natural gas, or nuclear power. Of course, it is also true that if wishes were horses, beggars would ride.

Over the past fifteen years, the federal government has poured tens of billions of dollars into "green" energy projects. The results have neither noticeably reduced our dependence on foreign oil nor cleaned our air and water of pollutants. They have not even made a dent in the atmospheric buildup of greenhouse gases. What we *have* accomplished by using up all of these scarce resources on solar, wind, and battery power is a convincing demonstration that while green energy may make for great politics, it also makes for lousy environmental and economic policy.

GREAT GOALS, BUT NOT MUCH SCIENCE OR ECONOMICS

Anyone who is worried about the environment—meaning each of us— is concerned about potential global warming as well as pollution that occurs with many sources of energy. Environmental quality is a valuable resource, and it is important that both environmental and economic policy treat it as such.

Enter the era of **green energy,** which refers to processes that can be harnessed to meet our energy needs with little pollution. Most observers would include in green energy, at a minimum, wind power, solar power, tidal and wave power, and geothermal power. Others might add hydroelectric and nuclear power to this list, although plenty of people would exclude these two on the grounds that (i) hydropower threatens the long-term survival of some fish species and (ii) nuclear power yields hazardous spent-fuel waste. More generally, green power is said to be a type of sustainable (or renewable) energy—although only rarely do people define what they mean by either "sustainable" or "renewable."[1]

A Problem with the Concept of *Needs*

Notice in the above definition of green energy the use of the word *needs*. One of the first concepts that anyone studying economics learns is that there is no useful definition of the term *need*. Even when we talk about the basics, such as food, water, and oxygen, it is possible to survive without them for roughly forty days, eight days, or eight minutes, respectively. And human tolerance for doing without clothing or shelter is, in many latitudes and seasons, remarkably high. It is thus much more useful to think in terms of the notion of **want** and people's **willingness to pay** for goods. Thus, we assert, no one *needs* to set a thermostat at 70 degrees Fahrenheit during a hot summer day, even though one might greatly enjoy the resulting cool air. Moreover, even if you might think you need such a cool environment, we are confident that if the price of achieving this outcome suddenly became $100 an hour, you would quickly agree that your needs were not what you thought they were.

The point is that the amount of energy we want to consume changes remarkably depending on the price of energy we face. In countries where the price of electricity is many times what it is in the United States, per-person electricity needs are miraculously less than in the United States. In the United States itself, as the price of natural gas falls, as it has over the last several years, we are finding more uses for natural gas. Trucks and busses are being converted to run on natural gas rather than gasoline, and those who heat with natural gas have discovered that it is okay to enjoy their home at 72 degrees in the winter, instead of, say, 68 degrees. With lower natural gas prices, propulsion with natural gas and a more comfortable thermostat setting in the winter both cost quite a bit less than they did ten years ago.

Indeed, without even considering sustainable or green energy issues, we know one thing for certain. If the energy used in factories, transportation, and heating and cooling leads to undesirable environmental

---

1 For example, it is commonplace to say that wind power is renewable but fossil fuel power is not, because the time it takes for natural processes to renew the fossil fuel is far beyond the human time horizon, whereas the wind renews itself as soon as we use it. But this ignores the fact that far more resources such as steel, glass, aluminum, and concrete are used to manufacture "renewable" power than fossil fuel power, and these resources are not themselves renewable.

results, we can reduce energy consumption and thus the magnitude of the environmental damage. How? We just make sure that the prices of conventional energy sources are higher than they are today. A large tax on energy will lead to a lower **quantity demanded** and consumed. This conclusion follows immediately from the **law of demand.**

GREEN ENERGY DECEPTION #1—WIND POWER

The wind is free, right? Perhaps when you think of a windy day, that's what you imagine. But wind power is definitely not free if we are generating "green" energy from large windmill turbines. In the first place, windmills require significant amounts of steel, fiberglass, and cement. So their creation is not free. Wind turbines also require the construction of new pylons for the transmission of the turbine-created electricity. Additionally, a widespread version of the wind turbine (called direct-drive) requires the use of neodymium—eight tons of the stuff in a typical wind farm. Almost all of this rare earth is produced in Inner Mongolia. To refine it, one must boil ore in a special acid. This production process leaves behind lakes of lethal radioactive debris.

There is also a problem of the visual pollution that comes with wind farms. Wind turbines must be put where there is lots of wind, often on the tops of hills, where they may be visible for up to forty miles. The ocean is another good place for wind farms, but because they must be close to the shore to make power transmission feasible, they again become a visual blight. (This was a key item in the controversial fight over a twenty-four-square-mile wind farm proposed for the middle of Nantucket Sound, off Martha's Vineyard.)

There is yet another issue: the problem of **intermittency.** The wind does not blow all the time, so city electric grids attached to wind farms require costly backup power stations. Under some circumstances, to replace a 500-megawatt conventional power plant with wind, one must have both a 500-megawatt wind power facility and a 375-megawatt conventional power plant. This backup power must start and stop as the wind blows—which generates much more pollution than if these power stations ran continuously. Hence, wind power is not a complete replacement for traditional energy sources and is more polluting than you might think. How then can a nation such as Denmark rely on wind power for 40 percent of the electricity it produces? Because it sits between (and relies upon) the hydropower stations of Norway and Sweden to the north and the coal-powered generating stations in Germany to the south.

Here is the big catch for wind power (and every other "green" source of energy): Despite recent reductions in the cost of wind power, it still uses up to three times as many resources as natural gas turbines, and off-shore wind farms use at least six times more resources than gas turbines. The enormous amount of resources gobbled up in the production of wind power means only one thing, and you probably have guessed what it is by now. Government has to subsidize wind power to get anyone to build wind farms. Such **subsidization**—taxpayer dollars—has created inefficiency in the use of our scarce resources. The bottom line is that the resources that go into generating wind power vastly exceed the value of the energy they produce. This simple fact means that wind power is in fact *not* sustainable, because it leaves us with fewer resources available for the future.

Green Energy Deception #2—Solar Power

Until the world exists no longer, the sun will shine on us. Doesn't that mean we should take advantage of nature's gift? Sure—as long as it is worth it. If we can harness the sun's power in a way that creates benefits that at least equal the cost of doing so, then that is what we should be doing. The costs of solar facilities are not trivial, though. Their manufacture and installation use large amounts of energy and other resources—far more than would be required for the implementation of conventional sources, such as natural gas turbines. They must be used where there is lots of sun, and because the solar panels take up so much land area, one has to cover a *lot* of desert to generate solar power in commercial quantities. Solar power also suffers from the intermittency problem, which means it must be accompanied by backup conventional sources that sit idle much of the time.

Consider one solar project built by NRG Energy halfway between Los Angeles and San Francisco. This company has installed a million solar panels, designed to produce electricity for about one hundred thousand homes. The cost of the project is $1.6 billion. But NRG Energy is not bearing this cost. Instead, the entire tab is being picked up by tax-payers and by electricity consumers in northern California (even those who are not consumers of NRG), who are getting a 50 percent surcharge added to their bills. Overall, taxpayers are forking over about $1.1 billion, while the electricity surcharge will extract almost $500 million from ratepayers—whether they get their electrons from NRG or not.

That it took $1.6 billion in subsidies to get this project off the ground is a clear signal that the project is unlikely to achieve its advertised objectives. We must remember that **wealth** (as that term is used by economists) simply means the sum total of productive capacity. The fact that the project must be subsidized to even exist implies that its costs exceed the benefits it yields. Hence, this project destroys wealth and is thus unsustainable.

WHAT ABOUT THE ENVIRONMENT?

Now, one might think that solar energy's great advantage is that it is "renewable." Indeed, the sun's rays will be there tomorrow for us, even if we use them for electricity generation today. But this ignores the fact that almost *none* of the nonhuman resources (such as silicon, aluminum, steel, concrete, and copper) going into constructing and maintaining the solar grid are renewable. And because it takes roughly *three times* as much of these other resources to generate electricity with solar power as it does with, say, natural gas, the claim that solar energy is more "renewable" than natural gas seems pretty unlikely.

But there is still the matter of air pollution and of carbon dioxide (which plays a role in determining the temperature of the earth's atmosphere). Here, at first blush, solar energy seems to have the big edge over even clean-burning natural gas. After all, burning natural gas to make electricity does produce carbon dioxide (about half as much as coal) and other air pollutants. With solar energy, we are not burning anything . . . until we remember all of those extra resources that go into turning the sun's rays into a usable form. All of the steel and aluminum and glass and other components have to be produced, and all of that production generates pollution and carbon dioxide. Again, taking this additional manufacturing into account, solar and wind power are environmentally dirtier than natural gas or nuclear power.

But, you might say, improvements in solar panels may lead to lower costs per panel and more output per panel and thus lower resource usage down the road. That is indeed what a cutting-edge solar technology firm called Solyndra told the government when it received a $528 million federal loan guarantee. Solyndra went bankrupt trying to prove this point, as have hundreds of other solar firms around the world. Make no mistake: The resource usage involved with solar power is coming down steadily, and there is little doubt that solar power will *eventually* be both economically and environmentally preferable in many applications. That time has not come and—significantly—there is *no* evidence that the pace of innovation in solar power has been accelerated in any way by expensive taxpayer subsidies.

INDUSTRIAL POLICY BY ANY OTHER NAME

When the government, any government, decides to subsidize, guarantee loans, or institute new regulations to support the growth of an industry, we call it **industrial policy.** Industrial policy means (an attempt at) picking winners, presumably because the private sector won't. History has shown, though, that industrial policy generally fails. As former Obama advisor economist Larry Summers said when he argued against federal loan guarantees to Solyndra, "the government is a crappy venture capitalist." Otherwise stated, politically directed investments rarely lead to the efficient use of resources.

This conclusion is hardly surprising. We actually design government institutions to *insulate* government decision makers from considerations of commercial feasibility and the demands of making a profit from what they do. Who, after all, wants the budget of the local police force to be dependent on its speeding ticket revenue? So here we have the basic flaw in every industrial policy: By design, governments, bureaucrats, and even elected officials have no "skin in the game," compared to a private entrepreneur or investor. Hence, the bureaucrats and politicians are far more likely to make an error when trying to pick winners in the marketplace.

GREEN ENERGY DECEPTION #3—ELECTRIC CARS

As part of the most recent push for technologies that are supposed to be pollution-free, the electric car has become the poster child. General Motors' Volt was heralded as a way to save both that company from decline and the environment. This and other electric cars (such as the Nissan Leaf and the luxury Tesla) are considered a centerpiece of the green energy revolution because, it is said, they conserve resources and cause less pollution.

But the cars have not lived up to expectations. Consider the Volt, which has a sticker price in the $40,000 to $45,000 range, depending on options. In the hopes of getting people to buy an otherwise ordinary Chevrolet priced like a Lexus, the federal government offers a $7,500 tax credit to buyers (paid for by you, the taxpayer). Even with the boost from this tax credit, sales were so slow that GM and its dealers had to offer discounts of up to 25 percent off the car's list price. Even this was not enough: In one year alone, GM had to shut down the Volt production line three times because of the car's lagging sales. The sad part of all this, according to the Congressional Budget Office, is that the Volt "will result in little or no reduction in the total gasoline use and greenhouse gas emissions of the nation's vehicle fleet."

Indeed, when one takes the broad view, electric cars are not really "green." Considering the full cycle of their production, including their large, expensive batteries, they create just as much carbon as do standard cars with internal-combustion engines for at least the first eighty thousand miles of operation. Even this calculation ignores what electric car advocates hate to talk about. Forty percent of the electricity used to charge the cars when they are plugged in is generated by coal-fired power plants—and coal generates far more carbon emissions and pollutants than does gasoline.

POLICY AND POLITICS

The essence of good politics lies in making costs and benefits *appear* to be whatever it takes to accomplish one's objectives. But the essence of good policy lies in making *accurate* evaluations of costs and benefits. Sometimes good politics and good policy coincide. But often they don't, and the case of green energy is one of those cases.

Politicians decided ahead of time that "doing something" about the environment was good politics. Given this objective, all that was left was to sell electric cars and wind and solar electricity generation as policies that had high environmental benefits and low resource costs. Green energy seems to offer neither of these promises. Someday this conclusion may change, but in the meantime we need to remind ourselves that this is an example of the simple adage that good politics is not always good policy.

DISCUSSION QUESTIONS

1. Can you think of any situation in which the use of taxpayer dollars to subsidize industrial production of one type or another might benefit the nation in the long run?

2. What do we mean when we say that industrial policy leads to inefficient use of resources?

3. Why does the federal government have to provide subsidies to entice private companies to build and maintain wind farms?

4. What are some of the arguments that you could use to justify the expansion of wind power and solar power?

5. What are the benefits to consumers who purchase electric cars?

6. Why don't drivers of conventional cars with internal-combustion engines care about whatever pollution they generate?

CHAPTER 21

The Fight over Genetically Modified Foods

If you've ever eaten popcorn, you've eaten a genetically modified organism (GMO). Actually, almost all of the foods we eat, many of the clothes we wear, and even the pages on which these words are printed come from plant or animal species that have been genetically modified. Virtually all living things that form a pivotal role in our lives, including our household pets, have genetic structures today that have been shaped by conscious human decisions to make them so. Why, then, did Congress pass a law that will require foods to be labeled accordingly if they contain GMOs?

THE EARLY HISTORY OF GMOs

Let's return to popcorn, because corn is probably the first organism whose genetic structure was consciously modified by humans to suit their wishes. Beginning about nine thousand years ago, the inhabitants of the Balsas River basin of southern Mexico began the process of transforming a plant called teosinte into corn (maize). Over the ensuing three thousand years, they undertook breeding experiments that

- softened the hull of the kernel, to make it more digestible;
- made the kernel stick more tightly to the cob, to reduce wastage; and
- transformed the structure of the plant from many branches to one stalk, to facilitate harvesting.

By six thousand years ago, teosinte had disappeared from fields, replaced with a crop very much identifiable as an ancestor of today's corn.

Although corn was first, human genetic experiments on cattle, rice, trees, horses, peas, wheat, cotton, pigs, and literally thousands of other plants and animals have formed the foundation for much of modern agriculture. The results of such genetic engineering, ranging from crossbreeding to plant grafting, now feed and clothe the world. In recent years, however, people around the globe have begun objecting to advances in the genetic modification of species. Genetically modified organisms are said to pose a threat to human health and to the ecological system in which we live. Why, after nine thousand years of success with genetic engineering, should people suddenly start to worry that it might yield catastrophic results? Just as importantly, what would be the likely results if we decided to bring genetic engineering to a halt or even just slow its pace significantly?

THE NEW GMOS

The answer to the first question centers on the relatively new methods that are being used to produce today's genetically modified plants (and even animals). Instead of crossbreeding two existing plants, scientists are selecting individual genes—sometimes from species far removed—and inserting them into a plant of interest.[1] The result is called a **transgenic species,** because its genes come from two or more different species. For example, so-called "Bt cotton" is a form of cotton that has had inserted into it a toxin-producing gene from a soil bacterium, known as *Bacillus thuringiensis*. The poison contained in the cotton is delivered only to bugs that eat cotton. The delivery of the toxin is so efficient that farmers who plant Bt cotton can use far fewer pesticides on their fields—pesticides that are toxic not merely to bugs, but also potentially life threatening to many other species, including *homo sapiens*.

THE THREAT FROM GMOS

The concern among people who object to the creation of modern GMOs is that they are unlike anything seen before in the nine thousand years of genetic engineering on record: There is simply no way to interbreed

---

1 The typical definition of what constitutes an objectionable GMO is not helpful. This, for example, is offered by Whole Foods as part of its campaign to label the GMO content of food: "Plants that have been altered through a technique that changes their genetic makeup, producing new combination[s] of genes and traits that do not occur in nature . . . , are called genetically modified organisms . . . ." By this definition, the maize that was created from teosinte was a GMO, which makes all "GMO-free" modern corn (descendant from maize) necessarily a GMO.

bacteria and plants. Unlike, say, peas, where crossbreeding of plants with red and white flowers reasonably can be expected to yield plants with pink flowers, when a gene from one species is inserted into another radically different species, there is no possible way of predicting what the result might be.

Thus, say the opponents of modern genetic engineering, the results of today's experiments might yield transgenic crops that spread from fields into forest or other wild lands, becoming environmental nuisances along the way. Or, they might cross-pollinate with neighboring wild plants, producing "superweeds" that could devastate huge swaths of previously productive agricultural lands. Indeed, say GMO opponents, we might even end up with transgenic killers, species capable of threatening the continued existence of entire species, perhaps even human beings.

How Likely Is the Danger?

Are such outcomes *possible*? Yes, say scientists, something very unpleasant and very costly *might* result from modern gene-splicing techniques. But according to leading medical, scientific, and regulatory bodies in the United States and Europe, the likelihood is very small, probably even smaller than with traditional methods of genetic engineering, including those dating back nine thousand years. The reason is that modern methods are highly targeted, involving the insertion of a single gene, with a known property, into a specific location in the genetic makeup of the recipient species. As a general rule, only *one* change in the recipient species is the result. This is in sharp contrast with older methods, in which a random "shotgun" approach is tried: Interbreed two plants and see what happens.[2] Sometimes nothing (observable) happens, and sometimes many things change—but it is very difficult to predict ahead of time just what will happen and whether or not it will be beneficial or harmful.

Even so, we have been in the business of modern gene-splicing for almost nine thousand years less than we have been interbreeding by traditional means. Thus, it is surely prudent to proceed with some caution, recognizing that there *may* be consequences of the new methods that we have not thought of yet. Indeed, we must also recognize that for many people there are costs of GMOs that transcend the scientific arguments.

---

2 Or animals: the 63-chromosome mule results from breeding two other species—a (male) 62-chromosome donkey and a (female) 64-chromosome horse.

THE GMO-FREE PREMIUM

No body of scientific evidence is infallible, and many consumers feel that the evidence supporting the safety of GMOs is insufficient for them. Hence, they try to avoid foods that contain GMOs, and some are even willing to pay a premium for GMO-free foods. This is presumably what is behind the decision by the Whole Foods supermarket chain to require GMO labeling on all their products by 2018. Consumer preference for non-GMO foods may also have led Congress in 2016 to pass a law that will require GMO labeling of food. The United Kingdom and Japan already have GMO labeling requirements, and some countries restrict or ban imports of GMOs that have not been approved by their relevant regulatory agencies. This is despite the fact that over the past twenty-five years, trillions of meals containing GMOs have been fed to billions of human beings, apparently without a single instance of harm resulting from any of the genetic modifications.

GMO-free food is generally more expensive to supply than is GMO food. Partly this is because of much more costly weed and pest control measures. But some of the higher costs arise because certification that an item is free of GMOs is a prolonged and arduous process. When these costs are combined with the preference among some consumers for GMO-free foods, the result has been the emergence of a price premium for such items. For soybeans and corn, for example, that premium has recently ranged from 15 to 20 percent. For those farmers and processors who wish to supply non-GMO foods, it is understandably important that they be able to prevent the contamination of their products with GMOs.

A QUESTION OF PROPERTY RIGHTS

For some crops and some processes, it is relatively easy to protect items from GMO contamination. But in other cases it is not. Alfalfa, for example, requires pollination, and bees simply do not know where one farmer's field begins and the other's ends. There are thus documented instances of non-GMO alfalfa crops having been pollinated by bees brought in to pollinate a neighbor's GMO crop. The result for the first farmer has been the loss of GMO-free certification and thus the forfeiture of the market price premium for her crops.

Not surprisingly, GMO-free farmers and processors regard GMOs as a threat to their property rights and to their livelihood. Hence, numerous lawsuits have been filed on this issue, which are now working their way through the courts. GMO farmers assert that they have a right to grow their crops without interference from their neighbors. Non-GMO farmers say they have a right to grow crops that are free of the threat of contamination. It is an important and contentious issue that seems likely to end up in the Supreme Court.

THE GREEN REVOLUTION

As disagreements over GMOs work their way through the market, the courts, and state legislatures, it is important to recognize a fundamental fact. Broadly construed, genetic engineering is central to the economic *and* environmental well-being of the world today, and its beneficial future is likely to grow, if we let it.

Let's first consider the history of the so-called "Green Revolution," which started fifty years ago. In the mid-1960s scientists used genetic engineering to develop high-yielding varieties of rice and wheat that were subsequently released to farmers in Asia and Latin America. These crops spread rapidly in tropical and subtropical climates that had good irrigation systems or reliable rainfall, literally transforming the state of agriculture—and human nutrition—in dozens of developing nations.

On the nutritional side of the equation, crop yields soared, food prices fell, and both the caloric and nutritional intake of hundreds of millions of people improved sharply. Had there been no Green Revolution, food prices would have been roughly 50 percent higher, and caloric intake in the affected developing nations would have been nearly 15 percent lower. Significantly, both malnutrition and infant and child mortality rates would have been markedly higher.

On the environmental side of matters, the impact of the Green Revolution may have been even more profound. Because the genetically modified rice, wheat, and other crops had much higher yields (in terms of bushels produced per acre), farmers were able to reduce the number of acres planted and still earn higher profits with the crops. Between about 1965 and 1990, for example, it is estimated that genetically engineered Green Revolution crops saved more than 100 million acres of wild lands in India. In recent years, the higher yields from modern GMO crops have reduced forest clearing in Honduras and the Philippines.

AROUND THE WORLD

On a global scale, estimates have been made of the total impact of farming techniques and changes in yields since 1950. One expert, Dennis Avery of the Hudson Institute, says that, absent these improvements, the world would have lost to agricultural cultivation an additional twenty million square *miles* of wildlife habitat, much of it forest. Given that there currently are sixteen million square miles of forests in the world today, this implies that improvements in techniques and crop yields "have saved every square mile of forest on the planet," according to Avery.

Now, not all of this was due to gene splicing in the laboratory, but a significant portion was, and the challenges we face in the future may be even greater. Many experts believe that most of the really big yield enhancements from traditional genetic engineering techniques have been exhausted. To be sure, improvements using crossbreeding are still being made, but no one believes they will be able to feed the *additional* three billion people who are likely to inhabit the earth by the year 2050. Modern gene splicing techniques have that potential, however. Perhaps just as importantly, modern GMO techniques promise to substantially *improve* the quality of the environment along the way.

The Environmental Benefits of GMOs

Consider Bt cotton, which we mentioned earlier. In the United States, where farmers successfully have used pesticides to protect cotton, switching to Bt cotton has not significantly improved yields. What it has done, however, is to permit farmers to sharply reduce their use of pesticides. This protects nontarget insects and other species in and around the cotton fields and also yields much less pesticide runoff into streams and lakes. In India, the benefits come in a different form. Cash-constrained farmers there use relatively few pesticides, so insect-caused crop losses in India historically have been huge. Thus, the key impact of Bt cotton in this nation is on the yield side: Crop yields per acre in India are pushed up 60 percent when Bt cotton is planted. This not only raises the income of farmers and helps push down prices for consumers but also protects wild lands from further agricultural intrusion.

Similarly, varieties of both soybeans and corn called Roundup Ready have transformed agricultural methods in the United States and elsewhere. These transgenic crops tolerate Roundup, an herbicide that kills many types of weeds and then quickly breaks down into environmentally harmless by-products. When farmers plant Roundup Ready soybeans and corn—which now amount to a substantial portion of United States crops of both—they are able to use Roundup instead of far more toxic alternatives. Moreover, they often no longer have to use plowing to aid them in controlling weeds. This in turn dramatically reduces soil erosion and damaging runoff into adjacent bodies of water.

PROMISE AND CAUTION

The promise of transgenic crops extends far beyond pesticides and plowing, however. For example, salt-resistant tomatoes and other crops have been developed that permit agriculture to be successful on otherwise-sterile lands, saving fertile savannahs and forests for wildlife. Similarly, crops are being developed that are able to tolerate aluminum, an element that is eminently useful in making airplanes but serves as a crop-killing contaminant in many soils around the world. There are even transgenic crops that are bred to thrive on the toxic wastes found in the worst industrial dump sites and are capable of transforming such areas from wastelands to wildlife habitats.

At the same time, however, it is important to recognize that Mother Nature fights back. Insects and weeds have already begun developing resistance to the Bt and Roundup Ready crops. And so, just as humans have had to devise new antibiotics to deal with the emergence of bacterial resistance to old drugs, geneticists and farmers may also be locked into a continuing "resistance race" with insects and weeds.

Given the uncertainties and unknowns in any new field of scientific inquiry, the potential costs of transgenic species—environmental as well as economic—must be carefully monitored and taken into account. Yet it is also important to remember the fate that likely would have befallen humankind had genetic manipulation been stopped in its tracks nine thousand years ago. Instead of munching popcorn in front of wide-screen televisions, we might well be tilling teosinte in southern Mexico.

DISCUSSION QUESTIONS

1. How do the potential (environmental and economic) costs of transgenic crops differ from most of the traditional costs associated with agriculture (such as tractors and labor)? *Hint:* Who bears the costs: the farmer or others in society? Does this difference mean that we should think and act differently regarding these costs?

2. How can the tools discussed in Chapters 1 through 3 help us understand some of the policy issues involved with GMOs?

3. Suppose one accurately took into account all of the costs and benefits of developing transgenic crops. Could you be sure that the economically efficient path to follow would be to permit the development of GMOs?

4. Suppose there are great benefits from transgenic crops, including improved nutrition, longer life spans, reduced infant mortality, and

the like. But also assume there are environmental costs, e.g., in the form of some species that are made extinct because they cannot compete with the new transgenic species. Should the existence of *some* environmental costs outweigh all other benefits combined, regardless of how great those benefits are?

5. The costs of GMO-free foods are said to be higher because these foods must be isolated from GMO crops during both growing and processing. But GMO crops also enable food to be grown on much less land than would otherwise be the case, thus reducing the price of that land. Is it possible that, on balance, the presence of GMO foods actually makes it *cheaper* to grow GMO-free crops?

6. GMO-free soybeans cost about $2 per bushel more than GMO soybeans. How many hours does someone have to work to pay that premium in the United States, where average wages are about $25 per hour? How many hours does someone have to work to pay that premium in those African nations where average wages are about 25 *cents* per hour? Are attitudes toward GMO-free crops likely to be different in Africa and the United States?

CHAPTER 22

Student Loans

"Massive and growing bigger by the day" is a phrase that aptly describes the current total of outstanding student loan debt in the United States. At around $1.3 trillion, this amount easily exceeds the total auto loan debt for all Americans. Indeed, student loan debt is the second-highest consumer debt in the nation (the only debt larger is from mortgage loans). As of 2017, more than 40 million Americans had an outstanding college loan debt. You might even be one of them. If so, did you make a good choice in taking out a student loan? Or, if you made a poor choice and cannot pay back your student loan, who will pay for it? We will attempt to answer these questions here.

WHY GO TO COLLEGE IN THE FIRST PLACE?

Every student has her or his reasons for pursuing a college education. For some, it is a path to a better economic future or an avenue to simply continue learning. Others are following a family tradition or want to enter a profession that has specific educational requirements. To be sure, venturing away from home and finding new friends is part of the allure of the college experience. But for most students, the main goal in obtaining a college degree involves a positive expected **rate of return** in terms of higher **lifetime earnings.** That expectation is often realized, because obtaining a college degree does have a positive expected rate of return. In fact, among people twenty-five to thirty-two years old, those with a college education earn an average of $18,000 per year more than those with only a high school degree. Moreover, based on past trends, this gap in earnings will likely grow in the future for this **cohort,** or age group.

Over their lifetime, those with a bachelor's degree will earn roughly 80 percent more than those with a high school diploma.

Notably, however, these figures are undiscounted—they do *not* take into account the fact that **interest** rates are positive, and so distant income is less valuable than income available immediately. Going to college means delaying employment income for four or five years, which cuts into the advantage of college over high school: That $25,000 per year you might make straight out of high school is the **opportunity cost** of spending your time in the college classroom. Moreover, college is expensive—with average tuition about $33,500 at private universities and $9,600 (in-state) at public institutions. Such costs are avoided by going to work right out of high school. Yet even with the delays and added costs, the extra education still pays off handsomely for most graduates.

It's Not for Everyone

Note that we say that "most" college graduates profit in the job market as a result of their education. The major a student pursues is a critical factor when determining the lifetime income available with a bachelor's degree. This is because, on average, jobs in the humanities, such as literature and art, pay much less than those in engineering, computer science, and economics. And then there is the differing ability and study habits of students, which help to determine the ultimate quality (and thus rate of return) of a college education. For some students, many of whom are in the humanities, especially those who go to third-tier colleges or spend their time playing rather than studying, obtaining a bachelor's degree may turn out to be a poor financial decision.

Does the High Cost of College Lead to More Student Loans, or Is It the Other Way Around?

Everyone knows that the **nominal price** of going to college has gone up over time. After all, we have had inflation for decades. Consider the following fact: If tuition at Harvard University had increased only at the **rate of inflation** over the last few decades, students would be paying about $15,500 today. Instead, tuition there is more than $45,000. And it's not just at Harvard: **Real, or inflation-adjusted,** tuition has also tripled over the last thirty-five years at other private colleges and universities. But if you pay in-state tuition at a public institution, don't pat yourself on the back too soon: Over the same period, inflation-adjusted tuition at these schools has risen by a factor of almost *four*.

Some argue that the rising **real price** of getting a degree has forced many students to take out ever-larger loans. In fact, careful research indicates that the increased *availability* (or **supply**) of student loans over this period has made it easier for students to finance their own higher education. Consequently, there has been an **increase in demand** for a college education, which in turn has caused the price (tuition) to rise. Indeed, professors Grey Gordon and Aaron Hedlund have found that the increased availability of cheap student loans accounts for fully *100 percent* of the increase in the cost of tuition over the last thirty-five years.

As a result, over this period we have seen in the United States a so-called "academic arms race." Specifically, universities have bid up the salaries of superstar professors, hoping to enhance school reputations and thus increase demand for their product. Moreover, the competition to enroll more students has caused university administrators to build bigger indoor swimming pools, more luxurious dorm rooms, and, of course, some of the finest athletic facilities money can buy. As long as college administrators know that they can pass on the greater cost of providing a higher education to students with access to cheap credit, they will do so. In turn, students oblige them by taking out larger and larger loans. The average college student who borrows funds will owe approximately $37,000 in loan debt when he or she graduates.

The Relationship Between Taking on Student Loans and Your GPA

At first blush, one would think that incurring student loan debt would create an incentive to work harder, to obtain a higher grade point average (GPA), and therefore land a higher paying job. But recent research by professors Peter Cappelli and Shinjae Won tells us otherwise.

In their study, Cappelli and Won compared the GPAs of college students who had received need-based grants (which have no required repayments) with students who took out student loans. The students who received grants achieved higher GPAs than those who took out loans. The researchers interpreted their research results using **behavioral economics.** In essence, because a grant is a type of financial gift, it creates a "sense of obligation to the giver that may make one feel uncomfortable, at least until the obligation has been discharged." In this case, say the authors, "discharging the obligation" comes about when the recipients of such grants do well in college—as demonstrated by earning a higher GPA.

STUDENT DEBT CAUSES OTHER DEMANDS FOR CREDIT TO FALL

Today, the percentage of Americans under the age of thirty-five who hold credit card debt is lower than it was in 1989. In a society in which credit card debt is common and widely accepted, this trend reveals an **inverse correlation** between rising student loan debts in the under-thirty-five population and their willingness to incur credit card debt. Because of their high student loans, Millennials—those individuals reaching young adulthood around the year 2000—do not want to incur even more debt. Oddly, their creditworthiness is suffering as a result.

Everyone has a credit score—a numerical expression of a person's credit files and history. To build a healthy credit score, you need to prove you can pay your debts. This is done best by purchasing "on credit." A person's credit card history makes up 15 percent of his or her creditworthiness score. By avoiding credit card debt, Millennials are not building strong credit scores. Weak credit scores limit loan amounts and mandate higher interest rates, all of which will make it more difficult for Millennials to borrow funds in the future for larger purchases, such as cars or homes.

This has already shown up in the housing market, where there is a negative relationship between student debt and home ownership. In the past, owning a home has represented a proverbial part of the American Dream. In the past ten years, however, home ownership for Americans under the age of thirty-five has decreased by almost 9 percent. When the National Association of Realtors did a survey on this decline, they found that outstanding student loan debt was listed as a principal reason why Millennials were not purchasing a house or condominium.

WHEN STUDENT LOANS AREN'T REPAID, WHO PAYS?

Another way Millennials and current students can hurt their credit scores is by not paying their student loan debts. Many people who owe on student loans are making their payments, and on time. But almost half of all borrowers have either (i) defaulted (stopped making payments altogether), or (ii) are delinquent on their loans (are behind on the payments, or (iii) have renegotiated with lenders to make smaller payment than originally agreed. Moreover, the number of borrowers who are paying what they agreed to is a dwindling percentage of the total each year: Delinquencies, defaults, and renegotiated repayments are all rising.

For many years, most students borrowed heavily from private lenders, with the federal government overseeing things and subsidizing some of the loans. The situation today is another story entirely. In 2010, the federal government forced commercial banks out of the federal loan market. Consequently, the federal government now backs most student loans: The U.S. Department of Education has a student loan portfolio of hundreds of billions of dollars. So, when student loans are not repaid today, who bears the burden? Increasingly, the answer is the U.S. taxpayer. The cost to taxpayer over the next decade is estimated to be more than $100 billion.

Student Loan Forgiveness—Who Benefits?

Seeing that many individuals were struggling or failing to pay off their large student loan debts, the federal government instituted a student loan forgiveness program that became fully effective in 2017. This program forgives *federal* student loan debt once a borrower has made a full decade of consistent payments. These payments are income-based. Thus, if a borrower works in a low-paying job, her or his repayment schedule will be adjusted to create a more modest monthly payment. Eventually, what remains of the debt can be forgiven.

There is a catch, though. This program is only for those graduates who work for government or nonprofit entities. Supposedly, the loan forgiveness program was designed to encourage young people to pursue traditionally lower paying jobs, such as social work and teaching. As a practical matter, the program covers about 25 percent of U.S. jobs, all either government or nonprofit, few of which look much like teaching or social work. Interestingly, most of the people taking advantage of this program are those who—based on the quality of the college they attended, or their socioeconomic characteristics—would be least likely to default on their loans.

Perhaps the biggest winners from this program are physicians. A typical medical student owes $180,000 when he or she graduates. Such graduates must undertake an additional three to ten years of training at hospitals, almost all of which are government or nonprofit. During this added training period, the physicians are hospital employees, getting paid salaries low enough to qualify for the forgiveness program. The doctors pay only 15 percent of their income on their student loans while in training. Ultimately, most of them will end up having 80 percent of their original loan balances forgiven. Then they go on to make annual six-figure salaries the rest of their lives. A recent survey of medical school graduates found that 40 percent planned to seek loan forgiveness. And of course, who wouldn't want to take advantage of such a good deal?

ARE STUDENT LOANS DIFFERENT?

The simple fact is that students differ in their abilities, some majors offer little preparation for top jobs, and not all colleges are the same quality. Low-ability students who have borrowed money to enroll in low-paying majors at weak colleges are most likely to have trouble repaying their debts, and they are the least likely to get any help in doing so. High-performing students in engineering, economics, and, of course, medicine at top schools—well, they are doing just fine. Few of them have trouble paying their bills, and whether they do or not, they are also most likely to get a hand from the government. So, all in all, student loans don't sound much different from the rest of life: Those that start with advantages usually figure out how to get more; everybody else, well, too bad for them.

DISCUSSION QUESTIONS

1. If graduating humanities majors can expect to earn lower lifetime incomes, why don't they major in something else?

2. Assume that Angela incurs $25,000 of student debt to obtain a bachelor's degree in business. Assume that Brian incurs no student debt to obtain the same bachelor's degree in business, but he incurs $25,000 in student loans to obtain an MBA. Which student has the *lower* probability of defaulting on student loans, and why?

3. Go to YouTube and find videos in which students are asked to discuss how big their student loans are. If you find that many do not know the actual size of their student loans or underestimate them, are you surprised? Why or why not? Under what circumstances would it be rational for student loan recipients to *not* know or care about the size of their financial obligations?

4. Jodi incurs $25,000 in student loans to obtain a bachelor's of science degree in engineering. Owen undertakes the same course of study, also incurring $25,000 in student loans, but he fails to graduate. Which student will have a higher probability of nonpayment of student loans, and why?

5. Critics of ever-expanding college enrollments argue that many students should not be going to college. Rather, they should be going to trade or vocational schools. That way, they could become electricians, plumbers, carpenters, or stonemasons. The reasoning is that skilled tradespeople often earn higher lifetime incomes than those who go to college and major in the humanities. The conclusion is,

therefore, that we should have fewer college graduates and more skilled tradespeople. Do you agree or disagree with this argument? What is your reasoning?

6. The inflation-corrected price of cars has gone up over time. But cars purchased today are quite different than those purchased thirty years ago. In particular, today's cars are much safer to drive because they have multiple airbags and more crash-resistant engineering. Additionally, they have sophisticated GPS systems. Consequently, if we correct our price statistics relating to automobiles to include the value of improvements in quality, the implied inflation-corrected price has not gone up as much as we think. Can the same argument apply to the inflation-corrected increase in the price of a college education? Why or why not?

CHAPTER 23

The Graying of America

America is aging. The seventy-eight million baby boomers who pushed the Beatles and the Rolling Stones into stardom are retiring. By 2030, roughly 20 percent of all Americans will be sixty-five or older. Just as the post–World War II baby boom presented both obstacles and opportunities, so does the graying of America. Let's see why.

THE ORIGINS OF THE "SENIOR BOOM"

Two principal forces are behind America's "senior boom." First, we're living longer. Average life expectancy in 1900 was forty-seven years; today, it is seventy-nine and is likely to reach eighty within the next decade. Second, the birthrate is near record-low levels. Today's mothers are having far fewer children than their mothers or grandmothers had. In short, the old are living longer, and the ranks of the young are growing too slowly to offset this fact. Together, these forces are pushing up the proportion of the population over age sixty-five. Indeed, the number of seniors is growing at twice the rate of the rest of the population. In 1970, the **median age** in the United States—the age that divides the older half of the population from the younger half—was twenty-eight. It is now thirty-eight and rising. Compounding these factors, the average age at retirement is low by historical standards. The result is more retirees relying on fewer workers to help ensure that their senior years are also golden years.

THE COSTS OF THE ELDERLY

Why should a person who is, say, college age be concerned with the age of the rest of the population? Well, old people are expensive. In fact, people over sixty-five now consume over 40 percent of the federal government's budget. **Social Security** payments to retirees are the biggest item, now running about $900 billion per year. Medicare, which pays hospital and doctors' bills for the elderly, costs over $600 billion per year and is increasing rapidly. Moreover, roughly one-quarter of the $550 billion annual budget for Medicaid, which helps pay medical bills for the poor of all ages, goes to people over the age of sixty-five.

Under current law, the elderly will likely consume *half* of all federal spending within the next decade: Medicare spending will double and the number of the very old will rise sharply—those over eighty-five and most in need of care. In a nutshell, senior citizens are the beneficiaries of an expensive and rapidly growing share of federal spending. What are they getting for our dollars?

Today's elderly are already more prosperous than any previous generation. Each year, inflation-adjusted Social Security benefits paid to new retirees are higher than the first-year benefits paid to people who retired the year before. In addition, for the past forty years, cost-of-living adjustments have protected Social Security benefits from inflation. The impact of Social Security is evident even at the lower end of the income scale: The poverty rate for people over sixty-five is much *lower* than for the population as a whole. Retired people today collect Social Security benefits that are two to five times what they and their employers contributed in payroll taxes plus interest earned.

Not surprisingly, medical expenses are a major concern for many elderly. Perhaps reflecting that concern, each person under the age of sixty-five in America currently pays an average of more than $2,000 per year in federal taxes to subsidize medical care for the elderly. Indeed, no other country in the world goes to the lengths that America does to preserve life. Some 30 percent of Medicare's budget goes to patients in their last year of life. Coronary bypass operations, costing over $80,000 apiece, are routinely performed on Americans in their sixties and seventies. For those over sixty-five, Medicare picks up the tab. Even heart transplants are now performed on people in their sixties and paid for by Medicare for those over sixty-five. Britain's National Health Service limits access to kidney dialysis for people over fifty-five. Yet Medicare subsidizes dialysis for more than one hundred thousand Americans, half of them over age sixty. The cost: over $8 billion per year. Overall, the elderly receive Medicare benefits worth five to twenty times the payroll taxes (plus interest) they paid for this program.

THE COSTS ARE PAID BY YOU

The responsibility for the huge and growing bills for Social Security and Medicare falls squarely on current and future workers because both programs are financed by payroll taxes. Thirty years ago, these programs were adequately financed with a payroll levy of less than 10 percent of the typical worker's earnings. Today, the tax rate exceeds 15 percent of median wages and is expected to grow rapidly.

By the year 2020, early baby boomers, born in the late 1940s and early 1950s, will have retired. Late baby boomers, born in the early 1960s, will be nearing retirement. Both groups will leave today's college students, and their children, a staggering bill to pay. For Social Security and Medicare to stay as they are, the payroll tax rate may have to rise to 25 percent of wages over the next decade. And a payroll tax rate of 40 percent is not unlikely by the middle of the twenty-first century.

One way to think of the immense bill facing today's college students and their successors is to consider the number of retirees each worker must support. In 1946, the burden of one Social Security recipient was shared by forty-two workers. By 1960, nine workers had to foot the bill for each retiree's Social Security benefits. Today, roughly three workers pick up the tab for each retiree's Social Security and Medicare benefits. By 2030, only two workers will be available to pay the Social Security and Medicare benefits due each recipient. Thus, a working couple will have to support not only themselves and their family but also someone outside the family who is receiving Social Security and Medicare benefits.

POLITICAL ECONOMY IN ACTION

Congress and the executive branch have seemed unwilling to face the pitfalls and promises of an aging America. Although the age of retirement for Social Security purposes is legislatively mandated to rise to sixty-seven, the best that politicians in Washington, D.C., appear able to do is appoint commissions to "study" the problems we face. And what changes are our politicians willing to make? We got a sample of this in 2003, with new legislation promising taxpayer-funded prescription drug benefits for senior citizens. Even people in favor of the new program called it the largest expansion in **entitlement programs** in forty years. Before passage of the law, President Bush claimed it was going to cost $35 billion per year, but within a couple of months, that estimate had been hiked to over $50 billion. In fact, the benefits of the program have been less than claimed, and the costs are even higher, because more than three-quarters of senior citizens had privately funded prescription drug plans *before* the new law took effect. Many of these private plans disappeared, leaving seniors with fewer choices and sticking younger taxpayers with a larger tax bill.

By now you may be wondering how we managed to commit ourselves to the huge budgetary burden of health and retirement benefits for senior citizens. There are three elements to the story. First, the cause is worthy: After all, who would want to deny the elderly decent medical care and a comfortable retirement? Second, the benefits of the programs are far more concentrated than the costs. A retired couple, for example, collects about $32,000 per year in Social Security and consumes another $20,000 in subsidized medical benefits. In contrast, the typical working couple pays less than one-fourth of this each year in Social Security and Medicare taxes. Hence, the retired couple has a stronger **incentive** to push for benefits than the working couple has to resist them. And finally, senior citizens vote at a far higher rate than members of any other age group, in no small part because they are retired and thus have fewer obligations on their time. They are thus much more likely to make it clear at the ballot box exactly how important their benefits are to them.

THE FUTURE PATH

It is possible for government to responsibly address the crisis in funding programs for senior citizens. A number of countries have privatized their social security systems, with varying degrees of success. Such a move is unlikely in the United States, but tangible and important reforms might be possible. When Social Security was founded, life expectancy in the United States was sixty-two, and people could not collect full benefits until age sixty-five. Today life expectancy is seventy-nine, but eligibility for full benefits comes at age sixty-seven. Moving the full retirement age to seventy is one clear potential reform. Then there is the fact that everyone is eligible to collect benefits. Bill Gates, for example, is worth $82 *billion*, yet in 2017 he became eligible to collect early retirement Social Security benefits. This is an extreme example, but many commentators have argued that Social Security benefits should be simply phased out for wealthy individuals.

In the meantime, if Social Security and Medicare are kept on their current paths and older workers continue to leave the workforce, the future burden on today's college students is likely to be unbearable. If we are to avoid the social tensions and enormous costs of such an outcome, the willingness and ability of older individuals to retain more of their self-sufficiency must be recognized. To do otherwise is to invite a future in which the golden years are but memories of the past.

DISCUSSION QUESTIONS

1. How do the payroll taxes levied on the earnings of workers affect their decisions about how much leisure they consume?

2. When the government taxes younger people to pay benefits to older people, how does this affect the amount of assistance that younger people might voluntarily choose to offer older people?

3. When the government taxes younger people to pay benefits to older people, how does this affect the size of the bequests that older people are likely to leave to their children or grandchildren when they die?

4. In general, people who are more productive earn higher incomes and thus pay higher taxes. How would a change in the immigration laws that favored more highly educated and skilled individuals affect the future tax burden of today's American college students? Would the admission of better-educated immigrants tend to raise or lower the wages of American college graduates? On balance, would an overhaul of the immigration system benefit or harm today's college students?

5. How would a change in immigration laws that allowed *more* legal immigration affect the budget crisis we face with Social Security and Medicare?

6. How does the promise of guaranteed Social Security and Medicare benefits affect an individual's decision to save during the years before retirement age?

CHAPTER 24

For Whom the Roads Are Tolled

If you've ever been caught in a rush-hour traffic jam, you understand what happens when a **scarce** good has a price of zero. In this case, the scarce good is highway travel, and when the money price of travel is zero, something else must be used to ration the quantity of the good demanded. During rush hour (and much of the rest of the day in places such as Los Angeles, New York, Seattle, and Atlanta) the "something" that rations travel demand is time—the time of the motorists caught in traffic.

THE COSTS OF DRIVING

When a person drives a car, he or she generates a variety of costs. First are the **private costs** of driving, including fuel, oil, vehicular wear and tear, and the value of the driver's time.[1] These are all borne by the driver, so when deciding whether and how much highway travel to consume, the driver weighs these costs against the benefits of that travel. If these were the only costs of driving, this discussion would end here. Drivers would bear the full cost of their activities, just as the consumers of pizza do, and there would be no other issues to consider. But in most of the world, during parts of most days, driving causes another cost that is not borne solely by the individuals responsible for it.

On any road, after traffic volume reaches some level, additional cars entering the road slow traffic. Once this process—called

---

1 Ideally, automobile licensing fees and excise taxes on fuel are set to accurately reflect the costs of maintaining and policing the road system. If so, drivers pay not only for their vehicles and their time but also for roads and the police necessary to keep them safe.

congestion—occurs, each added car slows traffic even more. Eventually, traffic can come to a complete halt. In these circumstances, each driver is implicitly using, without paying for it, a valuable resource: the time of other motorists. Unless drivers are made to bear the **congestion costs** they create, two things must be true. First, the money price of traveling on the road is so low that resources are being wasted. Second, the value of motorists' time spent in traffic is rationing the quantity of travel demanded.

THE BENEFITS OF LESS CONGESTION

Why do economists worry about congestion? Because its existence raises the possibility that the people using the road could be made *better off* if they were charged a money price for using the road. This money price (called a **toll**) would induce fewer motorists to drive. Some would carpool, others would use public transit, and still others might telecommute rather than come to the office at all.

The reduced driving would cut congestion and thus conserve the valuable time of those people who continued to drive. In fact, it is even possible that by charging drivers a toll, *more* people would succeed in reaching their destination in any given time period. It is easiest to see this when traffic is so bad that it comes to a grinding halt. The toll would discourage some people from entering the road, and permit the remaining traffic to move and thus reach its destination. But the general principle holds true even when traffic is just greatly slowed down by the congestion: Road tolls can both improve traffic flow and make drivers better off—surely a combination with plenty of appeal for those sick of being stuck in traffic.

WHY NOT TOLLS?

Why, then, don't we see more widespread use of tolls on highways? There are three reasons. First, toll collection is not free, and until recently, the costs were often large enough to offset many of the benefits. Early toll roads, such as the Pennsylvania and New Jersey turnpikes, were equipped with toll booths that were staffed by attendants twenty-four hours a day. Tolls were paid in cash and traffic had to come to a halt at the booths for payment. This, of course, *created* some of the congestion that the tolls were supposed to relieve.

But over the last two decades, almost all toll roads have switched to electronic toll collection systems that reduce such costs substantially. Small, inexpensive electronic devices called transponders can be installed in cars that use the toll road. The transponders send identifying information to receivers at toll stations that are suspended above the roadway. Toll stations also can be equipped with high-speed cameras to record the license plate numbers of cars passing through the stations. Either way, cars often need not slow down from cruising speeds to have their identification recorded as they pass through. Regular users keep accounts with the toll authority, from which tolls are deducted as they are incurred. Any motorist without an account receives a bill at the end of the month for her tolls, often with an additional service charge for the billing service.

Under both the camera and the transponder systems, electronic toll collection has drastically lowered the costs of using monetary prices to ration roadway usage. The result has been reduced congestion and improved economic efficiency. Drivers are better off and governments have extra revenue.

GETTING IT WRONG . . .

The second impediment to pricing highway travel is the sometimes unpredictable consequences of changes in the cost of travel. Unlike a typical privately provided good, each road is part of a network of roads. Thus, a change in costs on one segment of the system can sometimes have striking and substantial consequences elsewhere, which can significantly offset the benefits of the tolls.

The island nation of Singapore, for example, experienced some of the worst traffic in the world in the decades after World War II. Hence, its government began experimenting with pricing roads in 1975, starting with a special fee for vehicles entering the central business district during peak traffic periods. When combined with other traffic control measures, the fee helped cut traffic in central Singapore by 45 percent during peak hours, enabling traffic speed to almost double to about 22 miles per hour. But the system had problems, too. For example, just outside the central city, traffic jams got worse, as drivers sought routes they could use without paying. Moreover, on the roads leading into the central city, the drop in rush hour traffic was nearly matched by a sharp increase in traffic just before 7:30 and after 9:30.

Apart from such network issues, simply predicting how motorists will respond to a particular toll can be difficult. Atlanta, Georgia, for example, in 2011 implemented a "hot lane" on 15.5 miles of Interstate 85, northeast of downtown. Carpoolers can use the lane at no charge, but solo drivers must pay for the privilege. Initially, the city set fares too high to lure drivers from the free lanes, and revenues from the hot lane fell short of projections by almost 40 percent. Indeed, drivers were so irate at the high tolls that many set up Facebook pages to complain.

. . . OR RIGHT

Sometimes tolls meet with immediate success, as illustrated by the experience of London, England. Beginning in 2003, drivers entering the central area of London were charged a toll (called a "congestion fee") of £5, about $6. The result was a 20 percent reduction in traffic and a consequent increase in average speeds. London's population has steadily increased in the years since, so the congestion fee has been raised as well, and is now £11.50 ($14) per car. Despite having about 10 percent more residents now than in 2003, central London traffic congestion is still much lower than it was before the fee was implemented.

Stockholm, Sweden, instituted a permanent system of tolls in 2007. Motorists entering or leaving the central city between 6:30 AM and 6:30 PM must pay a congestion tax that varies by time from $2.00 to $4.00. The city estimates that traffic has been cut by 20 to 25 percent, and most residents seem to prefer paying, rather than enduring added congestion.

Despite their early toll woes, Atlanta and Singapore now seem to have sorted things out. In 2012 Atlanta reduced tolls from their high initial levels. Travel on the hot lane jumped in response, easing traffic in the other lanes. Revenues from the toll more than doubled and now exceed even the most optimistic early forecasts. Singapore has extended its tolls to cover roads more evenly. It also has smoothed out the large time-based toll hikes that originally had caused motorists to take extreme measures to avoid paying. (Some drivers were simply stopping on the highway to wait out the next scheduled drop in tolls.) And in both cities, complaints about the tolls dried up, as drivers came to appreciate the benefits of paying with money instead of with their time.

THE POLITICS OF PRICING

The third, and perhaps the biggest, impediment to efficient pricing of roads is that most roads are operated by governments rather than by private sector firms. Decisions to price roads must pass through the political process, which necessarily means that the efficiency concerns of the economist are likely to be outweighed by political concerns over who shall pay how much for what. Public opinion polls from densely populated and heavily congested Hong Kong help us understand the consequences.

Although motorists and non-motorists in Hong Kong are almost identical in agreeing that traffic congestion is serious (84.5 percent and 82.0 percent, respectively), they differ sharply in what they think should be done about it. Motorists favor new road construction, presumably because this would shift to taxpaying non-motorists part of the cost of relieving congestion. In contrast, non-motorists believe that financial disincentives to driving (such as tolls and licensing fees) should be given the top priority—presumably because this would shift more of the burden to drivers. These divergences of public opinion have slowed the use of private sector remedies for the congestion on publicly owned roads, just as they have elsewhere in the world. The result is too many roads on which monetary prices are too low (or nonexistent)—and thus congestion is too high.

Alternatives to Tolls

For many people, the notion of putting a price on roads seems alien. Many would argue that if we want to reduce automobile congestion on existing roads, two other methods should be used. The first is to simply build more roads, thus providing more capacity for the cars. The second method is to create or expand mass transit systems, in effect getting some motorists off the roads to leave more room for the remaining ones.

Indeed, both methods will cut congestion, but only temporarily. As soon as the new roads or mass transit become operational, traffic quickly begins to rise: Some people take more trips, others take longer trips, and still others change jobs or homes to take advantage of the improved traffic flow. Within a few years, congestion becomes as bad as it was before. Indeed, this process of re-congestion is sufficiently predictable that it now has a name: the Fundamental Law of Road Congestion. Adding 10 percent capacity to the transportation system, for example, simply results in 10 percent more travel, yielding no long-run change in congestion. (This doesn't mean that more roads or mass transit are bad—after all, they permit more travel. It just means that they produce no long-run cuts in congestion.)

The Long-Run Solution

Politicians probably will never give up road projects or mass transit systems, but the power of prices to cut congestion is becoming better recognized across the country. In the 1990s, Southern California began adding toll roads and hot lanes to its automotive infrastructure. The hot lanes spread elsewhere slowly at first, with only eleven in existence by 2009. But there are more than three hundred miles of them now, and many more, as well as entire new toll roads, are in the works. And the sophistication of the pricing schemes grows each year. The hot lane system in Fairfax, Virginia, is a good example. There, the price per mile traveled varies every fifteen minutes in response to traffic conditions. When traffic is light, the price is twenty cents per mile, but at the height of rush hour, motorists pay $1.00 per mile for the privilege of smooth, uncongested traveling.

Roughly six thousand miles of U.S. roads now require tolls, which is up 25 percent from a decade ago. As the operators of the toll roads gain more experience in adjusting tolls to traffic conditions, their ability to reduce congestion and spread travel more evenly across the day will grow. And as the experience of London and Singapore and elsewhere shows, pricing schemes can be adjusted to growing population pressures to yield permanent relief from road congestion. The spread of tolls has meant improved economic efficiency, and the revenues from them have reduced pressure to raise taxes to pay for roads. And so, just as the price system enables us to get the food and clothes and shelter we want, so too can it help us get to work on time and keep us cool under the collar.

DISCUSSION QUESTIONS

1. Rather than tolls, some localities use other means to reduce congestion on major routes, for example with access-limiting traffic lights at freeway on-ramps. From an economist's perspective, what are the disadvantages of such a system?

2. If the purpose of a toll is to bring the private costs of a driver's actions into equality with the total costs (including congestion), should the size of the toll depend on how many passengers are in the car? Should it depend on the size of the car (or differ between cars, trucks, and busses)? Should it depend on the time of day that it is collected?

3. Suppose that when you ate a pizza you only had to pay for the crust but not the toppings. What would happen to (i) the number of pizzas you ate, and (ii) the amount and quality of the toppings on each one? If you faced a price of zero for toppings, after you had fully adjusted to this new pricing, what would be the marginal value to you of the last topping consumed? (You can give an exact number.) Does this equal the marginal cost of the last topping, assuming that toppings are a scarce good? Are you consuming the efficient number of toppings? Of pizzas?

4. Assume that by paying a $5 toll to use a hot lane, you could save six minutes on your commute to work, time that could be used productively in your office. What would your hourly wage rate (or earnings) have to be to justify paying the toll from your perspective? Compare this wage to the average hourly earnings in the United States (www.bls.gov). Based on this comparison, what would you predict about the average price and age of single-occupant cars in hot lanes versus such cars in other lanes on the same road?

5. Suppose a suburb is connected to a central business district by a single two-lane road. One of these lanes has a toll of $5 for the trip, while the other lane has no toll. If everyone's time is worth $20 per hour, what is the minimum time savings in the toll lane to make it worthwhile for a motorist to pay the toll?

6. Consider a highway with a hot lane and a lane that has no toll. Assume that all cars in the hot lane must pay the toll, no matter how many people are riding in them. What can you predict about the average occupancy of vehicles in the hot lane compared to vehicles in the other lane during rush hour?

Property Rights and the Environment

PART SIX

Property Rights and the Environment

CHAPTER 25

What to Do About the Climate?

"You can't change the weather." Just about everyone knows that old adage. But in fact, humans *are* changing the weather, although because this is occurring slowly over long periods of time, we call it climate change.[1] We refer here, of course, to the greenhouse effect—the tendency of carbon dioxide (CO_2) and other gases to accumulate in the atmosphere, acting like a blanket that traps radiated heat, thereby increasing the earth's temperature. Before turning to the economics of the problem, let's take a brief look at the physical processes involved.

CO_2 AND CLIMATE

Certain gases in the atmosphere, chiefly water vapor and CO_2, trap heat radiating from the earth's surface. If they did not, the earth's average temperature would be roughly 0°F instead of just over 59°F, and everything would be frozen solid. Human activity helps create some so-called greenhouse gases, including CO_2 (mainly from combustion of fossil fuels) and methane (from landfills, livestock, and fossil fuel production). We have the potential, unmatched in any other species, to profoundly alter our ecosystem.

There seems little doubt that humankind has been producing these gases at a record rate and that they are steadily accumulating in the

---

1 The difference between weather and climate is the time scale. Weather is a description of atmospheric conditions (temperature, precipitation, and so forth) today, or this week, or this season. Climate refers to those same atmospheric conditions measured over decades, centuries, or millennia.

atmosphere. Airborne concentrations of CO_2, for example, are rising at the rate of about 0.5 percent per year. Over the past fifty years, the amount of CO_2 in the atmosphere has increased a total of about 25 percent. Laboratory analysis of glacial ice dating back at least 160,000 years indicates that global temperatures and CO_2 levels in the atmosphere do, in fact, tend to move together, suggesting that the effect of today's rising CO_2 levels may be higher global temperatures in the future. Indeed, the National Academy of Sciences (NAS) has suggested that by the end of the twenty-first century, greenhouse gases could be double the levels they were in 1860 and that global temperatures could rise by at least 2°F above today's average.

A couple of degrees may not sound like much, but it does not take much to alter the world as we know it. The global average temperature at the height of the last ice age eighteen thousand years ago—when Canada and most of Europe were covered with ice—was 51°F, a mere 8°F or so cooler than today. Thus, adding just a few degrees to today's global temperatures has the potential to cause a rise in the average sea level, inundating low-lying areas; life-threatening summer temperatures in tropical climes; and devastating changes in the worldwide distribution of precipitation.

SHOULD WE WORRY?

Over the last one hundred fifty years, global temperatures have risen about 1.5°F, with much of this increase likely due to human-caused accumulations of greenhouse gases such as CO_2. Despite the dire predictions for a hotter future, the warming process so far has actually been *beneficial* to humans. The biggest benefits have come in three areas.

1. *Mortality*—Extreme temperatures, either too hot or too cold, can kill. Worldwide, almost 8 percent of all deaths are due to ambient temperatures that are either too high or too low. Of the two extremes, being too cold (hypothermia) is far more dangerous; it causes 95 percent of temperature-related deaths. A warming climate has prevented far more cold weather deaths than it has caused extra hot weather deaths, and is expected to do so well into the future.

2. *Agriculture*—Accumulating CO_2 in the atmosphere has benefitted agriculture in two ways. First, warmer temperatures have extended growing seasons and thus improved crop yields. Second, all plants depend on CO_2 for photosynthesis, and from a plant's perspective, there is remarkably *little* CO_2 around (it is less than 0.04 percent

of the air). So when CO_2 levels go up, plants thrive and agricultural yields increase.[2] On both counts, agricultural output has risen, pushing down food prices, benefitting primarily the world's poorest people.

3. *Energy costs*—Global warming raises temperatures in cold areas and thus lowers heating costs there. Of course it also raises temperatures in warm areas, which increases the demand for air conditioning. Thus far the *net* effect has been to conserve resources, including fossil fuels, and thus drive down energy costs.

If global warming progresses as it is forecast to do, the net benefits of climate change are expected to turn into net costs: The incremental benefits of warming will diminish, while the incremental costs will rise. Eventually, probably late in this century, further global warming will generate added costs that exceed the added benefits. And once we get to this point, matters will likely stay that way a long time, because CO_2 stays in the air for one hundred years or more. It is the prospect of a much warmer future in which little can be done to reduce the high temperatures that has so many people worried about climate change.

MITIGATING CLIMATE CHANGE

There are two ways we might protect ourselves from the harms of climate change. We can, for example, seek to *mitigate* the problem by reducing emissions of greenhouse gases. We can also engage in *adaptation*, by adjusting to the climate. We'll look first at mitigation.

There are three broad strategies for mitigating climate change. The first of these, which we'll call piecemeal regulation, has thus far dominated the actions of most governments. For more than forty years, for example, automakers in many parts of the world have been required to produce cars that meet minimum standards for fuel economy. These rules were originally implemented to reduce dependence on foreign oil, but have evolved into a method of cutting CO_2 emissions by reducing the amount of gasoline consumed. Similarly, many local and national governments have imposed "green energy" standards (see Chapter 20) requiring that at least a certain percentage of energy be produced by renewable sources, most notably wind or solar. Finally, many national governments require that ethanol be blended with the gasoline burned by

---

2 The impact here is huge. Over the last thirty years the amount of green vegetation cover on the earth has grown 14 percent—an area twice the size of the contiguous United States.

cars, on the grounds that burning ethanol does not cause a net increase in greenhouse gases (see Chapter 27).

The problem with these and other piecemeal approaches is that they are inefficient ways of dealing with the problem. They put too much of the burden of reducing emissions on the targeted activities and not enough on other activities that generate greenhouse gases. Thus, for the sacrifices we make with these regulations, we get far less reduction in greenhouse gases than could be achieved with broader-based approaches.

The second key mitigation strategy is called "cap and trade." The relevant government sets an upper limit, or cap, on total emissions, and firms or individuals are sold or given percentage shares of this cap. These shares may be kept or bought and sold among willing traders. This system was used successfully in the United States for many years to limit sulfur dioxide (SO_2) and nitrogen oxide (NOx) by major utilities. Several years ago in Europe a cap and trade system for CO_2 emissions was tried on a wide scale, but it has been largely ineffective. Lobbying by the firms subject to the cap succeeded in getting a cap set so high that it had little impact on emissions.

The final major mitigation strategy is a tax on CO_2 emissions, called a carbon tax because the levy is based on the carbon content of the fuel being burned. Economists generally agree that it is important that such a tax be "revenue-neutral." That is, all proceeds of the tax should be automatically distributed to the citizenry in the form of direct payments or lower taxes elsewhere. Revenue neutrality prevents the tax from being used for purposes other than improving environmental quality.

The Canadian province of British Columbia (BC) implemented a revenue-neutral carbon tax in 2008, and it appears to be quite successful in reducing CO_2 emissions without adverse consequences. The tax started at $8 (in U.S. prices) per ton of carbon and was raised by $4 each year until it reached $24 per ton in 2012. That is now about 21 cents of the $4 per gallon BC residents pay for their gasoline. Gasoline consumption in the province has dropped relative to the rest of Canada since the tax was implemented, and there seems to have been little harm to the local economy. A great advantage of the carbon tax is its transparency: The 21 cents per gallon is well known to motorists. Despite this and the seeming effectiveness of the tax in British Columbia, there has been no rush to implement carbon taxes elsewhere.

THE PROBLEM WITH MITIGATION

There is a key problem with mitigation strategies, which you can see by examining your personal choices. Suppose you decide to help reduce climate change by giving up your automobile, setting your thermostat at 80°F in the summer and 60°F in the winter, and doing without your appliances and electronic devices. You would suffer all of the inconvenience and nuisance of these actions, but the resulting reduction in greenhouse gases would be immeasurably small: all pain, no gain. Even though you might be willing to endure this as a matter of principle, not many people are likely to follow your lead.

Very much the same problem plagues governments, even national governments, when it comes to climate change mitigation. All of the costs of such strategies fall at home, while (almost) all of the benefits are enjoyed by people elsewhere. Almost no one wants to take the lead alone, and when such actions are taken, they typically have little worldwide impact. For mitigation to be effective, there must be coordinated action on global scale. This starts with agreement, but nations have been *agreeing* to take action on climate change since 1988. Despite these agreements (most famously the 1991 Kyoto Protocol and most recently the 2016 Paris Agreement), virtually nothing has been done of substance, and so CO_2 levels continue to rise.

ADAPTING TO CLIMATE CHANGE

We can now see that greenhouse gases will continue to rise and so too will global temperatures. So let's consider *adaptation* to what is coming in the future. The good news is that adaptation is exactly how humans have *always* confronted environmental challenges. When early humans moved north out of Africa, they adapted to colder climates by devising clothes and shelter that would protect them. As glaciers retreated, humans moved to northern regions to occupy niches that once were uninhabitable. As warming continued, humans adapted by developing agriculture, and then they moved farming into harsher climates by developing new techniques and seed varieties.

So, how might we adapt? Consider first something as common as air conditioning. Around 1960, residential air conditioning began to become more common in the United States. Since then, the mortality impact of hot weather has fallen 70 percent. The adoption of residential air conditioning has thus saved the lives of about 14,000 people *per year*, just in the United States.

One of the major threats from warmer temperatures comes from rising sea levels as glaciers and ice sheets melt. The resulting inundation of low-lying areas will threaten both human lives and physical structures. But because this process will take place over decades, adaptation to it is not technically demanding. Aging buildings will not be replaced if threatened, and fewer new structures will be erected in vulnerable areas. Moreover, there already exist modern "Lego™-like" construction methods that permit the low-cost disassembly and movement of endangered structures.[3]

Agriculture is another area where adaptation will be profound and highly effective in mitigating the impacts of warming. The ability of farmers to fine tune their crops to changing environmental conditions is well documented, and the development of new methods of genetic modification of plants will accelerate and enhance that process. New varieties will be developed, growing areas in higher latitudes will open up, and different crops will be planted in areas closer to the equator.

None of this is free, of course, and there remain uncertainties about how global warming might affect species other than *Homo sapiens*. It is estimated, for example, that temperate forests can "migrate" only at a rate of about sixty miles per century, not fast enough to match the speed at which warming is expected to occur. Similarly, the anticipated rise in the sea level could wipe out much of today's coastal wetlands. Presumably, new wetlands would develop along our new coastline, but how well wetland-dwelling species would adapt is a question not yet resolved.

Of course mitigation is not free either, and it can come with its own set of environmental hazards. (As we note in Chapter 27, for example, the mandated use of ethanol in gasoline is estimated to have caused far more environmental damage that any benefits conferred by it.) The great advantage of adaptation is that its benefits accrue to those persons and entities that incur the costs. Hence individuals, firms, and local governments all have the appropriate incentives to adapt promptly and correctly to the changing climate. Eventually, international cooperation may produce significant mitigation. But until (and even after) then, adaptation is a powerful, immediate tool.

The Take Away

Atmospheric concentrations of greenhouse gases are rising and human actions are playing a key role. Global average temperatures almost surely will rise in the coming decades, regardless of what actions are taken today. Mitigation can ultimately reduce greenhouse gas concentrations and so eventually—far in the future—halt the rise in temperatures.

---

3 Over the last thirty years, despite rising temperatures, coastal areas have done just fine. Coastlines have gained more land (13,000 square miles) than they have lost (7,800 square miles).

But effective mitigation requires massive coordination on a global scale, something that seems unlikely in the foreseeable future. Adaptation requires no such collective action, and can bring immediate benefits in terms of sharply cutting adverse consequences of current and future warming. Humans have thrived like no other species precisely because we have adapted to the adversities we have faced. It is a lesson that will serve us well as we confront the climate change that lies ahead.

DISCUSSION QUESTIONS

1. Why will voluntary actions, undertaken at the individual level, be unlikely to bring about significant reductions in greenhouse gases such as CO_2? Does this mean that individuals are powerless over greenhouse gases?

2. Does the fact that the CO_2 produced by one nation results in adverse effects on other nations have any bearing on the likelihood that CO_2 emissions will be reduced to the optimal level? Would the problem be easier to solve if all the costs and benefits were concentrated within a single country? Within a single elevator or office?

3. The policy approach to greenhouse gases will almost certainly involve limits on emissions rather than taxes on emissions. Can you suggest why limits rather than taxes are likely to be used? (*Hint:* Under which system does a firm that emits one million tons of CO_2 pay more taxes? How will this affect the firm's lobbying efforts in Congress?)

4. It costs about $100,000 per acre to create wetlands. How reasonable is this number as an estimate of what wetlands are worth?

5. Suppose the United States decides to discourage CO_2 emissions by imposing a tax on them. How large should the tax on CO_2 emissions be?

6. Human-caused (anthropogenic) emissions of CO_2 are only about 3 percent of *total* CO_2 emissions each year. (Oceans are the biggest emitters.) Why is so much attention directed at anthropogenic emissions of CO_2?

CHAPTER 26

Save That Species

Codfish off the New England and eastern Canadian coasts were once so abundant, it was said, that a person could walk across the sea on their backs. The fish grew into six-foot-long, two hundred-pound giants, and generations of families from coastal communities knew they could count on the fish for a prosperous livelihood. Indeed, the northwestern Atlantic became known as the world's premier cod fishery (a **fishery** is an area where it is commercially feasible for fish or other aquatic animals to be harvested). Slowly over time, however, nature's bounty began to disappear. Fishing became more difficult, the number of fish caught each year diminished, and the average size of the fish shrank. In recent years, the problems accelerated. Between 1970 and 2000, the catch dropped more than 75 percent, and the weight of the typical fish caught dropped to twenty pounds. Since then, the Canadians have closed down their cod fishery, and the American fleet has shrunk to a ghost of its former self.

FISHERY COLLAPSE IS WIDESPREAD

The cod is not alone in its demise. The world's ocean fisheries are in decline. Since 1950, nearly 30 percent of all fisheries have collapsed, and some scientists project that in forty years, *all* of the world's fisheries could disappear. The problem, it is widely agreed, is a failure of humans to manage fisheries in a way that is consistent with both maximum economic benefit and long-term survival of ocean fish stocks. Of course, this wide agreement just begs the real question: Why have humans been able to manage wheat farms and cattle ranches, but failed so miserably in managing fisheries?

The answer starts here: In almost all of the world's fisheries, the governmentally established rules of fishing are such that to "own" a fish, someone must catch the fish, that is, remove it from the water, at which point it typically dies within minutes. This is unlike the rules for cattle, pigs, chickens, or sheep, under which to own an animal one need only put a brand on it, or surround it with a fence, or enclose it in a building. The peculiar rules imposed by governments on most fisheries lead to a peculiar and destructive set of incentives.

When the decision is made to harvest any living animal, biological issues are important in accurately gauging the true cost of the harvest. In particular, if harvest does *not* take place (i) the animal will continue growing, yielding a larger effective harvest in the future and (ii) it may reproduce, leaving offspring that will also contribute to a larger future yield. For cattle, pigs, and so forth, the harvesters (ranchers and farmers) take both of these facts into account, waiting until growth and reproduction rates have reached the point that it makes sense to harvest the animals now rather than waiting.

But with ocean fish, each harvester knows that if she doesn't take the fish now, the future benefits (from growth and reproduction) will be enjoyed by someone else who happens to catch the larger fish or its offspring later on. The fishers respond quite rationally to this incentive. They "race to fish," catching the fish before the fish have a chance to grow more fully and often before they have had a chance to reproduce. This causes declining fish stocks and, eventually, the collapse of the fishery.

THE FAILURE OF COMMAND AND CONTROL

Based on a growing body of evidence, however, it has become apparent that a simple change in the way fisheries are managed has the power to stop and even reverse these declines. Traditional management of fisheries by government is referred to as a "command and control" system, because in an effort to control the fishers, the government issues a series of commands about allowable behavior. These management systems limit, for example, the number of fishers, the size of boats they may use, the type of fishing gear, and season length, all in an effort to keep total harvests down.

Although command and control systems historically have held sway around the world, even the best of them suffer from a profound misalignment of **incentives:** The self-interest of the individual harvester is generally inconsistent with actions that would both maximize the value of the fishery and ensure its sustainability. Because individuals don't own any fish until they harvest them, they are motivated to out-compete other harvesters, taking fish that are too small and too young for long-term sustainability. The results are twofold. In the short run, the fishers harvest too many fish, and in the long run, they successfully lobby the government for more lenient rules, adding to the destruction. So far, no government has figured out how to use a command and control system to prevent excessive harvests, reduced stocks, and eventual collapse.

In recent years, the failure of command and control fishery management has become increasingly clear, but the question has been whether there is a viable alternative. Economists have suggested that catch shares assigned to individual harvesters offer such an alternative because property rights systems, of which catch shares are an example, are generally the most effective way to conserve resources.

CATCH SHARE SYSTEMS

Catch share systems combine two features. First, based on biological and other scientific criteria, a **total allowable catch (TAC)** size is determined. Then members of the fishing community (individuals or cooperatives, for example) are assigned shares of the TAC. Typically, the shares are granted to existing fishers in proportion to their historical fishing patterns. The shares, often called **individual transferable quotas (ITQs),** can then be used, sold, or leased to others. No one is permitted to harvest in excess of the amount specified in the harvester's **quota.** The catch shares give fishermen enforceable, transferable **property rights** to the fish, much as they have such property rights to their boats and gear. These owners of rights then have an incentive to protect and maintain the value of the fishery, just as they do to protect and maintain their other property.

Numerous studies of the use of catch shares show that this system can dramatically improve both the biological and the economic health of fisheries. Alaska, British Columbia, Iceland, and New Zealand all represent locations where catch shares, such as ITQs, are regarded as having succeeded. Recent research covering more than eleven thousand fisheries around the world reveals that catch shares are effective worldwide. In fact, the outcomes for fisheries with and without catch share systems have been studied systematically, accounting for factors (such as ecosystem characteristics and fish species) that might have played a role in the health and viability of the fish stocks. This research approach amounts to conducting a statistically controlled experiment—and the results are striking.

THE POWER OF INCENTIVES

A conventional measure of collapse for a fishery is a decline in catch to a level that is less than 10 percent of the maximum recorded catch for that fishery. By this criterion, an average of more than fifty fisheries have reached collapse each year since 1950, in a worldwide pattern that seems to be pointing toward the demise of all fisheries. But when a catch share system is implemented in fisheries, the process of collapse halts—completely. Moreover, in many of the ITQ fisheries, recovery of fish stocks begins soon after implementation, even as fishermen continue to profitably catch fish.

It is now estimated that had ITQs been implemented in all fisheries beginning in 1970, the incidence of collapse would have been cut by two-thirds. Moreover, instead of watching fisheries collapse today, we would be seeing them getting healthier, even as they were supporting harvesters and nourishing consumers. Most importantly, it appears that the power of ITQs to prevent and even reverse fishery collapse applies to species and ecosystems throughout the world.

TURFs WORK TOO

There is another property rights system that has proven effective for species that stay in one place (such as clams and oysters) or that migrate predictably and over only modest distances (such as lobsters and some fish). This system, called **territorial use rights for fishing (TURFs)**, is designed much like property rights to land. Each individual fisher, or cooperating group of fishers, receives the exclusive right to harvest the relevant species in a particular geographic area of the sea. No one else may lawfully harvest there, and if the species is overfished, the fishers assigned the area may not lawfully fish on other TURFs—they are out of business. Hence, just as farmers have the correct incentives to care for their crops, so too do fishers have the correct incentives to care for their species.

TURFs have been implemented in increasing numbers over the last decade, and it appears they are working just as advertised: Both the fish and the fishers are prospering. This is not a complete surprise, for fishers in traditional societies have been using TURFs for thousands of years to sustainably manage their fisheries. And because there has been so much experience with TURFs in traditional societies under so many different circumstances and with so many different species, there is every reason to believe that TURFs can be deployed successfully in many more fisheries in the future.

CAN WE SAVE THE WHALES, TOO?

Could a property rights system help protect whaling stocks around the world? In principle, the answer is "yes" for a catch share system, although three aspects of whales would make the task more difficult. Consider, for example, blue whales, which are believed to migrate thousands of miles each year. A blue whale, which can weigh almost one hundred tons, is difficult to kill even with the most modern equipment. Nevertheless, intensive hunting gradually reduced the stock from at least 300,000 to, at present, somewhere between five thousand and twelve thousand. Since 1965, an international treaty has banned all hunting of the blue whale, although sporadic hunting of blues by some nations, such as Brazil, Chile, and Peru, has continued.

The enormous range of the blue whales means that enforcing rules for their capture—and this includes a catch share system—would likely be quite expensive. It is one thing to enforce catch limits over several thousand square miles. It is quite another to enforce them over millions of square miles. The second difficulty with designing a catch share system for blue whales is that because of the long-standing ban on hunting and the sharp restrictions on hunting before that, little is known about their population or whether that population is shrinking or growing. Hence, setting the correct TAC would be extremely difficult.

The final tricky issue of designing a catch share program for whales is that they are a "charismatic" species—that is, people seem to like knowing they are out there swimming around. (We doubt, for example, whether you have ever seen a bumper sticker that says "Save the cod.") Thus, whales are said to have "existence value"—some people get great satisfaction just out of knowing that they exist, satisfaction that would be irreparably lost if the whales were hunted to extinction. Clearly, although harvesters and biologists might be quite knowledgeable about growth and reproduction rates of all sorts of fish and ocean-going mammals, they are unlikely to know the value that Uncle Fred or Aunt Jane in Peoria place on the survival of the blue whale species. So people worry that a catch share system for whales might yield an unacceptably low stock of them. As we'll see in a moment, however, the biologists and harvesters of whales might not have to know anything at all about Uncle Fred or Aunt Jane to make sure that there are plenty of whales to keep both them happy and the whales healthy.

SERVE THE BISON

Ted Turner, the founder of CNN and former owner of the Atlanta Braves baseball team, has eighteen ranches spanning two million acres. Ted also owns over fifty thousand head of bison spread out over many of these ranches. Simply put, Ted owns more bison than anyone else in the world. His bison holdings are obviously nowhere near as big as the enormous herds that once dominated the American plains. But they are big enough to ensure genetic diversity among the animals and also to make it a good bet that bison are not going to become extinct at any time in the foreseeable future.[1] There are no doubt many reasons Ted has so many bison hanging around, but of one of them we can be certain: He turns thousands of head into burgers and steaks every year, both for his own chain of restaurants and for many hundreds more restaurants that serve bison on their menus. And although Ted raises the most bison in America, there are plenty of other bison ranchers out there doing much the same thing and for the same reason. In North America alone, bison stocks are about four hundred thousand, with another one hundred thousand head scattered across the rest of the world.

So, just acting in their own self-interests, Ted and his fellow ranchers are able to keep bison stocks plenty big enough to ensure the survival of the species and thus big enough to satisfy the desires of Aunt Jane and Uncle Fred that the bison continue to exist. Moreover, Ted's herds are big enough to *simultaneously* satisfy the existence value demands of a million (or even 7.5 billion) people around the world, all without any of these demanders putting up a penny of their own money (unless they stop by for a burger, of course).

In effect, this is exactly what is happening in fisheries around the world where catch share and TURF systems are at work. The incentives of the harvesters to keep stocks large enough for profitable fishing are *also* sufficient to protect the fish from any threat of extinction. It thus seems likely that property rights systems have the potential to save the whales, too. Indeed, the consistent ability of such systems to enable recovery of fish stocks and of the profits from harvesting illustrates a compelling general message: The clear assignment of enforceable property rights remains the most effective way we know to protect other species from the depredations of *Homo sapiens*.

DISCUSSION QUESTIONS

1. Has there ever been a problem with the extinction of dogs, cats, or cattle? Why not?

2. Some people argue that the best way to save rare species is to set up private game reserves to which wealthy hunters can travel. How could this help save endangered species?

---

1 Note that we don't claim that this or any system can prevent extinction forever. Only about 0.02 percent (about one in five thousand) species that have ever existed are currently extant. There is no evidence to date that any species—*Homo sapiens* included—has any claim on immortality.

3. Is government *ownership* of animals needed to protect species from extinction?

4. In the United States, most fishing streams are public property, with access available to all. In Britain, most fishing streams are privately owned, with access restricted to those who are willing to pay for the right to fish. Anglers agree that over the past thirty years, the quality of fishing in the United States has declined, while the quality of fishing in Britain has risen. Can you suggest why?

5. Aquaculture is the business of raising water-dwelling animals, including fish, mollusks (such as oysters), and shellfish (such as shrimp) in enclosed areas. For fish, this means raising them in large net pens. Do you suppose there is a problem with "overfishing" with aquaculture? What is a key difference between aquaculture animals and wild animals that plays a role in your conclusion?

6. Although much credit is given to buffalo hunters for causing the near extinction of bison, there was another factor at work. Cattle are easily herded by men on horseback and readily contained by barbed-wire fences. Bison simply break through ordinary barbed wire and kill (by goring) horses used in any attempt to herd them. Explain how these characteristics of bison helped seal their fate on the Great Plains.

CHAPTER 27

Ethanol Madness

Henry Ford built his first automobile in 1896 to run on pure ethanol. If Congress has its way, the cars of the future will be built the same way. But what made good economic sense in the late nineteenth century doesn't necessarily make economic sense in the early twenty-first century—although it does make for good politics. Indeed, the ethanol story is a classic illustration of how good politics routinely trumps good economics to yield bad policies.

ETHANOL MANDATES AND SUBSIDIES

Ethanol is made in the Midwest just like moonshine whiskey is made in Appalachia. Corn and water are mixed into a mash, enzymes turn starch to sugar, yeast is added, and heat ferments the brew. Once this is distilled, the liquid portion is ethanol and the solids are used as a high-protein animal food. The high-proof ethanol is combustible but yields far less energy per gallon than gasoline does. Despite this inefficiency, federal law requires that ethanol be added to gasoline, in increasing amounts through 2022. This requirement is supposed to conserve resources and improve the environment. It does neither. Instead, it lines the pockets of American corn farmers and ethanol makers and, incidentally, enriches some Brazilian sugarcane farmers along the way.

Federal law has encouraged, subsidized, or mandated ethanol as a so-called alternative fuel for more than thirty years. But it was not until 2005 that ethanol really achieved national prominence. The use mandates of the Energy Policy Act, combined with surging gas prices and a hefty federal ethanol subsidy, created a boom in ethanol production. Soon ethanol refineries were springing up all over the Midwest, and imports of ethanol from Brazil reached record-high levels.

THE SUPPOSED VIRTUES OF ETHANOL

Three factors are typically used to justify federal policy that pushes ethanol. First, it is claimed that adding ethanol to gasoline reduces air pollution and so yields environmental benefits. That may have been true fifteen or twenty years ago, but even the Environmental Protection Agency (EPA) acknowledges that ethanol offers no environmental advantages over other modern methods of making reformulated gasoline. Hence, neither the congressional mandate to add ethanol nor the subsidy paid until 2012 for its use as a fuel additive can be justified on environmental grounds.

A second argument advanced on behalf of ethanol is that it is "renewable," in that fields on which corn is grown to produce ethanol this year can be replanted with more corn next year. This is true enough, but we are in little danger of running out of "nonrenewable" crude oil any time in the next century. Indeed, **proven reserves** of oil are at record-high levels and rising. Perhaps more to the point, the production of ethanol uses so much fossil fuel and other resources that, under most circumstances, its production actually *wastes* resources overall compared to gasoline. In part, this is because ethanol is about 25 percent less efficient than gasoline as a source of energy. But it is also because the corn used to make ethanol in the United States has a high **opportunity cost.** If it were not being used to make fuel, it would be used to feed humans and livestock. Moreover, because ethanol production is most efficiently conducted on a relatively small scale, ethanol must be transported by truck or rail, which is far more costly than the pipelines used for gasoline.

The third supposed advantage of ethanol is that its use reduces our dependence on imports of oil. In principle, this argument is correct, but its impact is tiny, and the likely consequences are not what you might expect. Total consumption of all **biofuels** in the United States amounts to only 3 percent of gasoline and diesel usage. To replace the oil we import from the Persian Gulf with corn-based ethanol, at least *50 percent* of the nation's total farmland would have to be devoted to corn for fuel. Moreover, any cuts in oil imports will likely *not* come from Persian Gulf sources. Canada and Mexico are two of the three biggest suppliers of crude oil to the United States, and both countries send almost 100 percent of their exports to the U.S. market.

THE POLITICAL ECONOMY OF ENVIRONMENTAL POLICY

All of this raises an interesting question. If ethanol doesn't protect the environment, conserve resources, or have any compelling foreign policy advantages, why do we mandate its use and, until recently, subsidize its production? The answer lies at the heart of **political economy,** the use of economics to study the causes and consequences of political decision making. It is true that a critical component of what the government does (such as providing for national defense and law enforcement) provides an institutional structure necessary for the creation and retention of our total wealth. Nevertheless, the essence of much government policymaking, especially in the environmental arena these days, has nothing to do with making the size of the economic pie larger (or with protecting the environment). Instead, many government policies are directed at dividing up the pie in new ways so that one group gets more resources at the expense of some other group. To do this successfully, politicians must be adept at concentrating the benefits of policies among a few favored recipients while dispersing the costs of those policies across a large number of disfavored individuals.

At first blush, such an approach sounds completely at odds with the essence of democracy. After all, under the principle of "one person, one vote," it seems that benefits should be widely spread (to gain votes from many grateful beneficiaries) and costs should be concentrated (so that only the votes of a few disfavored constituents are lost). The concept of **rational ignorance** explains what is really going on. It is costly for individuals to keep track of exactly how the decisions of their elected representatives affect them. When the consequences of political decisions are large enough to outweigh the **monitoring costs,** voters swiftly and surely express their pleasure or displeasure, both in the voting booth and in their campaign contributions. But when the consequences to each of them individually are small relative to the monitoring costs, people don't bother to keep track of them—they remain "rationally ignorant."

ETHANOL WINNERS AND LOSERS

About one-sixth of all U.S. ethanol for fuel is made by one company, Archer Daniels Midland (ADM). Clearly, even small changes in the price of ethanol are important to ADM. The federal mandate that ethanol be added to gasoline increases the profitability of making ethanol, so ADM has strong incentives to ensure that members of Congress are aware of the benefits (to ADM) of the use mandate. Similarly, corn farmers derive most of their income from sales of corn. Federal ethanol policy increases the demand for corn and thus increases its price. Because the resulting benefits are highly concentrated on corn farmers, each has a strong incentive to ensure that her members of Congress understand the benefits (to the farmer) of such policy.

Contrast this with the typical taxpayer or consumer of gasoline. It is true that the $20 billion spent on ethanol subsidies from 2004 through 2011 came out of taxpayers' pockets. Nevertheless, this amount was spread thinly across tens of millions of federal taxpayers. Similarly, although the mandated use of ethanol in gasoline is estimated to raise the cost of gas by about 8 cents per gallon, this amounts to no more than $50 per year for the typical driver. Neither taxpayer nor motorist is likely to spend much time complaining to his or her senator.

Thus, farmers and ethanol producers are willing to lobby hard for ethanol mandates and subsidies at the same time that taxpayers and drivers put up little effective resistance to having their pockets picked. It may make for bad economics and lousy environmental policy, but it is classic politics.

DISCUSSION QUESTIONS

1. Brazilian ethanol producers (who make ethanol from sugarcane) have lower production costs than U.S. producers. Until 2012, Congress protected U.S. producers from Brazilian competition by imposing an **import tariff** of nearly 60 cents per gallon on Brazilian ethanol. If Congress really cares about protecting the environment and reducing our reliance on foreign crude oil, why do you suppose we had a large import tariff on ethanol?

2. Ethanol in the European Union (EU) is made from beets. In 2013 the EU imposed a tariff of about 25 cents per gallon on imports of ethanol from the United States. Explain who wins and who loses due to this tariff. Consider both producers and consumers and consider not just the EU and the United States, but also Brazil, which exports ethanol to the EU.

3. Why do you suppose the federal government gives special treatment to owners of fertile farmland rather than, say, to automobile mechanics?

4. From 2004 through 2011, the federal subsidy on U.S. ethanol production was roughly 50 cents per gallon. Use the theory of rational ignorance to explain why the ethanol subsidy was only about 50 cents per gallon rather than, say, $5 per gallon.

5. The EPA has approved the use of up to 15 percent ethanol in fuel blends. Cars built before 2007 (especially those built before 2001) are at risk of considerable engine damage if they run on such "E15" fuel. Who will foot the bill for such damages, if they occur?

6. Why are foreign producers of products so often the subject of special taxes such as the tax on imported ethanol?

CHAPTER 28

The Death of Recycling

If you believe the media reports, recycling—once America's favorite environmental cause—is in deep trouble. Our nation's capital, Washington, DC, lost $1 million on its recycling program in just one year. It costs New York City an *extra* $300 per ton to recycle its trash than to simply send it to a landfill. And more than two thousand cities nationwide that once were paid for the recyclables in their trash now must pay companies to haul the stuff away. Recycling is in such bad shape that one prominent champion of the activity felt compelled to write an article entitled "Recycling Is Not Dead." Despite this article, plenty of people in the recycling industry act as if they are headed to a funeral. How did we get here, and what lies ahead?

THE MOBRO 4000

On March 22, 1987, a garbage barge named *Mobro 4000* set off with 3,200 tons of New York trash, originally intended for a cheap landfill in Louisiana. Hoping to cut transportation costs, the entrepreneur behind the barge's voyage tried to interest Jones County, North Carolina, in accepting the trash. But the *Mobro* arrived there before the deal could be finalized, causing county officials to wonder if the entrepreneur's haste signaled the presence of hazardous waste. They said "no thanks," and word soon spread, leading to rejection slips everywhere the *Mobro* went, including the original site in Louisiana. Eventually, the barge spent two months and 6,000 miles touring the Atlantic Ocean and the Gulf of Mexico looking for a home for its load, before finally returning to New York, where the trash was incinerated.

Although there was plenty of landfill space available for the trash, journalists covering the trash barge story claimed otherwise. The *Mobro*, said a reporter on a live TV feed from the barge itself, "really dramatizes the nationwide crisis we face with garbage disposal." Moreover, although the *Mobro* contained nothing but plain old household trash, print and broadcast media played up the (unfounded) fears of Jones County officials that New York was trying to unload hazardous waste in their backyard. Indeed, many observers concluded that if we were consuming so much that we could no longer find a home for our trash, this was undeniable proof that America was wasting **resources** at every turn.

By the end of that summer, recycling had become America's number one environmental cause, a position it held until it was displaced by fears of global warming (see Chapter 25). Even today, third-graders are routinely exhorted to recycle their trash to save the planet, a message that continues through most students' college careers. And across the country, many thousands of state and local governments have instituted recycling programs that cajole or force people to "use the blue bin" rather than just throwing their trash out.

ARE WE RUNNING OUT OF SPACE?

Beginning with the *Mobro* episode, claims about the lack of space for trash began to emerge, including from former Vice President Al Gore, who asserted that America was "running out of ways to dispose of our trash." The late science fiction author Isaac Asimov claimed that "almost all the existing landfills are reaching their maximum capacity, and we are running out of places to put new ones." Even the Environmental Protection Agency (EPA) joined in this chorus. But such claims are inconsistent with the facts, as EPA officials eventually came to admit. It is true that the *number* of landfills has shrunk by 90 percent since 1970. But the new landfills that have replaced them are so much larger that landfill capacity has *grown* substantially. In fact, since the *Mobro* sailed, America's landfill capacity has jumped 25 percent.

Just as importantly, trash takes up remarkably little space. Indeed, all of America's trash for the next *century* would fit in a single landfill, no more than ten miles on a side. For a different perspective, the noted sailor, entrepreneur, and environmentalist Ted Turner owns approximately two million acres of land. A century's worth of America's trash would fit comfortably on just 3 percent of Ted's land—leaving more than ample room for the 51,000 head of bison that graze on his properties.

HOW HAZARDOUS IS TRASH?

Despite the suspicions of Jones County officials that the *Mobro* might have hazardous waste on board, it did not. The barge's municipal solid waste (MSW), like all household trash, was remarkably harmless stuff. Federal and state laws prohibit dumping hazardous waste into MSW landfills, and so all such waste is sent to facilities designed to safely handle it.

As for our everyday trash, plastic and glass bottles and steel and aluminum cans pretty much do nothing once they are in a landfill. Organic material, including food and yard waste and paper and cardboard, decomposes initially, producing methane (a potent climate-warming gas) and leachate (a noxious liquid that is generated when fluids mix with rotting organics). But modern landfills collect the methane for use as a fuel in energy generation, while the leachate is pumped to the surface for transport to municipal water treatment plants to be cleaned and returned to the **hydrologic cycle** (see Chapter 9). To make sure that nothing escapes, the landfills are lined with clay and plastic, and surrounded by leachate monitoring wells and methane detection equipment. Moreover, once landfills reach the end of their useful life as repositories for new trash, they are covered with layers of clay and topsoil and then converted to golf courses, parks, or wildlife refuges.

RECYCLING AND RESOURCES

One of the supposed advantages of recycling is that it conserves resources. There is no doubt that it conserves *some* resources: Recycling aluminum cans conserves bauxite and energy, and recycling glass conserves sand. But paper products constitute 80 percent of the household trash recycled in America. Virtually all of the virgin pulp used to make paper comes from trees specifically grown for that purpose. Recycling paper reduces the demand for trees and encourages landowners to convert their property to parking lots or condominiums.

More generally, if we want to think about what to do with our trash, we can recycle it into something new, or we can toss it into a landfill.[1] Recycling has the advantage in that it yields valuable inputs to the production of other goods (used beverage cans become new ones, paper

---

1 There is a third option, incineration, which is used to dispose of 40 to 80 percent of trash throughout Europe and in Japan, chiefly in waste-to-energy facilities. Many years ago, trash incinerators created substantial air pollution and noxious residual by-products. Modern incinerators are clean, efficient producers of energy. Despite this, only about 12 percent of America's trash is incinerated, partly because land is relatively cheap, and partly because most Americans are unaware of how much incinerators have improved.

begats paper, and so forth). But recycling uses far more resources to collect, sort, and transport than landfilling does. Even after we adjust for resources recovered by recycling, the process of recycling everyday rubbish actually uses *more* resources than are expended when we send our trash to the landfill. In fact, on average we waste about $60 to $75 worth of resources for every ton of household trash that is recycled rather than sent to a landfill. To be sure, there are some locations where municipal recycling programs conserve resources, but the recycling programs in most American communities waste resources.

RECYCLING MANDATES

Even before the *Mobro* had hauled its load back to New York, observers said that because of the garbage crisis we should compel people to recycle. These mandates eventually took a variety of forms. For example, some products now must include a minimum amount of recycled content in their manufacture. Some communities mandated that curbside recycling programs be initiated. Others went so far as to ban items, such as cans and bottles, from trash bins, requiring (under penalty of fine) that they be separated and placed only in recycling containers.

Many of these mandates proved to be both misleading and wasteful, however. Curbside recycling programs, for example, have high costs because the volume of material recovered is low compared to the value of the human and physical resources devoted to collecting it. When Los Angeles instituted curbside recycling, for example, it had to double the number of sanitation trucks in its fleet, because the pickup routes effectively had to be run twice: once for the trash, once for the recyclables. Similarly, rules that require minimum recycled content force firms to use product mixes that fail to minimize the cost of production. Overall, recycling mandates have probably been the most important reason that municipal recycling programs waste resources.

RECYCLING AND THE ENVIRONMENT

Even so, many people feel that recycling programs are worthwhile, on the grounds that they protect the environment. It is certainly true that in many cases, recycling does this admirably. For example, recycling aluminum beverage containers conserves energy and so reduces pollution associated with energy use, and it does this with little offsetting environmental damage elsewhere. Similarly, under ideal manufacturing conditions, recycling paper or cardboard rather than making them from virgin pulp reduces the environmental damage of the manufacturing process.

"Life cycle analysis" (LCA) is the process by which analysts attempt to establish the environmental **trade-offs** involved in recycling versus using virgin materials. Such analysis is also the basis for the claims that recycling is environmentally superior. Yet the bloated sanitation truck fleet in Los Angeles—spewing diesel exhaust into the air—is just one example that the "ideal" recycling process is not always the *actual* process used. Hence, the environmental advantages of recycling are routinely less than are claimed.

Much of America's paper is recycled in China, where there is little, if any, effort to protect the environment. The Chinese are not inclined to reveal exactly how much environmental damage is done by this paper recycling, but there is little doubt that it is substantial. Similarly, much of America's metal and electronics recycling takes place in nations (including China, India, and others) where environmental protections are noted for their absence rather than their effectiveness. To date, no form of life cycle analysis accounts for the fact that much recycling takes places under environmentally catastrophic conditions in the developing world, and thus such analysis fails to inform us of the true environmental impacts of recycling programs.

Recycling Is as Old as Trash Itself

Although the voyage of the *Mobro* inspired many Americans (and people elsewhere) to begin or expand their recycling efforts, it is important to recognize that recycling is as old as trash itself. For as long as humans have been discarding rubbish, other humans have sifted through it for items of value. Indeed, contrary to what people say about prostitution, scavenging may well be the oldest profession.

During the Middle Ages, craftsmen recycled every bit of raw material not immediately used in crafting the item at hand, and gladly welcomed—and paid for—previously used items that could be refashioned into new ones. Long before state or local governments had contemplated the word *recycling*, the makers of steel, aluminum, and thousands of other products were recycling manufacturing scraps, and some were even operating convenient centers where consumers could drop off used items suitable for recycling. Indeed, entire industrial complexes routinely have been created expressly for the purpose of using one firm's castoff as the principal raw material in another's production process.

All of this recycling, including the recycling of much household trash, has been conducted voluntarily and by individuals and companies informed about the costs and benefits of what they were doing (even if they sometimes could not put precise monetary numbers on those costs and benefits). And all of this informed, voluntary recycling has conserved resources, raised our wealth, and typically had beneficial environmental outcomes. But such resource conservation and environmental protection does not necessarily extend to programs that are based on misinformation or government mandates.

THE PROBLEM

Voluntary recycling targets items that are of high value or that are low-cost to recycle. This means that what is left in the dregs of municipal solid waste—our trash—is both of low value and costly to recycle. Forcing people—or misleading them—to insensibly engage in recycling activities that have costs that exceed the benefits is bound to waste resources and reduce society's wealth.

It is true that individuals do not always have the correct knowledge and incentives to account for all of the environmental impacts of their actions (including impacts on the climate). But the correct way to address this problem is through environmental policy as a whole, including (see Chapter 25) the imposition of carbon taxes or other pollution taxes, where appropriate. Otherwise, we risk doing more harm than good, and perhaps even damaging the environment further.

THE REPORTS ARE EXAGGERATED

Two forces have been importantly responsible for the hard times recently experienced by the recycling industry. First, in 2013, China began demanding that the quality of the recyclable materials exported to its shores be improved substantially. This required recyclers in America and elsewhere to take greater care in collecting and sorting recyclables. That extra care raised the costs of recycling firms and also reduced their willingness to pay municipalities as much for recyclable items, especially paper and plastic. The effects of China's new policies were amplified by the sharp drop in the price of oil from 2014 to 2016, which helped push down commodities prices (and thus recyclables prices). The profitability of recycling fell even further, and so too did the amount of recycling that was undertaken.

But the recycling industry has been through down-cycles like this many times in the past, most recently in 2008–2009, when commodities prices collapsed during a major recession. But each time, economic conditions have improved, and so too have the profitability and volume of recycling. To paraphrase the great American humorist Mark Twain, reports of the death of recycling are an exaggeration. Recycling will bounce back. There is no need to try to force it back, just as there is typically no need to force or mislead people into recycling. Indeed, what is important in framing public policy toward recycling is to remember that too much of a good thing is not necessarily better than less of it.

DISCUSSION QUESTIONS

1. Some states require that retailers collect (refundable) deposits of a nickel or a dime on every can and bottle they sell. These deposits far exceed the economic value of the can or bottle. How do the deposits affect the incentives of individuals to recycle these products? Is it possible for bottle and can deposits to be *too high*, in the sense that they induce too much recycling or cause an increase in other undesirable activity? (*Hint:* Suppose the required deposits were, say $100 for each can or bottle.)

2. Why do many communities mandate recycling? (*Hint:* Could the incentives facing local governments and recycling companies differ from the incentives facing the average citizen?) Is it possible to induce people to recycle more without requiring that all residents recycle?

3. Some communities charge for trash pickup based on the number of garbage cans (or bags) that people put out for collection. How do hefty per-can trash pickup fees influence the decisions people make about what goods they will *consume*?

4. A community planning on charging a fee for trash pickup might structure the fee in any of several ways. It might, for example, charge a fixed amount per garbage can, a certain amount per pound of garbage, or a flat fee per month without regard to the amount of garbage collected. How would each of these affect the amount and type of garbage produced? Which system would lead to an increase in the use of trash compactors? Which would lead to the most garbage?

5. Forty-eight states import garbage from other states or from Canada, while forty-nine states export at least some of their trash. How does interstate trade in trash differ (if at all) from interstate trade in other products?

6. The population concentrations of most counties in the United States tend to be located in the middle of each county. Where do you think most landfills are located within each county?

PART SEVEN

Globalization and Economic Prosperity

CHAPTER 29

The Economics of the Big Mac

The notion that two all-beef patties might be deliciously combined with condiments on a sesame-seed bun was first proposed in an advertising jingle for the Big Mac. The world's favorite monster burger was born in Uniontown, Pennsylvania, created by Jim Delligatti in August 1967. Delligatti's family has operated McDonald's restaurants since the earliest days of the company and now owns eighteen of those restaurants. The family even opened a Big Mac Museum Restaurant near that burger's birthplace. A Big Mac contains twenty-eight grams of fat, or about one ounce of artery-clogging substances. But we are not here to attack the Big Mac. Rather, we wish to see how economists can use this standardized product to help compare the cost of living and the levels of real incomes around the world.

SOME ARE POOR, SOME ARE RICH, AND MANY ARE IN BETWEEN

It seems obvious that the average European or American or Canadian earns a higher income than the average resident of countries such as China and India. What is more difficult to estimate is how *much* better off the citizens are in one nation compared to another. If we want to make such an estimate, some obstacles must be overcome. First there is the matter of national currencies. In the United States, for example, we probably want to make income comparisons in dollars. But dollars are not the national currency in China or India or most other nations, so we must somehow convert from one currency to another.

FOREIGN EXCHANGE RATES

Travel within another country requires that payments be made in the currency of that nation. If you go to Europe, in nineteen countries, you will buy goods with euros. If you go to India, you will pay in rupees. If you go to Russia, you will make purchases using rubles.

So, to compare the average Russian's income in rubles with the average American's income in dollars, we must convert the rubles to the equivalent amount of dollars. The data for converting are readily available on a daily basis, because there is a worldwide market in **foreign exchange,** or national currencies. You might find that it takes sixty rubles (or sixty rupees) to buy one dollar. So, as a first approximation, this means that to compare incomes across the world, simple arithmetic is involved. We convert, via **foreign exchange rate** tables—found on hundreds of Internet sites—other nations' average incomes in their own currencies to what they are in U.S. currency: dollars.

For example, if the average income in France is 34,000 euros, we multiply the current euro exchange rate by that number. Suppose the exchange rate is such that one euro equals 1.10 dollars, then the average income in France is 34,000 euros times 1.1 dollars per euro, or $37,400.

When we do such calculations, we find that on an exchange-rate basis, the average American is thirty-five times richer than the average Indian, seven times richer than the average citizen of China, and about six times richer than the average Russian.

PROBLEMS WITH USING MARKET EXCHANGE RATES

Foreign exchange rates are a function of world **supply** and **demand** (sound familiar?). But the demand and supply of currencies are ultimately derived from (or determined by) the demand and supply of, among other things, **traded goods.** Traded goods (and services) are those that, as the name suggests, are traded across national borders. Some examples of traded goods are wines, automobiles, wheat, and shoes. If all goods were traded and if that trade occurred with no distortions, then exchange rates would permit us to perfectly compare incomes around the world.

But there is a complication: Not all goods and services that we consume are traded goods. **Non-traded goods** include houses, haircuts, house-cleaning services, and landscaping, as well as many others. Non-traded goods and services are not involved in exchange across countries' borders.

The existence of non-traded goods implies that bias will result if we use only exchange rates to make international comparisons. This is because in poorer countries, wages are low and so non-traded goods (made with that low-cost labor) are likely to be the cheapest. That is, in low-income nations we expect restaurant meals, beauty salon services, and house cleaning to be much less expensive than those same items in high-income nations. Hence, if we use current exchange rates—based on traded goods—to convert incomes to a common currency, differences in average incomes between low-wage nations and high-wage nations are going to be exaggerated.

Often you will read newspaper stories about a developing country in which the average income, say, is $1,000 a year. That number is derived from current foreign exchange rates. It does not take account of how cheaply residents in that country can buy basic foods and services that are not traded in international markets.

Purchasing Power Parity—A Solution?

Somehow, we have to adjust current exchange rates to account for differences in the true cost of living across countries. To do so, we may use a concept known as **purchasing power parity,** which creates a type of adjusted foreign exchange rate.[1] The details of how the World Bank and other organizations calculate various purchasing power parity measures for two hundred countries are not important here. Suffice it to say that in doing so, attempts are made to adjust market foreign exchange rates for the relative cost of living in each country. So, on a purchasing power parity basis—taking into account the lower cost of living in India, China, and Russia—average American income is only nine times higher than in India, three times higher than in China, and 2.5 times as high as in Russia.

A major problem remains, nonetheless. **Purchasing power** adjustments are difficult to calculate in each country. The residents of each nation buy different combinations of goods and services or, in the alternative, they buy similar goods and services but with subtle variations in quality. Not only are the calculations difficult, but also there are disputes over the best way to do them for each country, leading to doubts about whether the measures *really* account for differences in the cost of living.

It is here that the ubiquitous Big Mac proves its worth.

---

1 Obviously, there is no market for anything measured in units of purchasing power parity.

Big Mac to the Rescue

A typical Big Mac is created using virtually identical ingredients around the world (although substitution occurs where religious or cultural norms rule out beef). Big Macs are produced according to a uniform process detailed in the McDonald's six-hundred-page manual. As well as being a "standard product," local prices of Big Macs are not distorted by international transportation and distribution costs.

In light of these facts, since 1986, the magazine *The Economist* has developed a Big Mac Index. By using one good only—a Big Mac—*The Economist* has thereby created a means of comparing the cost of living around the world and also a means of determining how much exchange rates fail to account for non-traded goods.

Keeping in mind that the methods of production and the ingredients are the same in Big Macs everywhere, if we convert international Big Mac prices using exchange rates, we "should" get exactly the same price everywhere. But if, using exchange rates, we calculate that a Big Mac costs $6.60 in Switzerland, but only $5.00 in America, this says that a dollar doesn't go very far in Switzerland. That is, the cost of living in Switzerland is relatively high, most likely because non-traded goods (such as housing) are quite expensive there. Similarly, if we also find that, at current exchange rates, a Big Mac costs the equivalent of $2.80 in China, we have found that the dollar goes a long way there: The cost of living is low in China compared to that in the United States. Again, this is most likely because non-traded goods made with low-wage labor are quite cheap in China.

The upshot is that if we adjust incomes using the Big Mac Index to correct for differences in the cost of living, we can get a much better idea of relative real incomes. In one recent year, for example, using exchange rates, income in Switzerland was about $80,000, compared to about $56,000 in the United States. After correcting with the aid of the Big Mac, however, we find that real income in Switzerland is only about $60,000—still higher than in the United States but not by much.

McWages, Real Wages, and Well-Being

Now consider creating a McWage. Given that the talent necessary to make a Big Mac is about the same everywhere, we can collect information on the wages of Big Mac preparers throughout the world. This will enable us to compare the cost of hiring this particular quality of labor across countries. If we then take McWages and divide them by the local price of a Big Mac, we can discern how many Big Mac equivalents each worker is paid per hour. This is a simple, albeit one-good-specific, measure of the **real wage** for low-skill workers that is, the wage adjusted for the cost of living in each nation. And this measure—"Big Macs per hour"—can be constructed without worrying about biases in exchange rates or complicated purchasing power parity calculations.

That is exactly what economists Orley Ashenfelter and Stepan Jurajda have done. They have found that low-skill workers in America earn about 2.5 Big Macs per hour (or BMPH), compared to 3.1 BMPH earned in Japan. In Canada and Western Europe, workers are paid about 2.2 BMPH. Using the same calculations, the authors found that workers in Russia earn about 1.2 BMPH, while Eastern European workers collect about 0.8. Workers in China earn about 0.6 BMPH, while those in India earn only about 0.4. The bottom line is that using the BMPH index, we see that standards of living vary greatly around the world, but not nearly to the extent that is suggested by exchange rates.

Trends in Productivity

A basic tenet of economics is that in competitive labor markets (and that is certainly where McDonald's gets its workers) people are paid based on what they produce. Thus, using the data mentioned above, we can infer that low-skill workers in America are only about 10 percent more productive than those in Canada or Western Europe, but they are about four times as productive as those in China.

We can also look at the patterns of change in the BMPH index over time, to give us an idea of how **productivity,** and thus standards of living, are evolving around the world. As one example, between 2000 and 2007, McWages in the United States rose by 13 percent, while the price of a Big Mac jumped by 21 percent. That means that real wages for low-skill workers *fell* in the United States by about 8 percent over this period. Doing the same calculation for the same period, productivity, and thus real wages, rose 60 percent in China and by over 50 percent in India. Clearly, average productivity was rising sharply in these two countries.

Between 2007 and 2016, real wages continued to fall (but more slowly) in developed nations such as the United States, Canada, and Western Europe. In most developing nations, real wages have been rising, although much more slowly than before. The good news of this story is that developing nations are generally closing the standard of living gap. The bad news is that the world financial crisis and its aftermath have diminished opportunities for low-skill workers around the world, a development that is surely worth monitoring in the future.

DISCUSSION QUESTIONS

1. Assume you are going to take a trip to Paris. You buy euros at your local bank or at the airport. Then you start spending them once you are in Paris. Every time you buy something there, you explicitly or implicitly translate the euro price into dollars. Often, you might say to yourself, "How do Parisians afford such high prices?" What is wrong with this line of reasoning? (*Hint*: In what currency do Parisians earn their income?)

2. Why don't the local prices of restaurant meals, haircuts, and gardening services affect a country's exchange rate?

3. If the same amount of materials and the same methods are used to produce Big Macs in over one hundred twenty countries, why aren't the prices of Big Macs all the same, expressed in dollars?

4. Is there anything that a Big Mac preparer in a developing country can do to earn a higher real wage rate?

5. Why does McDonald's provide a six-hundred-page manual to the company's franchises in every country? (*Hint*: What are the ways that any franchisor can monitor quality of its franchisees?)

6. In a wealthy country, wages are not only high in the traded-goods and services sector, but also high in the non-traded goods and services sector. Why? (*Hint*: Are there two separate labor markets or just one?)

CHAPTER 30

Globalization and the Wealth of America

The past twenty-five years have been a time of great change for international trade and **globalization.** The North American Free Trade Agreement (NAFTA), for example, substantially reduced the **trade barriers** among citizens of Canada, the United States, and Mexico. On a global scale, the Uruguay Round of the General Agreement on Tariffs and Trade (GATT) was ratified by 117 nations, including the United States. Under the terms of this agreement, GATT was replaced by the **World Trade Organization (WTO),** whose membership now numbers over 150, and **tariffs** were cut worldwide. Agricultural **subsidies** were reduced, patent protections were extended, and the WTO established a set of arbitration boards to settle international disputes over trade issues.

Many economists believe that both NAFTA and the agreements reached during the Uruguay Round were victories not only for free trade and globalization, but also for the citizens of the participating nations. Nevertheless, many noneconomists, particularly politicians, have opposed these agreements. Indeed, a centerpiece of President Trump's 2016 campaign was a promise to dismantle NAFTA and start a trade war with China. In light of the chasm between economic evidence and political rhetoric, it is important that we understand what is beneficial about NAFTA, the Uruguay Round, and free trade in general.

GAINS FROM TRADE

Voluntary trade creates new wealth. In voluntary trade, both parties in an exchange gain. They give up something of lesser value in return for something of greater value. In this sense, exchanges are always unequal.

But it is this unequal nature of exchange that is the source of the increased **productivity** and higher wealth that occurs whenever trade takes place. When we engage in exchange, what we give up is worth less than what we get—for if this were not true, we would not have traded. And what is true for us is also true for our trading partner, meaning that both partners end up better off.

Free trade encourages individuals to use their abilities in the most productive manner possible and to exchange the fruits of their efforts. The **gains from trade** lie in one of the most fundamental ideas in economics: A nation gains from doing what it can do best *relative to other nations*, that is, by specializing in endeavors in which it has a **comparative advantage.** Trade encourages individuals and nations to discover ways to specialize so that they can become more productive and enjoy higher incomes. Increased productivity and the subsequent increase in economic growth are exactly what the signatories of the Uruguay Round and NAFTA sought—and are obtaining—by reducing trade barriers.

GLOBALIZATION AND THE OPPOSITION TO IT

Globalization differs from free trade chiefly in the degree of integration across nations. For example, although there is free trade in wine, the wines produced in Australia, California, and France are each created wholly within the geopolitical borders indicated by their labels. Moreover, each remains a distinct economic entity, in that significant relative price changes between, say, French and California wines are observed. In contrast, the market for automobiles has become truly "global." If you purchase a "Japanese" automobile in the United States, assembly of the vehicle may have taken place in Japan, the United States, or even Mexico, and the components of the car may have come from a half-dozen or more different nations. And if you call for customer support for your car, the person answering the phone may be at a call center located in any of a variety of English-speaking nations. Globalization thus means that trade between nations becomes as seamless as trade between states, provinces, or cities within a given nation.

Despite the enormous gains from exchange, globalization is routinely opposed by some people. Many excuses are offered for this opposition, but they all basically come down to one issue: When our borders are fully open to trade with other nations, some individuals and businesses in our nation face more competition. As you saw in Chapter 18, most firms and workers hate competition, and who can blame them? After all, if a firm can keep the competition out, **profits** are sure to rise. And if workers can prevent competition from other sources, they can enjoy higher wages and greater selection among jobs. So the real source of most opposition to globalization is that the opponents to trade dislike the competition that comes with it. There is nothing immoral or unethical about this—but there is nothing altruistic or noble about it, either. It is self-interest, pure and simple.

BEGGAR-THY-NEIGHBOR

Because of this, opposition to globalization is nothing new. One of the most famous examples of such opposition led to passage of the Smoot–Hawley Tariff of 1930. This major federal statute was a classic example of **protectionism**—an effort to protect a subset of American producers at the expense of consumers and other producers. It included tariff schedules for more than twenty thousand products, raising taxes on affected imports by an average of 52 percent.

The Smoot–Hawley Tariff encouraged beggar-thy-neighbor policies by the rest of the world. Such policies represent an attempt to improve (a portion of) one's domestic economy at the expense of foreign countries' economies. In this case, tariffs were imposed to discourage **imports** so that domestic import-competing industries would benefit. The beggar-thy-neighbor policy at the heart of Smoot–Hawley was soon adopted by the United Kingdom, France, the Netherlands, and Switzerland. The result was a halt to globalization and a massive reduction in international trade that almost certainly worsened the worldwide depression of the 1930s.

Opponents of globalization sometimes claim that beggar-thy-neighbor policies benefit the United States by protecting import-competing industries. In general, this claim is not correct. It is true that some Americans benefit from such policies, but two large groups of Americans lose. First, there are the purchasers of imports and import-competing goods. They suffer from higher prices and reduced selection of goods and suppliers caused by tariffs and import **quotas.** Second, the decline in imports caused by protectionism also causes a decline in **exports,** thereby harming firms and employees in these industries. This follows directly from one of the most fundamental propositions in international trade: *In the long run, imports are paid for by exports.* This proposition simply states that when one country buys goods and services from the rest of the world (imports), the rest of the world eventually wants goods from that country (exports) in exchange. Given this fundamental proposition, a corollary becomes obvious: *Any restriction on imports leads to a reduction in exports.* Thus, any business for import-competing industries gained as a result of tariffs or quotas means at least as much business lost for exporting industries.

THE TRUMP PROMISE

When Donald Trump promised to "Make America Great Again," he had things exactly wrong, at least when it came to his pledge to reduce America's participation in world trade. Restricting imports reduces the wealth of Americans who consume imports, and those (like truck drivers) who participate in the import business. Moreover, as we just saw, restricting imports means that *exports* must decline as well. This reduces the wealth of the Americans who produce and transport goods for export.

Now, you might say, this will all be more than made up for by an expansion of trade *within* the United States. But it won't, because the reduction in trade with the rest of the world reduces our overall wealth, and thereby contributes to a reduction in domestic consumption, and thus production. To see why this is true, consider what would happen if we restricted or eliminated *interstate* trade within America. (After all, those autoworkers in Detroit are taking jobs away from people in Miami, Chicago, and Dallas who might otherwise be making cars.) Indeed, let's also eliminate trade between people in different *counties*. Or, perhaps we should carry the argument to its logical ending, by eliminating all trade between people, so that each of us can be fully employed producing whatever it is we might hope to consume in such a world.

The promise of protectionism is a promise of impoverishment—and it is one that will hurt the disadvantaged the most. A study of forty countries found that the richest citizens would lose 28 percent of their wealth if international trade were halted. But the poorest 10 percent of the populations would lose 68 percent of their meager incomes without international trade. It is difficult to see how a policy that harms people at every point in the income distribution will make us "great."

DUMPING

Opponents of globalization raise a variety of objections in their efforts to restrict international trade. For example, it is sometimes said that foreign companies engage in **dumping,** selling their goods in America below cost. The first question to ask is: Below *whose* cost? Clearly, if the foreign firm is selling in America, it must be offering the good for sale at a price that is at or below the cost of buying from American firms or else it could not induce American consumers to buy it. But the ability of individuals or firms to get goods at lower cost is one of the *benefits* of free trade, not one of its negatives.

What about claims that import sales are taking place at prices below the foreign company's costs? This amounts to arguing that the owners of the foreign company are voluntarily giving some of their wealth to us, namely, the difference between their costs and the lower price they charge us. It is possible, though unlikely, that they might wish to do this as a way of getting us to try a product that we would not otherwise purchase. But if so, why would we want to refuse this gift? As a nation, we are richer if we accept it. Moreover, it is a gift that will be offered for only a short while, for there is no point in selling below one's cost unless one hopes soon to raise price profitably above cost!

LABOR AND ENVIRONMENTAL STANDARDS

Another argument sometimes raised against globalization is that the goods are produced abroad using unfair labor practices (such as the use of child labor) or using production processes that do not meet American environmental standards. Such charges are sometimes correct. But we must remember two things. First, although we may find the use of child labor (or perhaps sixty-hour work weeks with no overtime pay) objectionable, such practices were once common in the United States. They used to be prevalent in America for the same reason they are now practiced abroad. The people involved were (or are) too poor to do otherwise. Some families in developing nations cannot survive unless all members of the family contribute. As unfortunate as this is, if we insist on imposing our attitudes—shaped in part by our great wealth—on peoples whose wealth is far less than ours, we run the risk of making them worse off even as we think we are helping them.

Similar considerations apply to environmental standards. It is well established that individuals' and nations' willingness to pay for environmental quality is very much shaped by their wealth. Environmental quality is a **luxury good.** That is, people who are rich (such as Americans) want to consume much more of it per capita than people who are poor. Insisting that other nations meet environmental standards that we find acceptable is much like insisting that they wear the clothes we wear, use the modes of transportation we prefer, and consume the foods we like.[1] The few people who manage to comply will indeed be living in the style to which we are accustomed, but most people will simply be impoverished by the attempt.

Our point is not that foreign labor or environmental standards are, or should be, irrelevant to Americans. Our point is that achieving high standards of either is costly, and trade restrictions are unlikely to be the most efficient or most effective way to achieve them. Just as important,

---

1 There is one important exception to this argument. In the case of foreign air or water pollution generated near enough to our borders (for example, with Mexico or Canada) to cause harm to Americans, good public policy presumably dictates that we seek to treat such pollution as though it were being generated inside our borders.

labor standards and environmental standards are all too often raised as smoke screens to hide the real motive—keeping the competition out.

THE POLITICAL ECONOMY OF TRADE BARRIERS

If it is true that globalization is beneficial and that restrictions on trade are generally harmful, we must surely raise the question of how legislation such as the Smoot–Hawley Tariff (or any other such restriction) ever gets passed. As Mark Twain noted many years ago, the reason the free traders win the arguments and the protectionists win the votes is simple. Foreign competition often clearly affects a narrow and specific import-competing industry such as textiles, shoes, or automobiles, and thus trade restrictions benefit a narrow, well-defined group of economic agents.

Restrictions on imports of Japanese automobiles in the 1980s chiefly benefited the Big Three automakers in this country—General Motors, Ford, and Chrysler. Similarly, long-standing quotas on the imports of sugar benefit a handful of large American sugar producers. When tariffs of up to 30 percent were slapped on many steel imports in 2002, an even smaller number of American steelmakers and their employees benefited. And when Barack Obama slapped tariffs on Chinese tires in 2009, it cost American consumers $1.1 billion, or $900,000 for each of the 1,200 jobs supposedly "saved" in the U.S. tire industry. Because of the concentrated benefits that accrue when Congress votes in favor of trade restrictions, sufficient lobbying and campaign funds can be raised in those industries to convince members of Congress to impose those restrictions.

The eventual reduction in exports that must follow is normally spread in small doses throughout all export industries. Thus, no specific group of workers, managers, or shareholders in export industries will feel that it should contribute money to convince Congress to reduce barriers to globalization. Furthermore, although consumers of imports and import-competing goods lose due to trade restrictions, they too are typically a diffuse group of individuals, none of whom will be individually affected much because of any single import restriction. It is the simultaneous existence of concentrated benefits and diffuse costs that led to Mark Twain's conclusion that the protectionists would often win the votes. (Concentrated benefits and dispersed costs are at the heart of Chapters 20, 23, and 27 in explaining some U.S. domestic policies.)

Of course, the protectionists don't win all the votes—after all, roughly one-sixth of the U.S. economy is based on international trade. Despite the opposition to globalization that comes from many quarters, its benefits to the economy as a whole are so great that it is unthinkable that we might do away with international trade altogether. Thus, when we think about developments, such as NAFTA and the WTO, it is clear that both economic theory and empirical evidence indicate that Americans are better off because of globalization.

DISCUSSION QUESTIONS

1. During the late 1980s and early 1990s, American automobile manufacturers greatly increased the quality of the cars they produced relative to the quality of the cars produced in other nations. What effect do you think this had on American imports of Japanese cars, Japanese imports of American cars, and American exports of goods and services other than automobiles?

2. Over the past thirty-five years, some Japanese automakers have opened plants in the United States so that they could produce (and sell) "Japanese" cars here. What effect do you think this had on American imports of Japanese cars, Japanese imports of American cars, and American exports of goods and services other than automobiles?

3. For a number of years, Japanese carmakers voluntarily limited the number of cars they exported to the United States. What effect do you think this had on Japanese imports of American cars and on American exports of goods and services other than automobiles?

4. Until recently, American cars exported to Japan had driver controls on the left side (as in the United States), even though Japanese cars sold in Japan have driver controls on the *right* side, because the Japanese (like the British) drive on the left side of the road. Suppose the Japanese tried to sell their cars in the United States with the driver controls on the right side. What impact would this likely have on their sales in this country? Do you think the unwillingness of American carmakers to put the driver controls on the correct side for exports to Japan had any effect on their sales of cars in that country?

5. The U.S. government subsidizes the export of U.S.-manufactured commercial aircraft. What effect do you think this policy has on American imports of foreign goods and American exports of products other than commercial aircraft? Explain.

6. Who bears the costs and enjoys the benefits of the subsidies mentioned in the previous question?

CHAPTER 31

The $750,000
Steelworker

In even-numbered years, particularly years evenly divisible by 4, politicians are apt to give speeches about the need to protect U.S. jobs from the evils of **globalization.** We are thus encouraged to buy American. If further encouragement is needed, we are told that if we do not voluntarily reduce the amount of imported goods we purchase, the government will impose (or make more onerous) either **tariffs** (taxes) on imported goods or **quotas** (quantity restrictions) that will physically limit **imports.** The objective is to save U.S. jobs.

Unlike black rhinos or blue whales, U.S. jobs are in no danger of becoming extinct. There are an infinite number of potential jobs in the American economy, and there always will be. Some of these jobs are not very pleasant, and many others do not pay very well, but there will always be employment of some sort as long as there is **scarcity.** Thus, when steelworkers making $72,000 per year say that imports of foreign steel should be reduced to save their jobs, what they really mean is this: They want to be protected from **competition** so they can continue their present employment at the same or higher salary rather than move to a different job that has less desirable working conditions or pays a lower salary. There is nothing wrong with the steelworkers' goal (better working conditions and higher pay), but it has nothing to do with saving jobs.

THE NATURE OF TRADE

In any discussion of the consequences of restrictions on international trade, it is essential to remember two facts. First, *we pay for imports with* **exports.** It is true that in the short run, we can sell off assets or borrow from abroad if we happen to import more goods and services than we export. But we have only a finite amount of assets to sell, and foreigners do not want to wait forever before we pay our bills. Ultimately, our accounts can be settled only if we provide (export) goods and services to the trading partners from whom we purchase (import) goods and services. Trade, after all, involves *quid pro quo* (literally, something for something). The second point to remember is that *voluntary trade is mutually beneficial to the trading partners.* If we restrict international trade, we reduce those benefits, both for our trading partners and for ourselves. One way these reduced benefits are manifested is in the form of curtailed employment opportunities for workers. In a nutshell, even though tariffs and quotas enhance job opportunities in import-competing industries, they also cost us jobs in export industries; the net effect seems to be *reduced* employment overall.

What is true for the United States is also true for other countries: They will buy our goods only if they can market theirs, because they too must export goods to pay for their imports. Thus, any U.S. restrictions on imports—via tariffs, quotas, or other means—ultimately cause a reduction in our exports, because other countries will be unable to pay for our goods. Hence, import restrictions must inevitably decrease the size of our export sector. So imposing trade restrictions to save jobs in import-competing industries has the effect of costing jobs in export industries.

PROTECTION FOR AUTOMOBILES

Import restrictions also impose costs on U.S. consumers. By reducing competition from abroad, quotas, tariffs, and other trade restraints push up the prices of foreign goods and enable U.S. producers to hike their own prices. One of the best-documented examples of this is the automobile industry.

Due in part to the enhanced quality of imported cars, sales of domestically produced automobiles fell from nine million units in 1978 to an average of six million units per year between 1980 and 1982. **Profits** for U.S. automobile manufacturers plummeted as well, turning into substantial losses for some of them. American automakers and autoworkers' unions demanded protection from import competition. They were joined in their cries by politicians from automobile-producing states. The result was a voluntary agreement by Japanese car companies (the most important competitors of U.S. firms) that restricted U.S. sales of Japanese cars to 1.68 million units per year. This agreement—which amounted to a quota even though it never officially bore that name—began in April 1981 and continued into the 1990s in various forms.

Robert W. Crandall, an economist with the Brookings Institution, has estimated how much this voluntary trade restriction cost U.S. consumers in terms of higher car prices. According to his estimates, the reduced supply of Japanese cars pushed their prices up by $5,200 apiece, measured in 2017 dollars. The higher price of Japanese imports in turn enabled domestic producers to hike their prices an average of $2,100 per car. The total tab in the first full year of the program was over $11 billion. Crandall also estimated the number of jobs in automobile-related industries that were preserved by the voluntary import restrictions at about twenty-six thousand. Dividing $11 billion by twenty-six thousand jobs yields a cost to consumers of about $420,000 *per year* for every job preserved in the automobile industry. U.S. consumers could have saved over $8 billion on their car purchases each year if instead of implicitly agreeing to import restrictions, they had simply given $100,000 to every autoworker whose job was preserved by the voluntary import restraints.

PROTECTION FOR OTHER INDUSTRIES

The same types of calculations have been made for other industries. Tariffs in the apparel industry were increased between 1977 and 1981, preserving the jobs of about 116,000 U.S. apparel workers at a cost of $50,000 per job each year. At about the same time, the producers of Citizens' Band radios also managed to get tariffs raised. Approximately six hundred workers in the industry kept their jobs as a result, at an annual cost to consumers of over $90,000 per job.

The cost of **protectionism** has been even higher in other industries. Jobs preserved in the glassware industry due to trade restrictions cost $200,000 apiece each year. In the maritime industry, the yearly cost of trade protection is $290,000 per job. In the steel industry, the cost of preserving a job has been estimated at an astounding $750,000 per year. If free trade were permitted, each worker moving to employment elsewhere could be given a cash payment of half that amount each year, and consumers would still save a lot of money.

The current record holder for squandering resources to cater to a handful of workers, however, goes to Barack Obama. In 2009, in response to claims of **dumping** (see Chapter 30) by Chinese tire makers, he imposed a special tariff on tire imports from China. The cost to Americans of this policy was $1.1 billion per year. This amounts to $900,000 per year for each of the 1,200 jobs that were "saved." Of course, President Trump campaigned on the promise of even more protectionism, so perhaps by the time you read this, we'll have a new record holder.

TOTAL EMPLOYMENT FALLS

Even so, this is not the full story. None of these studies estimating the cost to consumers of preserving jobs in import-competing industries has attempted to estimate the ultimate impact of import restrictions on the flow of exports, the number of jobs lost in the export sector, and thus the total number of jobs gained or lost.

When imports to the United States are restricted, our trading partners will necessarily buy less of what we produce. The resulting decline in export sales means fewer jobs in exporting industries. And the total reduction in trade leads to fewer jobs for workers, such as stevedores (who load and unload ships) and truck drivers (who carry goods to and from ports). On both counts—the overall cut in trade and the accompanying decline in exports—protectionism leads to job losses that might not be immediately obvious.

Several years ago, Congress tried to pass a domestic-content bill for automobiles. In effect, the legislation would have required that cars sold in the United States have a minimum percentage of their components manufactured and assembled in this country. Proponents of the legislation argued that it would protect 300,000 jobs in the U.S. automobile manufacturing and auto parts supply industries. Yet the legislation's supporters failed to recognize the negative impact of the bill on trade in general and on U.S. export industries. A U.S. Department of Labor study did recognize these impacts, estimating that the domestic-content legislation would actually cost more jobs in trade-related and export industries than it protected in import-competing businesses. Congress ultimately decided not to impose a domestic-content requirement for cars sold in the United States.

When President Bush decided in 2002 to impose tariffs of up to 30 percent on steel imports, the adverse effects on the economy were substantial and soon apparent. To take but one example, prior to the tariffs, the Port of New Orleans relied on steel imports for more than 40 percent of its revenues, in part because once steel coming into the port is offloaded, the ships are cleaned and refilled with U.S. grain for export. By reducing imports, the tariffs slashed economic activity at the port and also reduced U.S. grain exports. Businesses and farms all up and down the Mississippi River were adversely affected. More broadly, the higher costs of imported steel produced a decline in employment in U.S. industries that use steel as an input. Indeed, one study estimated that due to the tariffs, about 200,000 people lost their jobs in 2002 in these industries alone—a number that exceeded the total number of people actually employed by the steel manufacturing firms protected by the tariff.

THE IMPOSSIBILITY OF REAL PROTECTION

In principle, trade restrictions are imposed to provide economic help to specific industries and to increase employment in those industries. Ironically, in the long term, restrictions may be totally ineffective in protecting an industry's employment. Researchers at the **World Trade Organization (WTO)** examined employment in three industries that have been heavily protected throughout the world: textiles, clothing, and iron and steel. Despite stringent trade protection for these industries, employment *declined* during the period of protection, in some cases dramatically. In textiles, employment fell 22 percent in the United States and 46 percent in the European Union. The clothing industry had employment losses ranging from 18 percent in the United States to 56 percent in Sweden. Declines in employment in the iron and steel industry ranged anywhere from 10 percent in Canada to 54 percent in the United States. In short, restrictions on free trade are no guarantee against job losses, even in the industries supposedly being protected.

The evidence seems clear: The cost of protecting jobs in the short run is huge. In the long run, it appears that jobs cannot be protected, especially if one considers all aspects of protectionism. Free trade is a tough platform on which to run for office. But it is the one that yields the most general benefits if implemented. Of course, this does not mean that politicians will embrace it, and so we end up "saving" jobs at a cost of $750,000 each—or more.

DISCUSSION QUESTIONS

1. Who gains and who loses from import restrictions?

2. What motivates politicians to impose trade restrictions?

3. If it would be cheaper to give each steelworker $375,000 per year in cash than to impose restrictions on imports of steel, why do we have the import restrictions rather than the cash payments?

4. Most U.S. imports and exports travel through our seaports at some point. How do you predict that members of Congress from coastal states would vote on proposals to restrict international trade? What

other information would you want to know when making such a prediction?

5. When you go shopping for a new computer, is your real objective to "import" a computer into your apartment or is it to "export" cash from your wallet? What does this tell you about the true object of international trade—is it imports or exports?

6. Some U.S. policy is designed to subsidize exports and thus increase employment in export industries. What effect does such policy have on our imports of foreign goods and thus on employment in industries that compete with imports?

GLOSSARY

adverse selection: a process in which "undesirable" (high-cost or high-risk) participants tend to dominate one side of the market, causing adverse effects for the other side; often results from asymmetric information

algorithms: processes or rules to be followed in calculations or other problem-solving operations, especially by a computer

amenities: desirable or useful features of a person, good, or location

antitrust laws: federal and state legislation that prohibits anticompetitive behavior by firms; examples of such behavior include collusion, monopolization, and vertical foreclosure

assets: all tangible and intangible items to which an individual or institution holds a legal claim of ownership

asymmetric information: circumstance in which participants on one side of a market have more information than participants on the other side of the market; often results in adverse selection

bankruptcy: a legal status that permits an individual or firm to escape responsibility for many or all of their debts

behavioral economics: the study of psychology as it relates to the economic decision making processes of individuals

biofuels: fuels made from recently-living organisms or their by-products

body mass index (BMI): a measure of a person's weight relative to the person's height; it equals the person's weight in pounds multiplied by 703, and then divided by the square of the person's height in inches; BMI scores between 25 and 30 indicate that a person is overweight, a BMI score of more than 30 indicates obesity, and a score above 35 indicates *clinical obesity*

capital, or capital stock: the collection of productive assets that can be combined with other inputs, such as labor, to produce goods and services

capital gains: increases in the value of capital assets that are captured upon sale of the assets; when the value of the assets decreases, these are called capital losses

capitalist system: an economic system in which there is large-scale private ownership of resources and in which market incentives play a dominant role in allocating those resources

cartel: a group of independent businesses, often on an international scale, that agree to restrict trade, to their mutual benefit

civil law system: a legal system in which statutes passed by legislatures and executive decrees, rather than judicial decisions based on precedent, form the basis for most legal rules

clinically obese: characterized by a *body mass index* above 35

closed access: an element of the property right to a good, ensuring that the owner can effectively exclude other people from using the good

cohort: a group of people with a common defining characteristic, such as age

common law system: a legal system in which judicial decisions based on precedent, rather than executive decrees or statutes passed by legislatures, form the basis for most legal rules

common property resource: a good jointly owned by a group of individuals who cannot (for legal or physical reasons) divide the good into pieces and dispose of them separately

comparative advantage: the ability to produce a good at a lower opportunity cost than others; the principle of comparative advantage implies that individuals, firms, and nations will specialize in producing goods for which they have the lowest opportunity cost compared to other entities

compensating differential: additional pay given to workers employed in particularly hazardous or unpleasant jobs

competition: rivalry among buyers or sellers of outputs or among buyers or sellers of inputs

complement: a good having the property that a change in its price will cause the demand for another good to change in the opposite direction

congestion: overuse of a resource to the point that one person's use impedes use by other individuals

congestion costs: alternatives forgone (costs incurred) by drivers whose travel time is slowed by highway congestion

constant-dollar price: price corrected for changes in the purchasing power of the dollar, taking inflation and deflation into account

constant-quality price: the price of a good adjusted upward or downward to reflect the higher- or lower-than-average quality of that good

consume: the act of enjoying or using up a service or good

consumer price index: a measure of the dollar cost of a typical bundle of consumer goods relative to the cost of that bundle in a base year

cost: the highest-valued (best) forgone alternative; the most valuable option that is sacrificed when a choice is made

demand: the willingness and ability to purchase goods

demand curve: a graphic representation of demand—a negatively sloped line showing the inverse relationship between the price and the quantity demanded

discount rate: the time value of money, typically expressed as a percentage per year

disposable income: the maximum amount of spending that consumers can undertake after they have paid direct taxes, such as income taxes

dominant firm oligopoly: an *oligopoly* in which one of the small number of firms in the industry accounts for a much larger share of transactions than do other firms

dumping: the sale of a product in another country at a price either below the price charged in the product's home country or below the product's cost of production

dynamic analysis: an assessment of the economic impact of a policy that takes into account the induced responses to that policy

earned income tax credit: a tax policy that offers payments from the government to people who earn relatively low wages

earnings premium: the excess in the pay for one employment compared to another

economic efficiency: the case in which a given level of inputs is used to produce the maximum output possible (or, equivalently, a given level of output is produced with the minimum amount of inputs)

economic good: any good or service that is scarce

economic growth: sustained increases over time in real per capita income

economic profits: profits in excess of competitive profits that are the minimum necessary to keep resources employed in an industry

elastic demand: characteristic of a demand curve in which a given percentage change in price will result in a larger inverse percentage change in quantity demanded; total revenues and price are inversely related in the elastic portion of the demand curve

elasticity: a measure of the responsiveness of one variable to a change in another variable; it is the ratio of two percentage changes

elasticity of demand: responsiveness of the quantity of a commodity demanded to a change in its price per unit

elasticity of supply: responsiveness of the quantity of a commodity supplied to a change in its price per unit

entitlement program: a government program that guarantees a certain level of benefits to persons who meet the requirements set by law

equilibrium price: the price that clears the market when there is no excess quantity demanded or supplied; the price at which the demand curve intersects the supply curve; also called *market-clearing price*

excess quantity demanded: the difference, at the current price, between the *quantity demanded* and the *quantity supplied*; in *equilibrium* this difference is zero

exports: sales of goods or services to a foreign country

externalities: benefits or costs of an economic activity that spill over to a third party; pollution is a negative spillover or externality

fishery: a fishing ground or area where fish are caught

fixed exchange rates: a system of legally fixed prices (rates) at which two or more national currencies trade (exchange) for one another

foreign exchange: national currencies

foreign exchange rate: the relative price at which two national currencies trade

free good: any good or service available in larger quantities than desired at a zero price

full cost: the combined measure of all of the things that must be given up to undertake an activity; includes both the money price (other goods that must be sacrificed) and the value of the time that must be sacrificed

full price: see *full cost*

gains from trade: the extent to which individuals, firms, or nations benefit by engaging in exchange

globalization: the integration of national economies into an international economy as a result of lower trade barriers, reduced transportation, and communication costs

green energy: source of energy that can be harnessed with little direct pollution

human capital: the accumulated training, education, and knowledge of workers

hydrologic cycle: the process that begins with evaporation of water from the earth's surface; as moist air is lifted, it cools and water vapor condenses to form clouds, eventually returning the water to the surface as precipitation

import tariff: a tax applied specifically to imports of goods or services from another nation

imports: purchases of goods or services from a foreign country

in-kind transfers: grants of goods and services rather than cash to recipients who meet certain criteria; examples include Medicare, Medicaid, subsidized housing, food stamps, and school lunches

incentives: perceived consequences of actions or decisions; they may be positive or negative, monetary or nonmonetary

income elasticity of demand: a measure of the responsiveness of demand to changes in income, calculated as the percentage change in demand for a good divided by the percentage change in consumer income

income inequality: differences in the share of total income accruing across individuals or groups of individuals

income mobility: the tendency of individuals to move around in the income distribution over time

increase in demand: a rise in the amount demanded at each price of the good; a shift to the right of the market *demand* curve

increase in supply: a rise in the amount supplied at each price of the good; a shift to the right of the market supply curve

individual mandate: the requirement under the Affordable Care Act of 2010 that individuals purchase health care insurance or face an income-related fine; many people refusing insurance under the Act have been granted exemptions from the mandate

individual transferable quota (ITQ): the share of a *total allowable catch* that the owner of the ITQ may catch

industrial policy: government laws or regulations designed to induce particular economic outcomes, often directed at stimulating the output of a specific manufacturing sector

industry concentration: a measure of the percentage share of transactions accounted for by the largest firms; it is most often calculated for the biggest four or eight firms, but can be calculated for any number of the biggest companies

inelastic: relatively unresponsive

inelastic demand: characteristic of a demand curve in which a given change in price will result in a less than proportionate inverse change in the quantity demanded; total revenue and price are directly related in the inelastic region of the demand curve

inflation: a rise in the dollar cost of achieving a given level of satisfaction, often measured in terms of the dollar cost of a particular standard bundle of goods

inflation-corrected: adjusted for the *inflation* that has taken place since a *nominal price* was originally measured

innovation: the transformation of something new, such as an invention, into something that creates economic benefits

insolvent: in a financial condition in which the value of one's assets is less than the value of one's liabilities

institutions: the basic rules, customs, and practices of society

intellectual property: creative ideas and expressions of the human mind that have commercial value and receive the legal protection of a property right, as through the issuance of a patent, copyright, or trademark

interest: the charge for the privilege of borrowing money, typically expressed as an annual percentage rate

intermediary firms: companies that provide services that enable buyers and sellers to engage in trade

intermittency: when used in the context of renewable energy sources, refers to the fact that because wind, solar, and tides are not consistent sources of energy, they require costly backup conventionally fueled power plants, such as coal, nuclear, or natural gas

invention: a novel product, process, or application that is clearly distinguishable from existing products, processes, or applications

inverse correlation: a contrary relationship between two variables, in which they move in opposite directions

investment: the acquisition of or addition to a property for the purpose of generating additional future services or goods

investment bankers: companies that specialize in helping other firms acquire the funds needed to expand their businesses

labor force participation rate: the sum of all people who are working or are available for and looking for work, divided by the population; both numerator and denominator are generally restricted to persons aged sixteen and above

law of demand: law stating that quantity demanded and price are inversely related—more is bought at a lower price and less at a higher price (other things being equal)

law of supply: law stating that a direct relationship exists between price and quantity supplied (other things being equal)

liabilities: amounts owed; monetary claims against an individual or an institution

luxury good: a good for which the income elasticity of demand is greater than one, meaning that people spend an increasing proportion of their income on the good as they get richer

marginal analysis: analysis of what happens when small changes take place relative to the status quo

marginal benefits: additional benefits associated with one more unit of a good or action; the change in total benefits due to the addition of one more unit of production

marginal costs: changes in total costs due to a change in one unit of production

marginal tax rate: the fraction of the last dollar of income that is paid in taxes

market-clearing price: *see* equilibrium price

market share: the proportion of total sales in an industry accounted for by a specific firm or group of firms in that industry

market supply: total quantities of a good offered for sale by suppliers at various prices

market valuation: the economic worth of a company, typically as revealed by the stock market

median age: age that exactly separates the younger half of the population from the older half

menu mandates: legal requirements that the caloric content (and perhaps other nutritional content) of food items be reported on menus in restaurants

minimum wage: the lowest hourly wage that firms may legally pay their workers

models, or theories: simplified representations of the real world used to make predictions or to better understand the real world

monitoring costs: costs that must be incurred to observe the behavior of a politician or other agent to whom responsibilities have been delegated

monopolistic competition: the situation that exists when producers and sellers offer for sale similar products with slight variations in features or quality; although the products are priced above their average minimum cost, competition among firms reduces long-run economic profits to zero

monopoly: a single supplier; a firm that faces a downward-sloping demand curve for its output and therefore can choose the price at which it will sell the good; an example of a price searcher

monopoly power: the ability of a company to charge a price for its product that is in excess of the marginal cost of producing the product

monopsonist: a firm operating as a monopsony

monopsony: a single buyer; a firm that faces an upward-sloping supply curve for its input and therefore can choose the price at which it will buy the good; an example of a price searcher

moral hazard: the tendency of an entity insulated from risk to behave differently than it would behave if it were fully exposed to the risk

natural resource endowments: the collection of naturally occurring minerals (such as oil and iron ore) and living things (such as forests and fish stocks) that can be used to produce goods and services

negative externality: a cost associated with an economic activity that is paid by third parties; pollution is a negative externality because, for example, someone other than the driver of an automobile bears part of the cost of the car's exhaust emissions

negative tax: a payment from the government made to supplement the incomes of people who earn low wages

network effects: increases in the value of a good or service that occur when more people use it

nominal prices: the costs of goods, expressed in terms of a nation's currency, such as the dollar

nonprice competition: offering additional services or higher product quality to attract business instead of cutting prices to do so

non-traded goods: those items and services traded only within a country and not across its national borders

oligopoly: a firm that is one of a very few sellers (or buyers) in a market; in such a situation, each firm reacts to changes in the prices and quantities of its rivals

open access: an element of the property rights to a good that prevents the owner from excluding people from using the good; in effect, anyone who wishes to use the good is legally free to do so

opportunity cost: the highest-valued alternative that must be sacrificed to attain something or to satisfy a want

outsourcing: the practice of having workers located in foreign lands perform tasks (typically services) that have traditionally been performed by domestic workers

patent: legal protection for an invention that prevents others imitating the invention without compensating the inventor

per capita income: average income per person

perfectly elastic: characterized by an infinite value for the ratio of the percentage change in quantity over the percentage change in price; visually, a perfectly inelastic curve appears horizontal

perfectly inelastic: characterized by a zero value for the ratio of the percentage change in quantity over the percentage change in price; visually, a perfectly inelastic curve appears vertical

physical capital: nonhuman productive resources

platform economy: an economic system in which *platform firms* account for a substantial portion of economic activity

platform firms: companies whose sole business is to create and service *two-sided markets*, typically using computer software and hardware to accomplish this

political economy: the study of the causes and consequences of political decision making

price discrimination: selling at prices that do not reflect differences in marginal costs; different prices with the same marginal costs, for example, or the same prices with different marginal costs

price elasticity of demand: the percentage change in quantity demanded divided by the percentage change in price; *see also* elasticity of demand

price elasticity of supply: the percentage change in quantity supplied divided by the percentage change in price; *see also* elasticity of supply

price searcher: a firm that must search for the profit-maximizing price because it faces a downward-sloping demand curve (if it is a seller) or an upward-sloping supply curve (if it is a buyer); often used as a synonym for monopoly or monopsony

price taker: any economic agent that takes the market price as given; often used as a synonym for a firm operating in a market characterized by pure competition

private costs: alternatives forgone (costs incurred) by the relevant decision maker

product differentiation: distinguishing products by brand name, color, and other minor attributes

productivity: output produced per unit of input

profit: income generated by selling something for a higher price than was paid for it; in production, the income generated is the difference between total revenues received from consumers who purchase the goods and the total cost of producing those goods

property and contract rights: legal rules governing the use and exchange of property, and enforceable agreements between people or businesses

property rights: set of rules specifying how a good may be used and exchanged

protectionism: the imposition of rules designed to protect certain individuals or firms from competition, usually competition from imported goods

proven reserves: estimated quantities of oil and gas that geological and engineering data demonstrate with reasonable certainty to be recoverable in future years from known reservoirs under existing economic and operating conditions

purchasing power: ability or means to acquire goods and services

purchasing power parity: the principle that, in long-run equilibrium, all goods traded internationally must trade at the same price, adjusted for exchange rates

pure competition: a market structure in which participants individually have no influence over market prices; all act as price takers

quantity demanded: the amount of a good or service chosen at a particular price for that item

quantity supplied: the amount of a good or service offered at a particular price for that item

quota: a limit on the amount of a good or an activity; often used in international trade to limit the amount of some foreign good that may be imported into a country

rate of return: the net benefit, in percentage terms, of engaging in an activity; for example, if the investment of $1.00 yields a gross return of $1.20, the net benefit is $0.20 and the rate of return is $0.20/$1.00 = 5 or 20 percent

rational ignorance: a state in which knowledge is incomplete because obtaining perfect information is too costly

real income: income adjusted for inflation (or, equivalently, income expressed in terms of goods and services)

real, or inflation-adjusted, cost: the cost of an item adjusted for changes in the overall price level

real per capita income: gross domestic product (GDP) corrected for inflation and divided by population

real price: a price that is adjusted for inflation and is expressed in terms of some base year

real wage: a wage that is adjusted for inflation and is expressed in terms of some base year

real property: land, those structures and equipment firmly attached thereto, and all resources under the land

relative prices: the costs of goods, expressed in terms of other goods or in terms of a basic bundle of goods

rent control: a system in which the government tells building owners how much they can charge for rent

resource: any input used in the production of desired goods and services

revealed preferences: the likes and dislikes of consumers, as demonstrated by the choices they make in the marketplace

rule of law: the principle that relations between individuals, businesses, and the government are governed by clearly enumerated rules that apply to everyone in society

scarce: not free; something must be sacrificed to obtain

scarce good: any good that commands a positive price

scarcity: state of nature in which resources are limited even though wants are unlimited; scarcity means that nature does not freely provide as much of everything as people want

shortage: situation in which an excess quantity is demanded or an insufficient quantity is supplied; the difference between the quantity demanded and the quantity supplied at a specific price below the market-clearing price

social cost: the full cost that society bears when a resource-using action occurs; for example, the social cost of driving a car is equal to all private costs plus any additional cost that other members of society bear (such as air pollution and traffic congestion)

Social Security: an entitlement program operated by the federal government in which taxes are levied on workers to enable payment of pensions to retirees

static analysis: any assessment of the economic impact of a policy that does not fully take into account the induced responses to that policy

stock: the quantity of something at a particular point in time; an inventory of goods is a stock, as is a bank account at a point in time; stocks are defined independent of time, although they are assessed at a point in time

subsidies: government payments for the production of specific goods, generally designed to raise the profits of the firms receiving the subsidies and often intended to increase the output of the subsidized goods

subsidization: the act of providing subsidies

substitute: a good having the property that a change in its price will cause the demand for another good to change in the same direction

supply: the willingness and ability to sell goods

supply curve: a graphic representation of supply, which slopes upward (has a positive slope), reflecting the positive relationship between price and quantity supplied

supply schedule: a set of prices and the quantity supplied at each price; a schedule showing the rate of planned production at each relative price for a specified time period

surplus: excess quantity supplied or an insufficient quantity demanded; the difference between the quantity supplied and the quantity demanded at a price above the market-clearing price; as applied to the government budget, an excess of tax receipts over expenditures

target price: the minimum price that farmers are guaranteed to receive for their crop, as set by the federal government; if the market price falls below the target price, farmers receive a payment equal to the difference between the two (multiplied by their production of the crop)

tariff: a tax levied on imports

tax credit: an offset against current or future income taxes

tax rate: proportion of the value of the taxed item that is collected in taxes

tax revenue: total dollar value of taxes collected

technological change: a change in the set of feasible production possibilities, typically the result of the productive implementation of new knowledge

time cost: the economic value of the time a person must sacrifice to engage in an activity

toll: a money price paid for the right to drive on a road or bridge or in a designated lane of either

total allowable catch (TAC): government-established limit on the total number of or number of pounds of fish that may lawfully be taken from a *fishery* during a given period; often used in conjunction with *individual transferable quotas (ITQs)*

trade barriers: any rules having the effect of reducing the amount of international exchange; tariffs and quotas are trade barriers

traded goods: those exchanged across national borders

trade-off: term relating to opportunity cost. To get a desired economic good, it is necessary to trade-off (give up) some other desired economic good in a situation of scarcity; a trade-off involves making a sacrifice to obtain something

transaction costs: costs of conducting exchanges of goods

transgenic species: one that contains genetic material from two or more distinct species; examples include mules and Bt cotton

territorial use rights for fishing (TURF): a property rights system for fisheries, in which individual fishers, or cooperating groups of fishers, receive the exclusive right to harvest the relevant species in a particular geographic area of the sea

two-sided market: any trading environment in which the value of being able to participate depends positively on the number of *other* participants

Type I error: an error of commission, such as might arise when an unsafe drug is mistakenly permitted to be sold

Type II error: an error of omission, such as might arise if a beneficial drug is mistakenly prevented from reaching the market

unemployment rate: the percentage of the labor force that is looking for and able to work, but is not currently working

user fees: charges imposed for the use of a good or service; often applied to the charges assigned by governments for the use of government-owned resources, ranging from roads to parks

venture capital: funds invested in high-risk, generally new, companies

voucher: a document that authorizes a person to receive a specified dollar amount of services at no charge

want: the amount of a good or service that would be chosen if the price of that good or service were zero

wealth: the total value of all human and nonhuman assets, tangible or intangible

white-collar jobs: employment in which workers rely chiefly on their intellect and knowledge rather than their physical skills

willingness to pay: the maximum price someone would voluntarily pay for a good or service

World Trade Organization (WTO): an association of more than 145 nations that helps reduce trade barriers among its members and settles international trade disputes among them

SELECTED REFERENCES

CHAPTER 1   Death by Bureaucrat

Howes, Matthew. "The Global Drug-Lag Problem." *CenterWatch News Online,* May 26, 2015.

Kazman, Sam. "Deadly Overcaution: FDA's Drug Approval Process." *Journal of Regulation and Social Cost* 1, no. 1 (1990): 35–54.

Peltzman, Sam. "An Evaluation of Consumer Protection Legislation: The 1962 Drug Amendments." *Journal of Political Economy* 81, no. 1 (1973): 1049–1091.

Philipson, Tomas, Ernst R. Berndt, Adrian H. B. Gottschalk, and Eric Sun. "Cost-Benefit Analysis of the FDA: The Case of the Prescription Drug User Fee Acts." *Journal of Public Economics* 92 no. 5-6 (2008): 1306–1325.

CHAPTER 2   Innovation

Aeppel, Timothy. "Economists Debate: Has All the Important Stuff Already Been Invented?" *Wall Street Journal,* June 15, 2014.

Ip, Greg, et al. "The Economy's Hidden Problem: We're Out of New Ideas," *The Wall Street Journal,* December 6, 2016. Retrieved from http://www.wsj.com /articles/the-economys-hidden-problem-were-out-of-big-ideas-1481042066

Ridley, Matt. *The Evolution of Everything.* New York: HarperCollins, 2015.

Van Dyke, Raymond. "Caveat Emptor: The New Patent Paradigm," *E-Commerce Times,* March 15, 2014.

CHAPTER 3   Flying the Friendly Skies?

Mitchell, Mark L., and Michael T. Maloney. "Crisis in the Cockpit? The Role of Market Forces in Promoting Air Travel Safety." *Journal of Law and Economics* 32, no. 2 (1989): 139–184.

Steele, Jason. "How Safe Is Air Travel? The Statistical Truth," February 18, 2015. Retrieved from https://thepointsguy.com/2015/02/how-safe-is-air-travel-the-statistical-truth/

www.airsafe.com. A wide range of informative statistics on airline safety around the world.

www1.faa.gov. Official Web site of the Federal Aviation Administration.

CHAPTER 4   The Mystery of Wealth

Acemoglu, Daron, and James Robinson. *Why Nations Fail.* New York: Crown. 2012.

Easterly, William, and Ross Levine. "Tropics, Germs, and Crops: How Endowments Influence Economic Development." *Journal of Monetary Economics* 50, no. 1 (2003): 3–39.

Jones, Charles I. "The Facts of Economic Growth," December 18, 2015—Version 2.0. A revised version of NBER Working Paper No. 21142, May 2015.

Mahoney, Paul G. "The Common Law and Economic Growth: Hayek Might Be Right." *Journal of Legal Studies* 30, no. 3 (2001): 503–525.

Chapter 5   The Economics of Exclusion

Acheson, James M. *The Lobster Gangs of Maine*. Hanover, NH: University Press of New England, 1988.

Demsetz, Harold. "Towards a Theory of Property Rights." *American Economic Review* 57, no. 2 (1967): 347–357.

Kaffine, Daniel T. "Quality and the Commons: The Surf Gangs of California." *Journal of Law and Economics* 52, no. 4 (October 2009): 727–743.

Chapter 6   Sex, Booze, and Drugs

American Society of Addiction Medicine. "Opioid Addiction 2016 Facts and Figures." Retrieved from http://www.asam.org/docs/default-source/advocacy/opioid-addiction-disease-facts-figures.pdf

Becker, Gary, Kevin M. Murphy, and Michael Grossman. "The Market for Illegal Goods: The Case of Drugs." *Journal of Political Economy* 114, no. 1 (2006): 38–60.

Benjamin, Daniel K., and Roger LeRoy Miller. *Undoing Drugs: Beyond Legalization*. New York: Basic Books, 1993.

Miron, Jeffrey A., and Jeffrey Zwiebel. "Alcohol Consumption during Prohibition." *American Economic Review* 81, no. 2 (1991): 242–247.

"More Bang for your Buck," *The Economist*, August 9, 2014: 15–19.

Chapter 7   The Economics of Obesity

"Behavioral Risk Factors Surveillance System." *www.CDD.gov*. Centers for Disease Control and Prevention, 1 Feb. 2016. Retrieved from http://www.cdc.gov/brfss/

"Body-Mass Index and All-Cause Mortality." www.thelancet.com. The Global BMI Mortality Collaboration, 388 no. 10046 (August 20, 2016): 776–786. Retrieved from http://www.thelancet.com/pdfs/journals/lancet/PIIS0140-6736(16)30175-1.pdf

Siegel, Karen R., et al. "Association of Higher Consumption of Foods Derived from Subsidized Commodities with Adverse Cardiometabolic Risk among U.S. Adults." *Journal of the American Medical Association, Internal Medicine*. July 5, 2016. Retrieved from http://jamanetwork.com/journals/jamainternalmedicine/article-abstract/2530901

Yelowitz, Aaron. "Menu Mandates and Obesity: A Futile Effort," *Cato Institute Policy Analysis* No. 789, April 13, 2016.

Chapter 8   Kidneys for Sale

"The Gap between Supply and Demand." *The Economist*, October 9, 2008. Retrieved from http://www.economist.com/node/12380981

Harrington, David E., and Edward A. Sayre. "Paying for Bodies, But Not for Organs." *Regulation* Winter 2006–2007, 14–19.

Held, P. J., F, McCormick, A. Ojo, and J. P. Roberts. "A Cost-Benefit Analysis of Government Compensation of Kidney Donors," *American Journal of Transplantation*, 16, no. 3 (2016): 877–885.

Mahdavi-Mazdeh, Mitra. "The Iranian Model of Living Renal Transplantation." *Kidney International* 82 (2012): 627–634.

Rosenberg, Tina. "Need a Kidney? Not Iranian? You'll Wait. *New York Times*, July 31, 2015. Retrieved from http://opinionator.blogs.nytimes.com/2015/07/31/need-a-kidney-not-iranian-youll-wait/

Rosenberg, Tina. "It's Time to Compensate Kidney Donors," *New York Times*, August 7, 2015. Retrieved from http://opinionator.blogs.nytimes.com/2015/08/07/its-time-to-compensate-kidney-donors/

CHAPTER 9   Are We Running Out of Water?

Anderson, Terry L., Brandon Scarborough, and Lawrence R. Watson. *Tapping Water Markets*. New York: Routledge, 2012.

Brat, Ilan. "California Drought Spurs Technology on the Farm." *The Wall Street Journal*, July 16, 2015.

Casselman, Ben. "Desperate Sprinklers." *The Wall Street Journal*, July 20, 2007.

Libecap, Gary. *Owens Valley Revisited: A Reassessment of the West's First Great Water Transfer*. Stanford, CA: Stanford University Press, 2007.

Morelle, Rebecca. "Surface water shifting around the Earth," August 25, 2016. Retrieved from http://www.bbc.com/news/science-environment-37187100

Olmstead, Sheila M., and Robert N. Stavins. "Comparing Price and Nonprice Approaches to Urban Water Conservation." *Water Resources Research* 45 (2009): W04301 (doi:10.1029/2008WR007227).

Yardley, Jim. "Beneath Booming Cities, China's Future Is Drying Up." *New York Times*, September 28, 2007.

CHAPTER 10   Bankrupt Landlords, from Sea to Shining Sea

Downs, Anthony. *Residential Rent Controls: An Evaluation*. Washington, DC: Urban Land Institute, 1988.

Glaeser, Edward L., and Erzo F. P. Luttmer. "The Misallocation of Housing under Rent Control." *American Economic Review* 93, no. 4 (2003): 1027–1046.

www.nycrgb.org/html/guidelines/guidelines.html. Official Web site of the New York City Rent Guidelines Board.

www.smgov.net/Summary_of_Regulations.aspx. Official Web site of the City of Santa Monica Rent Control Board.

CHAPTER 11   *Das Kapital* in the Twenty-First Century

Auerbach, Alan, and Laurence J. Kotlikoff. "We've Been Measuring Inequality Wrong," *New Republic*, March 14, 2016. Retrieved from https://newrepublic.com/article/131517/weve-measuring-inequality-wrong

Burkhauser, Richard V., Jeff Larrimore, and Kosali I. Simon."A 'Second Opinion' on the Economic Health of the American Middle Class," *National Tax Journal*, 65 no. 1 (2012): 7–32.

Chetty, Raj, et al. "Where is the Land of Opportunity? The Geography of Intergenerational Mobility in the United States." *The Quarterly Journal of Economics*, 129, no. 4 (2014): 1553–1623.

Congressional Budget Office, *The Distribution of Household Income and Federal Taxes, 2010*. Washington DC, December 2013.

Marx, Karl. *Capital: A Critique of Political Economy*. London England: Penguin Classics, 2004 (translation of the original from 1867).

Zumbrun, Josh. "Why Wealth Equality Is Way More Complicated Than Just Rich and Poor," *The Wall Street Journal*, October 12, 2015. Retrieved from http://blogs.wsj.com/economics/2015/10/12/why-wealth-inequality-is-way-more-complicated-than-just-rich-and-poor/tab/print/

CHAPTER 12   (Why) Are Women Paid Less?

Becker, Elizabeth, and Cotton M. Lindsay. "The Limits of the Wage Impact of Discrimination." *Managerial and Decision Economics* 26 (2005): 513–525.

Becker, Gary. *The Economics of Discrimination*. Chicago: University of Chicago Press, 1957.

Goldin, Claudia. "A Grand Gender Convergence: Its Last Chapter." *American Economic Review* 104, no. 4 (2014): 1091–1119.

Heckman, James J. "Detecting Discrimination." *Journal of Economic Perspectives* 12, no. 1 (1998): 101–116.

CHAPTER 13   The Effects of the Minimum Wage

Baker, Michael, Dwayne Benjamin, and Shuchita Stanger. "The Highs and Lows of the Minimum Wage Effects: A Time-Series Cross-Section Study of the Canadian Law." *Journal of Labor Economics* 17, no. 2 (1999): 318–350.

Card, David, and Alan Krueger. "Minimum Wages and Employment: A Case Study of the Fast-Food Industry in New Jersey and Pennsylvania." *American Economic Review* 84, no. 3 (1994): 772–793.

DeSilver, Drew. "Who Makes Minimum Wage?" Pew Research Center, September 8, 2014. Retrieved from http://www.pewresearch.org/fact-tank/2014/09/08/who-makes-minimum-wage

Neumark, David, "Who Really Gets the Minimum Wage," *Wall Street Journal*, July 6, 2014.

Neumark, David, and William Wascher. "Minimum Wages and Employment: A Case Study of the Fast-Food Industry in New Jersey and Pennsylvania: Comment." *American Economic Review* 90, no. 5 (2000): 1362–1396.

Neumark, David. "Employment Effects of Minimum Wages." *IZA World of Labor*. May, 2014.

CHAPTER 14   The (Dis)Incentives of Higher Taxes

Feenberg, Daniel R,. and James M. Poterba. "The Alternative Minimum Tax and Effective Marginal Tax Rates." *National Tax Journal* 57, no. 2 (2004): 407–427.

Harberger. Arnold. *Taxation and Welfare*. New York: Little, Brown and Company, 1974.

Mitchell, Daniel J. "What Can the United States Learn from the Nordic Model?" *Cato Institute Policy Analysis*, November 5, 2007.

CHAPTER 15   The Platform Economy

Diehl, Mark A., Joris Drayer, and Joel G. Maxcy, "On the Demand for Live Sport Contests: Insights from the Secondary Market for National Football League Tickets," *Journal of Sport Management*, 30, no. 1 (2016): 82–94.

Kenney, Martin, and John Zysman, "Choosing a Future in the Platform Economy: The Implications and Consequences of Digital Platforms," *Issues in Science and Technology*, National Academies of Sciences, Engineering, and Medicine, Spring 2016, pp. 61–69.

Rysman, Mark, "The Economics of Two-Sided Markets," *The Journal of Economic Perspectives*, 23, no. 3 (2009): 125–143.

CHAPTER 16   Contracts, Combinations, and Conspiracies

Kanfer, Steven. *The Last Empire: DeBeers, Diamonds, and the World*. New York: Farrar, Straus & Giroux, 1993.

www.eia.doe.gov. Official Web site of the Energy Information Administration.

www.ncaa-ea-likeness-settlement.com Site for potential claimants in the NCAA-EA Sports video likeness lawsuit.

Zimbalist, Andrew. *Unpaid Professionals: Commercialism and Conflict in Big-Time College Sports*. Princeton, NJ: Princeton University Press, 2001.

CHAPTER 17   Coffee, Tea, or Tuition-Free?

Chevalier, Judith, and Austan Goolsbee. "Measuring Prices and Price Competition Online: Amazon.com versus BarnesandNoble.com." *Quantitative Marketing and Economics* 1, no. 2 (2003): 203–222.

McCartney, Scott. "How Airlines Spend Your Airfare." *Wall Street Journal,* June 6, 2012. Retrieved from http://online.wsj.com/article/SB10001424052702303296604577450581396602106.html

Odlyzko, Andrew. *Privacy, Economics, and Price Discrimination on the Internet*. St. Paul: University of Minnesota, Digital Technology Center, 2003.

"They're Watching You." *The Economist*, October 18, 2003, p. 77.

CHAPTER 18   Keeping the Competition Out

Brustein, Joshua. "Uber's Fare War on New York Puts Million-Dollar Medallions at Risk." BloombergBusinessWeek, July 7, 2014. Retrieved from http://www.

businessweek.com/articles/2014-07-07/ubers-fare-war-on-new-york-taxis-puts-million-dollar-medallions-at-risk

Carpenter, Dick M., II, Lisa Knepper, Angela C. Erickson, and John K. Koss. "License to Work: A National Study of Burdens from Occupational Licensing." Institute for Justice: Arlington, VA, 2012.

Kravis, Marie-Josee. "What's Killing Jobs and Stalling the Economy," *The Wall Street Journal*, June 3, 2016.

Lipton, Eric. "Finding the Intersection of Supply and Demand." *New York Times*, November 23, 2003, p. 31.

"Tap to Hail." *The Economist*, October 19, 2013, p. 72.

www.schallerconsult.com/taxi/topics.htm. Facts on the New York City taxicab and taxi medallion markets.

CHAPTER 19   Health Insurance for All . . . Or Maybe Not

Cox, Cynthia, Michelle Long, Ashley Semanskee, Rabah Kamal, Gary Claxton, and Larry Levitt. "2017 Premium Changes and Insurer Participation in the Affordable Care Act's Health Insurance Marketplaces." The Henry J. Kaiser Foundation, November 1, 2016. Retrieved from http://kff.org/health-reform/issue-brief/2017-premium-changes-and-insurer-participation-in-the-affordable-care-acts-health-insurance-marketplaces/

Goodnough, Abby. "Many See I.R.S Penalties as More Affordable Than Insurance," *The New York Times*, November 7, 2016.

Ip, Greg. "The Unstable Economics in Obama's Health Care Law." *The Wall Street Journal.* August 19, 2016.

Radnofsky, Louise. "Number of Uninsured in U.S. Dropped Below 10% for First Time in 2015." *The Wall Street Journal*, May 17, 2016.

Somashekhar, Sandhya, and Ariana Eunjung Cha. "Insurers Restricting Choice of Doctors and Hospitals to Keep Costs Down." *Washington Post*, November 20, 2013.

CHAPTER 20   The Deception of Green Energy

Conca, James. "The Direct Costs of Energy: Why Solar Will Continue to Lag Hydro and Nukes." *Forbes*, July 8, 2012. Retrieved from www.forbes.com/sites/jamesconca/2012/07/08/the-direct-costs-of-energy-hydronuclear-best-solar-still-lagging/

Congressional Budget Office. "Effects of Federal Tax Credits for the Purchase of Electric Vehicles." Retrieved from www.cbo.gov/publication/43576

Frank, Charles R., Jr. "The Net Benefits of Low and No-Carbon Electricity Technologies," *Global Economy & Development Working Paper,* No. 73, Brookings Institution: Washington DC, May 2014.

Jacobson, Mark, and Mark Delucchi. "Providing all Global Energy with Wind, Water, and Solar Power, Part 1: Technologies, Energy Resources, Quantities and Areas of Infrastructure, and Materials." *Energy Policy* 39 (2011): 1154–1169.

Joskow, Paul L. "Comparing the Costs of Intermittent and Dispatchable Electricity Generating Technologies." *American Economic Review* 101, no. 3 (2011): 238–241.

Lantz, Eric, Ryan Wisser, and Maureen Hand. "IES Wind Task 26: The Past and Future of Wind Energy." National Renewable Energy Laboratory, Golden, CO, May 2012.

Lipton Eric and Clifford Krause. "A Gold Rush of Subsidies in the Search for Clean Energy." *New York Times*, November 11, 2011.

CHAPTER 21   The Fight over Genetically Modified Foods

Evenson, R. E., and D. Gollin. "Assessing the Impact of the Green Revolution, 1960 to 2000." *Science* 300 (May 2, 2003), 758–762.

Federoff, Nina. "Prehistoric GM Corn." *Science* 302 (November 14, 2003), 1158–1159.

Genetically Engineered Crops: Experiences and Prospects. Washington, DC: The National Academies Press, 2016. Retrieved from http://www.nap.edu/23395

Hakim, Danny. "Doubts About the Promised Bounty of Genetically Modified Crops." *The New York Times*, October 29, 2016.

Harmon, Amy. "Golden Rice: A Lifesaver?" *New York Times*, August 24, 2013.

Lomborg, Bjorn. "Think Organic Food Is Better for You, Animals, and the Planet? Think Again," *The Guardian*, June 12, 2016.

Qain, Matin, and David Zilberman. "Yield Effects of Genetically Modified Crops in Developing Countries." *Science* 299 (February 7, 2003), 900–902.

CHAPTER 22   Student Loans

Berman, Jullian. "America's Growing Student-Loan-Debt Crisis." *Market Watch*. Jan. 19, 2016.

Cappelli, Peter, and Shinjae Won. "How You Pay Affects How You Do: Financial Aid Type and Student Performance In College." *National Bureau of Economic Research*. Working Paper 22604, Sept. 2016.

Glater, Jonathan D. "Student Debt and the Siren Song of Systemic Risk." *Harvard Journal on Legislation*. 53, No. 99 (2016).

Gordon, Grey, and Aaron Hedlund. "Accounting for the Rise in College Tuition." NBER Working Paper c13711, September 28, 2015.

Lucca, D. O., et al. "Credit Supply and the Rise In College Tuition: Evidence from the Expansion in Federal Student Aid Programs." *Federal Reserve Bank of New York*. Staff Papers, No. 733. Oct. 2016.

Price, Eric William. "Does Post-Recessionary Student Loan Debt Negatively Impact the Likelihood of Homeownership More Than Pre-Recessionary Student Loan Debt?" *Graduate School of Arts and Sciences*. Georgetown University, Apr. 12, 2015.

Webber, Douglas A. "Is College Worth It? How Ability, Major, and Debt Affect the Rate of Return." *Economics of Education Review*, Vol. 53, Aug. 2016: 296–310.

CHAPTER 23   The Graying of America

Council of Economic Advisers. "Restoring Solvency to Social Security." *Economic Report of the President*. Washington, DC: Government Printing Office, 2004, Ch. 6.

Ip, Greg. "For Economy, Aging Population Poses a Double Whammy," *The Wall Street Journal*, August 3, 2016.

Miron, Jeffrey A., and David N. Weil. "The Genesis and Evolution of Social Security." In *The Defining Moment: The Great Depression and the American Economy in the Twentieth Century*, eds. Michael D. Bordo, Claudia Goldin, and Eugene N. White. Chicago: University of Chicago Press, 1998, pp. 297–322.

"Policy Basics: Where Do Our Federal Tax Dollars Go?" Center on Budget and Policy Priorities, March 31, 2014. Retrieved from www.cbpp.org/cms/?fa=view&id=1258

CHAPTER 24   For Whom the Roads Are Tolled

Christainsen, Gregory B. "Road Pricing in Singapore after 30 Years," *Cato Journal*, 26, no. 1 (2006): 71–88.

McWhirter, Cameron. "On U.S. Highways, More Fast Lanes Aren't Free," *Wall Street Journal*, November 28, 2013.

Turner, Matthew A., and Gilles Duranton. "The Fundamental Law of Highway Congestion: Evidence from the U.S." *American Economic Review* 101, no. 6 (2011): 2616–2652.

Wheatley, Malcolm. "How IT Fixed London's Traffic Woes," *CIO Magazine*, July 15, 2003.

CHAPTER 25   What to Do About the Climate?

Barreca, Alan, Karen Clay, Olivier Deschenes, Michael Greenstone, and Joseph S. Shapiro. "Adapting to Climate Change: The Remarkable Decline in the US Temperature-Mortality Relationship over the Twentieth Century." *Journal of Political Economy* 124, no. 1 (February 2016): 105–159.

Gasparrini, Antonio, et al. "Mortality Risk Attributable to High and Low Ambient Temperature: A Multicountry Observational Study," *The Lancet*, 386 (July 25, 2015): 369–375.

Morelle, Rebecca. "Surface Water Shifting around the Earth," August 25, 2016. Retrieved from http://www.bbc.com/news/science-environment-37187100

Olmstead, Alan L., and Paul W. Rhode. *Creating Abundance: Biological Innovation and American Agricultural Development*. New York: Cambridge University Press, 2008.

Ridley, Matt. "Global Warming versus Global Greening," 2016 Annual GWPF Lecture, The Royal Society, London, 2016.

CHAPTER 26   Save That Species

Anderson, Terry L., and Peter J. Hill. *The Not So Wild, Wild West: Property Rights on the Frontier*. Stanford: Stanford University Press, 2004.

Coase, Ronald. "The Problem of Social Cost." *Journal of Law and Economics* 3 (1960): 1–44.

Costello, Christopher, Steven D. Gaines, and John Lyman. "Can Catch Shares Prevent Fisheries Collapse?" *Science* 321, no. 5826 (September 2008): 1678–1681.

Costello, Christopher, and Daniel Kaffine. "Private Conservation in TURF-Managed Fisheries," *Natural Resource Modeling*, July 2016. Retrieved from http://dx.doi.org/10.1111/nrm.12103 DO - 10.1111/nrm.12103

Gates, C. Cormack, Curtis H. Freese, Peter J. P. Gogan, and Mandy Kotzman. *American Bison: Status Survey and Conservation Guidelines*. Gland, Switzerland: International Union for Conservation of Nature, 2010.

Grafton, R., Quentin, Dale Squires, and Kevin J. Fox. "Private Property and Economic Efficiency: A Study of a Common-Pool Resource." *Journal of Law & Economics* 43, no. 2 (2000): 679–713.

CHAPTER 27   Ethanol Madness

Barrionuevo, Alexei. "Boom in Ethanol Reshapes Economy of Heart-land." *New York Times*, June 25, 2006, p. 1.

Cappiello, Dina, and Matt Apuzzo. "The Secret Environmental Cost of Ethanol Policy." *Associated Press*, November 12, 2013.

Environmental Protection Agency. *Regulatory Announcement: Removal of Reformulated Gasoline Oxygen Content Requirement and Revision of Commingling Prohibition to Address Non-Oxygenated Reformulated Gasoline*. Document no. EPA420-F-06–020. Washington, DC: Environmental Protection Agency, February 2006.

www.eia.doe.gov. Official Web site of the Energy Information Administration.

CHAPTER 28   The Death of Recycling

Benjamin, Daniel K. *Recycling Myths Revisited*. No. PS-47. Bozeman, MT: Property and Environment Research Center, 2010.

Bohm, Robert A., David H. Folz, Thomas C. Kinnaman, and Michael J. Podolsky. "The Costs of Municipal Waste and Recycling Programs," *Resources, Conservation, and Recycling* 54 (2010): 864-871.

Kinnaman, Thomas C., Takayoshi Shinkuma, and Masashi Yamamoto. "The Socially Optimal Recycling Rate: Evidence from Japan," *Journal of Environmental Economics and Management* 68, no. 1 (2014): 54–70.

Porter, Richard C. *The Economics of Waste*. Washington, DC: Resources for the Future, 2002.

Rathje, William, and Cullen Murphy. *Rubbish: The Archeology of Garbage*. New York: HarperCollins, 1992.

Tierney, John. "The Reign of Recycling," *New York Times*, October 3, 2015. Retrieved from http://mobile.nytimes.com/2015/10/04/opinion/sunday/the-reign-of-recycling.html?_r=0

CHAPTER 29   The Economics of the Big Mac

Ashenfelter, Orley, "Comparing Real Wages." NBER Working Paper No. 18006, April, 2012. Retrieved from www.nber.org/papers/w18006

Ashenfelter, Orley, and Stepan Jurajda, "Cross-Country Comparisons of Wage Rates: The McWage Index." Princeton, NJ: Industrial Relations Section, Princeton University, August 2009.

Clementi, Fabio, et al., "A Big Mac Test of Price Dynamics and Dispersion of Across Euro Area." *Economic Bulletin* 30, no. 3, (August 2010): 2037–2053.

www.economist.com/content/big-mac-index Website for the Big Mac index

https://www.statista.com/statistics/275235/big-mac-worldwide-cities-working-time/ Recent data on the number of minutes of work required to pay for a Big Mac

CHAPTER 30   Globalization and the Wealth of America

Althaus, Dudley, and Christina Rogers. "Donald Trump's NAFTA Plan Would Confront Globalized Auto Industry," *The Wall Street Journal*, November 10, 2016.

Eichengreen, Barry. "The Political Economy of the Smoot–Hawley Tariff." *Research in Economic History* 12, no. 1 (1989): 1–43.

Federal Reserve Bank of Dallas. *The Fruits of Free Trade.* Annual Report. Dallas, TX: Federal Reserve Bank, 2002.

Irwin, Douglas A. "From Smoot–Hawley to Reciprocal Trade Agreements: Changing the Course of U.S. Trade Policy in the 1930s." In *The Defining Moment: The Great Depression and the American Economy in the Twentieth Century*, eds. Michael D. Bordo, Claudia Goldin, and Eugene N. White. Chicago: University of Chicago Press, 1998, pp. 325–352.

Reynolds, Alan. "What the China Trade Warriors Get Wrong," *The Wall Street Journal*, October 26, 2016.

CHAPTER 31   The $750,000 Steelworker

Berry, Steven, James Levinsohn, and Ariel Pakes. "Voluntary Export Restraints on Automobiles: Evaluating a Trade Policy." *American Economic Review* 89, no. 3 (1999): 400–430.

Crandall, Robert W. "The Effects of U.S. Trade Protection for Autos and Steel." *Brookings Papers on Economic Activity*, no. 1 (1987): 271–288.

Eberstadt, Nicholas. "The Idle Army: America's Unworking Men," *The Wall Street Journal*, September 1, 2016.

INDEX